Medical Tourism
Facilitator's Handbook

Medical Tourism Facilitator's Handbook

Maria K. Todd

CRC Press
Taylor & Francis Group
Boca Raton London New York

CRC Press is an imprint of the
Taylor & Francis Group, an **informa** business

A PRODUCTIVITY PRESS BOOK

CRC Press
Taylor & Francis Group
6000 Broken Sound Parkway NW, Suite 300
Boca Raton, FL 33487-2742

© 2012 by Taylor & Francis Group, LLC
CRC Press is an imprint of Taylor & Francis Group, an Informa business

No claim to original U.S. Government works

Printed in the United States of America on acid-free paper
Version Date: 20111012

International Standard Book Number: 978-1-4398-1283-9 (Hardback)

Visit the Taylor & Francis Web site at
http://www.taylorandfrancis.com

and the CRC Press Web site at
http://www.crcpress.com

Contents

Acknowledgments

This book was by far the hardest to write of the books I've written. I didn't realize how much the industry would change and evolve while I was writing it, nor did I estimate how practicing what I wrote as part of the refinement of the message would create such innovation and success. As a result, my writing time was constantly set secondary to client needs, provider relations, and business development. Writing a book of this caliber took hard work not only on my part, but on the part of those who have assisted along the way.

First off, I want to thank my husband, Alan. You have provided support and encouragement even if from time to time, it came in the form of pouting and complaining that you wanted some "Ria time." You have sacrificed that "Ria time" so that I could meet the commitments of a growing business and the authorship of this book. You've cooked, helped out, fetched tissues when I cried that I couldn't handle the stress of so much going on at once, and you've rubbed my shoulders and neck when I've spent too many hours in the chair working.

Thanks to everyone at my company, Mercury Healthcare, who had a hand in the editing process, the sounding board, and best and better practices. Our collective wisdom is reflected in this book, and while it may be my name on the cover, I know who helped me get here. You rock! In addition, I want to thank our clients and our global health network providers and other facilitators whom I trust. It has been an honor to serve you, to work with you and to include you in my extended family. Many times, you have let me make you my "guinea pigs," and I am grateful you trusted me to lead the way. I was able to use many of you as case studies in the book, adding a sense of reality and "nuts and bolts" to the examples, so thank you for allowing me to do that.

I want to give special thanks to Derek Hedden. You were an amazing and patient collaborative internal editor. Thanks for assisting with the research and authorship of the Medical Spa chapter.

Thanks also to Lisa Beichl, a trusted colleague and collaborator, for your contribution of Chapter 9, Quality and Safety Transparency.

Lastly, this book would not have been possible without the patience and support of Productivity Press and my publisher, Kristine Mednansky (AKA Jimmy the Squirrel). You knew when and how to push and when to back off and trust me to get the job done. It was a pleasure and an honor to get to work with such a talented team of people. I am ever grateful for this book; it is truly a dream come true!

The *Medical Tourism Facilitator's Handbook* evolved out of an awareness that arose while I attended a conference associated with the Medical Tourism Association (MTA) held in San Francisco in September 2008. What I witnessed was not only comical, but sad and, to my trained eye, frightening.

In preparation for attending the event, I was provided a list of attendees and organizations. I used this list to do some due diligence. More than 40 of the vendors and facilitators listed had websites that were parking spaces for a Uniform Resource Locator (URL) without content. Many others were home pages with links to nowhere. I labeled all those as "not ready for primetime."

I met several individuals who identified themselves as new facilitators. Each paid several thousands of dollars in combined admissions, airfares, hotel and other travel expenses to this expensive city to attend the conference. While there, everyone did their best to meet medical providers, attend showcase presentations by the providers, negotiate representation agreements, and close business deals.

Some of these new facilitators had no business cards and were embarrassed when asked to exchange cards with hospital personnel or medical providers. For example, I stood next to an individual at one booth sponsored by a hospital and heard the following: "We just started our business last week so we don't have any cards, but my partner is at Kinko's right now getting some printed for us because we didn't know if we would need them for this."

At another booth from a hospital in Malaysia, a gentleman in his 50s came up and introduced himself. When the person at the booth asked him his background and experience as a facilitator, the gent stated that he had been a truck driver until the previous six months when he injured his back. The hospital representative chuckled and said, "Well, I guess you know orthopedics then, eh?" to which the gent replied, "Them are bones, right?" I had to step away or risk being labeled rude as I could not contain my amusement. This comically demonstrates how not everyone seeking to be involved in medical tourism is a medical or travel expert.

I also encountered hospital personnel and other providers who were not ready for medical tourism business but had high hopes of establishing a foothold in the industry. Also present were foreign government economic development representatives and travel and tourism development representatives, all hoping to promote their countries as medical tourism destinations, but they had representatives who themselves could not speak enough English to win my confidence as to their level of preparation.

All in all, according to the Medical Tourism Association spokesperson, the attendance at that event was over 800 individuals. The sponsors generated a lot of revenue at that event and many press releases. More of these have been scheduled, and many more thousands of dollars in revenue will be produced.

What I did not see was a venue or forum to host or present the intense training necessary to combine four very distinct roles—that of travel planner, case manager, concierge, and web portal developer—into that of a professional medical travel facilitator.

I sat at a table with Susanne Sapa, RN, CCM, of Maryland, and Gerald Milden, a seasoned veteran producer in the trade show industry (PC Expo, MacWorld Expo, E3, and Microsoft's Windows World), and we shared our observations and discussed what was missing over coffee.

Sapa was planning to become a facilitator and was there to explore the industry. Her background included being a traveler nurse in Washington, DC, who accompanied patients being repatriated back to the United States. She was also a nurse in a large, integrated health delivery system in Virginia and a certified case manager and registered nurse. She had a business partner who was a surgeon, and together they planned to activate a business sometime in 2009. She has since activated her business after months of planning, legal expense, travel, and provider network development.

Milden, on the other hand, was there to explore the business potential of the trade show and determine if his model would be successful in that domain. He started work on a company called International Medical Expositions, and had booked four venues in Canada under the brand MedExpos. As a seasoned entrepreneur and investor, he put the project on hold when the economy soured. As the Kenny Rogers song goes, "You got to know when to hold 'em, know when to fold 'em, know when to walk away and know when to run." I respect him for having the courage to postpone, knowing what I know as an experienced meeting planner. He forfeited many thousands of dollars but cut his losses and those of his investors. If and when he tries again, I will be there to support him 100%.

I was there in the capacity of managing partner of my consultancy in global health care program development (Global Health Sources, LLC) to determine the state of the industry, the potential need for our consulting services, and to perhaps do some networking. I never went there with the intention of writing a book such as this or its provider compendium, *Medical Tourism Program Development*, or to establish another nonprofit in this space—The Council on the Global Integration of Health Care (www.cgih.org).

Upon my return from the conference, I immediately called Kristine Mednansky, my longtime friend and editor at Productivity Press, who was also my publisher at McGraw Hill Health Care Education Group for my first three books. I proposed this book and she brought it forth to the review committee, along with the companion book, *Medical Tourism Program Development*, and both were accepted.

I am indebted to several others, including many physicians and hospital providers who gave their wisdom and time in critique, resources, and generosity to bring this book to reality.

Josef Woodman is the author of *Patients Beyond Borders: Everybody's Guide to Affordable, World-Class Medical Tourism,* second edition. His books have emerged as the leading books for the growing market of Americans seeking an alternative to the pricing quagmire, uncertain insurance coverage, and inconsistent delivery of health care services in the United States. It's been praised by ABC News, the *Washington Post,* travel guru Arthur Frommer and *Travel + Leisure Magazine.*

Barbara Baker, a dear friend and new facilitator, helped me prove concepts as I wrote the book by actually going through the processes suggested to establish her new business. Together, we inspected hospitals as potential providers for her network, reviewed representation contracts, toured hotels and museums, and met with dignitaries interested in promoting medical tourism in Mexico. My research and planning and theories came to life as we validated the suggested preparation, policies, procedures, activities, and investigations outlined in this book to ensure they were based in reality, not just theory.

Lorna Greenwood, WCS, CRM, CIC, CISR, ACSR, program manager at US Risk Underwriters, Inc. in Dallas, Texas, provided assistance with the technical aspects of professional liability coverage available to medical travel facilitators.

Lisa Beichl, BA, MBA, an international health care expert with Milliman Care Guidelines, was very generous with her assistance, providing an overview of and insight into how other insurance programs outside the United States treated medical tourism and globally integrated health care. Her concentration in non-U.S. markets began in Germany with United Health Care, where she consulted on metrics development with a large German public health fund developing a disease management program, and later she worked on improving metrics with a third-party administrator (TPA) operating in the Middle East. Subsequent leadership positions in Switzerland with Swiss Re Life and Health and in Germany with Allianz and Munich Re focused on health insurance/reinsurance strategy and operational development in Latin America, Central and Eastern Europe, the Middle East, and Southeast Asia. Lisa has extensive insight and experience in managed care projects in global markets and served as an excellent complementary resource in the preparation of this manuscript.

Introduction

In a nutshell, medical tourism is the practice of traveling outside one's hometown to access medical or dental care, or costly and sophisticated diagnostic testing. For most medical travelers, depending on the destination location and procedure sought, the savings can be from 50% to as great as 90% of the price paid at home.

It amazes me when people in the health care and insurance industries look at me dumbfounded when I speak about medical tourism. Some furrow their eyebrows, others shake their heads in bewilderment, and still others dismiss the idea with some offhand comment that if they ignore it, it will not exist. I have a cat that does the last response to many things, but she's a cat.

Most of the folks I hang out with are executives in health care or insurance, health law attorneys, academics, or health care professionals. Not cats! So when they dismiss this growing trend, I have to wonder where they will be in the next 5 years. In the United States, there are around 7,500 hospitals with their doors still open. That, too, amazes me when I see who is at the helm, and their leadership style, market awareness, and lack of strategic planning. According to a study done by Dr. Paul Keckley of Deloitte in 2008, each one of those U.S. hospitals lost an average of 10 cases from their community to somewhere else on the planet. Worse yet, each hospital lost an average of $21,000 in revenue (not billed charges) to hospitals elsewhere in the world—hospitals that collected 100% of their fees on those cases, from cash paying customers who went there with U.S. dollars in hand, ready to pay their bill in advance for the high-quality and high-tech health care services not yet rendered. Although the Deloitte Center for Health Care Solutions' volume estimates do not appear to be based on hard data, they do show evidence of an undeniable trending pattern.

What other industry segment anticipates the growth that medical tourism is likely to experience in the next few years and beyond? Even when travel costs are factored in, most medical tourism packages are substantially more affordable that hometown health care. In reality, the media hype does not factor in the aftercare that is generally accessed in the hometown into those figures, but suffice it to say that the savings are real and access to lifesaving procedures that may not be available in one's home country may also incentivize the medical traveler to seek care abroad.

In the last 10 to 15 years, and even before (I began facilitating medical travel on a casual basis for clients in the 1970s when I was a travel agent), most medical tourism was for cosmetic, gender reassignment, or dental procedures. More recently, it has grown to include medically necessary and lifesaving procedures as well as procedures to improve one's quality of life or family planning. All throughout the world, medical tourism has grown over recent years beyond all expectations and is entering a new phase where key issues and questions are being raised, not only by the traveling patients, but also by government health ministries, public and private hospitals, facilitators, medical organizations, international corporations, and insurance companies all over the world.

Little doubt remains about the future of medical tourism and globally integrated health care. The truths are self-evident: We are all individuals, not populations; we all have illnesses; and we require options and solutions. There are qualified providers all over the world. Health care costs often exceed one's ability to pay for necessary care from local hometown providers. Why shouldn't we source diagnostics, medical and wellness services, treatments, and interventions from resources that offer affordable, high-quality health care regardless of where it is located? In fact, what will it take to globally integrate care so that, as individuals, we have the right to seek coordinated care and interventions in which we believe, whether experimental, investigative, or the current standard of care worldwide?

Currently, the United States spends more than $2 trillion a year on health care, or at least 16% of the gross domestic product. Spending rose 6.1% in 2007. The great debate in the United States exists about how, when, and for what purpose health care services outside of one's hometown should be utilized, and from whom they should be sourced. In other countries, the debate has been settled. Some countries actually outsource specific disease management to climates better suited to handle rheumatologic patients' needs, while others simply don't have the medical specialists, hospitals, or other equipment in their home country and have decided that it is appropriate to seek care outside their geopolitical borders. I've met representatives from these countries, physicians mainly, who are charged with the responsibility to visit facilities abroad and report back to governments, employers, and health care insurance programs about their findings and the qualifications of the providers abroad.

When patients are moved from one locale to another, someone has to be in charge of the logistics, coordination of care, credentials vetting and privileging of the health care professionals, and the appropriateness to determine fitness for travel to the locality where care will be rendered, and back. This job of a coordinator is generally referred to as *medical tourism facilitator* or *medical travel facilitator*. I prefer the latter, as not all medical travel is associated with tourism and leisure activities. As a part of this industry that has gained popularity in recent years but has been ongoing for decades, several questions need to be asked and answered, including an understanding of the structures and dynamics of the current medical tourism marketplace, how medical tourism is marketed and what can be done to improve the image, how collaborations will be implemented for globally integrated, cross-border health care, the establishment and recognition and acceptance of regulating authorities in the industry, and how the medicolegal risks involving patients, facilitators, and hospitals will be mitigated and dealt with when they occur. Finally, what is the future for medical tourism in the current economic climate and, more specifically, how will that future affect the role for a professional medical travel facilitator who wishes to develop a business strategy that ensures a sustainable, competitive advantage?

Congratulations on your decision to become a medical tourism facilitator. Your role will be varied and will have many dimensions in this emerging market. Your responsibility will be high, your compassion tested, your patience tried, and your intelligence insulted. That's all part of the job. It's not personal.

- On the bright side, your service will most often be appreciated and rewarded, not just with remuneration but with endless gratitude from your clients, their families, and friends who are aware of your service, dedication, and hard work to see them through a challenge, remain at the ready, on call, responsive, as the voice of calm, the go-to person, and the virtual or physical hand-holder.
- The word "facilitate" means to make easier. You will do this by being prepared, thinking ahead, imagining and rehearsing your processes, systems, procedures, and troubleshooting one step ahead for a client who should be focused on getting well, eliminating pain, or improving health. For the casual medical tourist who has gathered together a gaggle of girlfriends to jet off to a spa, your job is to be like the maid of honor at a wedding. Think of everything, have solutions, smooth the wrinkles, deal with the unexpected, and never let them see you "perspire."
- You also have some new skills to refine if you've never been a travel agent or health care worker before. You are going to need to learn about airline routings, and regional and international hubs. If a flight is canceled due to weather, you need to run all the possible scenarios to get your clients to their destination, on time, with as little stress as possible. They may be stranded in a huge airport that you have never been in yourself. You owe it to them to think ahead, have a backup plan, know which airlines go where, when, how frequently and to be able to coach them as to what to say to the gate agent that will reroute them. If they misconnect, and are not experienced travelers, this alone could be the one thing that ruins an otherwise perfect episode of clinical care and earns you demerits on customer satisfaction.

- Other knowledge you will need is of anatomy and physiology: the structure and function of the parts of the body. Everything is connected. You have to understand *how*. For example, how stress can affect blood pressure, how altitude can affect swelling and inflammation, and increase pain. How clots form after travel, after surgery. You have to be the trusted voice of reason, even if you only read aloud to clients what the recommendations from the doctor say on paper. Even if only to remind them. You have to understand the language of medicine, to speak to physicians and nurses and hospital personnel so that they will respect you. You have to spell and pronounce medical words accurately and appropriately. You have to have the courage to tell people that you don't understand something but that you are willing to learn if they will explain it until you "get it."

I didn't just wake up one day knowing all of this. I attended college courses for anatomy and physiology, medical terminology, chemistry, biochemistry, zoology, physics, and organic chemistry. I learned microbiology and how viruses and other microorganisms can cause infections. I learned instrumentation of the operating theater as a scrub nurse. I was taught the routine of surgical cases so that when someone tells me he or she plans to have an arthroscopy of the left knee to correct disruption of the anterior cruciate ligament, I know what will probably happen in that case from start to finish and afterward. (It also helps that I have had seven similar procedures and can relate to the crutches, the pain, flying with crutches, falling down from the crutches in snow, down stairs, on sidewalks, and having someone accidentally kick the crutches out from underneath me in the airport, when flying two days after surgery—and so forth!)

In the 1970s, I worked for the American Automobile Association's East Florida Division in the domestic and then in the worldwide travel agency. I attended school at night to become a travel agent. I learned geography, and airline and travel terminology. I learned about minimum connecting times, visa, passport, and immigration procedures, airline routings, seating configurations on the various aircrafts, hubs, tours (both escorted and unescorted), commissionable rates, rating systems, amenities, meal plans, inclusions and exclusions, and so forth. As a medical tourism facilitator, the last thing you want to do is have someone tend to his or her own travel plans. If you are unskilled and unprepared for this, affiliate with a professional travel agent who can be your go-to troubleshooter 24/7.

As a professional health care industry speaker and consultant, I have flown over 10 million miles since 1989 when I started to consult and speak professionally. I know some airports so well I can tell you if they replaced the carpet or recently developed new scuff marks on the walls in a particular concourse. The gate agents know me in cities that are not my hometown.

Still, travel causes stress on occasion. Thoughts that run through my head include Will my bags arrive? Will we arrive on time? Will I misconnect? I am hungry, I have a dead cell phone, my charger is in my checked luggage, I have to go to the bathroom, and my knee hurts. How far is it? Will it be clean? Is there food that is edible? Oh crap, we're circling the airport again. I really need to get up to the restroom; the seat belt sign is on. I hope we land soon. Wow—the turbulence is bad! This is kind of bumpy. The lady in 4A is white knuckling her husband, poor thing. I have to get to my destination on time. I'll miss my appointments. What if the flight I am supposed to connect to doesn't arrive? Who is going to advise the driver scheduled to pick me up? Will he speak English? How will I let him know I am not going to be on that flight? And when I do arrive, who will pick me up? Maybe they will be busy with someone else. If they send my bags on without me, what am I going to sleep in tonight? Where will I sleep tonight? Oh, I really need to go to the bathroom and I am hungry! Are we ever going to land? I wonder how difficult it will be to communicate with the airport staff. What hotel will they put me in? Oh, this is a weather delay, that's right...they don't cover hotels and expenses when the delay is caused by weather. I am on my own here.

Those are the fleeting thoughts that cover about 90 seconds' time for me quite often when bad things happen. Could you imagine if this was my first time out of the country? And, if I were medically challenged, can you imagine the added stress?

I speak a smattering of about 12 languages, enough to get food, shelter, safety, and medical care. Can you imagine if I were your client who only spoke English? Once we land (and I've been able to go to the bathroom), if I call you, will you be able to sort things out? Will you answer the phone? Will you be able to calm me down? Will you handle things so I can just sit in a corner and wait until I am told what is going to happen and what to do next?

Consider that all part of the job you signed on for.

A Note to the Reader

Dearest Reader,

This may be the first book of its kind: the first "living" book on medical tourism facilitation. What this means is that I have posted additional tools, reference materials, worksheets, and updated information at http://www.mercury-healthcare.com. (You can access it using the passphrase "thank you.") Medical tourism is a living, evolving industry, and this copy of the *Handbook of Medical Tourism Facilitation* will be updated regularly to reflect changes as they occur, making it the last medical tourism facilitation professional book you'll ever need. The book you hold in your hand is your key to accessing that digital toolkit and more.

There are two ways to use this book, and how you choose depends on your learning style and personal preference:

1. Read it from cover to cover and come away with a solid understanding of medical tourism facilitation and how to become a professional in this domain, or
2. Use it as a guide and create your own business strategy as you read. Eventually, I will develop a workbook and you can find that and much more guidance at http://www .mercury-healthcare.com.

Either way you choose to proceed, my sincerest intention is for you to come away with a thorough understanding of how to succeed as a medical tourism facilitator.

Thank you for picking up this book. Thank you for wanting to learn more about this evolving sector in health care. And most of all, thank you for trusting me and my associates and co-authors to be your guide.

Best regards,

Maria K. Todd
Founder and CEO
Mercury Healthcare

1 Defining the Role of the Facilitator

A medical travel facilitator is a new role in the health care industry, and also in the travel industry. As such, there are no clearly defined job descriptions published in the industry that have been accepted by any accrediting body, certification body, or official entity. The role is as dynamic as the medical tourism and global health sector itself. With its evolution, we can see four clearly defined subordinate roles and responsibilities within it that have emerged in the last five to six years: travel planner, medical case manager, destination medical concierge, and marketing and Web portal developer.

As these four roles already have professional designations and responsibilities, those incumbent in the positions are bound to be merciless in their criticism of a newcomer who attempts to commingle the four distinct disciplines without the requisite training or possession of the bodies of knowledge necessary to do them well as a "professional." There is also bound to be a bit of jealousy if they are well-entrenched and invested in an established business model that is more narrowly defined than one of these other professionals, especially if they are too busy to learn the new complementary skills necessary to transition into this newly evolved composite role. There may be readers of this book who are in a position to expand their professional scope, such as an established nurse case manager, a professional concierge, a destination management professional, a professional travel agent, or a Web developer specializing in search engine optimization (SEO), e-commerce, or other online services. This chapter will address these roles and how their responsibilities intersect as a facilitator of medical travel.

PROFESSIONAL MEDICAL TRAVEL FACILITATOR

The main responsibility of a medical travel facilitator is to make the process of traveling—whether for work or pleasure—as stress-free and as positive an experience as possible. While a travel agent performs some of the same functions as a reservations sales agent at an airline, hotel, or car rental agency, the medical tourism facilitator adds the health care travel planning component to that scope and responsibility. The facilitator's value is in the relationship and peace of mind they develop with and for their customer.

Medical travel facilitators provide personalized service to each of their clients. These personalized services have regulatory implications for the security of personally identifiable health information, confidentiality, and privacy.

Facilitators should understand their customer, and recognize their medical and travel needs and preferences. In this age of impersonal and poor customer service, Web-based reservation systems, and the innumerable choices of providers worldwide, medical travelers appreciate the reliability and attention to detail a professional facilitator brings to the entire medical travel experience.

As the medical travel facilitator's role continues to evolve, it will reflect the growth and the changes within the medical travel industry, as well as the way people access and pay for care outside their hometown. One could argue that the Internet has enabled consumers to be far more educated and savvy about purchasing medical travel than just 5 years ago. One could also argue just as easily that the innumerable choices, accreditation systems, packages, and pricing could easily overwhelm a non-medical person with all the options available for care, quality, access, and price. Therefore, customers who turn to a medical travel facilitator require a professional who can make sense of the complicated and changing world of today's medical tourism and globally integrated health care industry.

A medical travel facilitator must provide their client with:

- Knowledge of the medical tourism and global health industry
- Knowledge of medical terminology, anatomy, and how the body works (physiology)
- Knowledge of all aspects and rules of the travel industry equivalent to that of a professional travel agent
- Knowledge of health care resource management (often referred to as medical case management)
- An understanding of travel insurance and health insurance programs available worldwide
- Extensive information about the products you sell and how travel products are a part of medical tourism
- The ability to perform a competitive analysis
- Understanding of clarifications in a supplier's fine print including restrictions and cancellation penalties
- Recommendations, personal experience, and expertise regarding vacation and tourism planning
- Simplified travel and medical services planning
- Confidential and personalized service
- Exceptional problem-solving skills and preparation for the unexpected

CASE MANAGEMENT

Medical case management is a specialty that is most often associated with nursing professionals and others, such as social workers, with experience in resource management for patients who require coordination of complex medical treatment. Case managers are advocates who help patients understand their health status, treatment options, and why they are important. The Case Management Society of America (www.cmsa.org) is an international nonprofit association. The association was formed in 1990 and is the leading nonprofit association dedicated to the professional development of case managers worldwide. At this time, they have more than 11,000 members in 70 chapters. They offer many educational programs to members and nonmembers alike.

CMSA offers a Certified Case Manager credential that is recognized by many, and that confirms that the case manager possesses the education, skills, and experience required to render appropriate services based on accepted principles of practice. Case managers work in a variety of specialties, including health care, mental health care, addictions, long-term care, aging, HIV/AIDS, disabilities, occupational services, child welfare, and immigrant/refugee services. They are employed in the public, nonprofit, and for-profit sectors. They are also moving into medical tourism as case managers for individuals and for companies who elect to offer a global option to employees as part of their health care coverage options, and also for insurance companies that include global care access to health plan members as a part of their benefit options.

At insurance companies, case managers have the role of gatekeeper, or medical travel facilitator, which assists the patient with travel to a specialty care provider who may be located at a university teaching hospital or research facility outside of patients' hometowns. In some cases, the case manager will coordinate the travel personally while, in other cases, a contracted travel planner may be retained to handle the travel planning that may be paid either by the health plan or by the patient. In some cases, the health plan contracts with a provider who may have their own in-house travel coordinator or facilitator who arranges travel and housing.

The CMSA has developed a nationally recognized publication titled *Standards of Practice for Case Management*. It was officially released in early 1995 and is a forerunner in establishing formal, written standards of practice from a variety of disciplines. During that same year, the National

Board approved the Ethics Statement on Case Management Practice, a peer-reviewed foundation from which to apply ethical principles to the practice of case management. Both of the aforementioned publications are available from CMSA National. Expect that, as the professional medical travel facilitator role evolves, these standards may be adopted or similar standards will be developed based upon this body of knowledge that serve the industry well.

CMSA developed the Council for Case Management Accountability (CCMA) in response to payer and purchaser expectations for demonstrating value in the marketplace. This new division of CMSA will establish evidence-based standards of practice and help its members achieve those standards through the measurement, evaluation, and reporting of outcomes. The medical tourism industry would do well to partner with CCMA to develop efficient and sound principles and practices based on the experience of nearly 20 years of development by CMSA in this area of expertise.

Through the support of a certification program, CMSA continues to enhance the level of case manager professionalism, furthering the development of a new, higher level of industry expertise. For more information, please contact the Commission for Case Manager Certification at (847) 818-0292. CCMC is a separate entity independent from CMSA.

As you develop your business model and business plan, keep in mind that a certified case manager who receives training and experience as a travel agent will become a tough competitor to your business with the proper marketing and industry knowledge. This is especially true if you have neither the medical or travel background and intend to enter this market without the necessary training and experience. If you don't have time to undertake this training on your own, you would be wise to consider a partnership with a CCM or have one as an advisor to your business in a consulting or advisory capacity.

TRAVEL PLANNER

Medical travel is more complicated than tourism without a health care objective. Professional travel agents who engage in medical travel facilitation take on a new role for which they may not have been trained. No travel agent wants their client to get hurt or suffer needlessly due to lack of understanding or planning for the nature of the illness or the recuperation comfort of the client. Travel counselors have to think beyond the basics to have a plan and a procedure in the event that their client has an unrelated complication such as a security issue, unrelated illness or injury, unplanned trip interruptions, or cultural surprises they didn't expect or for which they were unprepared.

Professional travel counselors are probably among the best coordinators for arranging health travel and tourism, but they must learn best practices, medical terminology, and know about the procedures they will coordinate. Since few have experience with medical procedures, they need a little professional development training to develop policies and procedures for this strategic addition to their business.

The American Society of Travel Agents (ASTA) and its affiliates are the world's largest and most influential travel trade association, representing over 20,000 members in more than 140 countries. ASTA is committed to upholding the professionalism and profitability of the travel agent community. In addition, ASTA promotes ethical business practices through effective representation in industry and government affairs, education, and training, and by identifying and meeting the needs of the traveling public. Members include travel agencies and agents, suppliers, tour operators, hotels, car rental firms, travel schools, and future travel professionals.

There are two categories of travel agents: Airline Reporting Corporation (ARC) accredited and non-ARC accredited sellers of travel. As of March 2007, there were 18,856 ARC-accredited agency locations. Unfortunately, non-ARC sellers of travel are extremely difficult to quantify, as no industry standard is in effect, thus making it impossible to accurately portray the size of this portion of the travel agent market.

When beginning a competitive analysis for your business plan, consider for a moment that the U.S. Bureau of Labor Statistics data from 2006 indicated that there were 87,600 workers employed in the travel agent industry. These folks, with the addition of a body of knowledge in medical terminology and how the medical side of the business works, can easily establish themselves as direct competitors and many already have established clientele who trust them.

Travel agents make money as sales agents, whereby revenue is comprised of commissions paid by the supplier and/or service fees paid by its customer. In recent years, agencies have developed different models such as the "consultant" model and "retail" model. Many travel agencies do not adhere to one model or the other but are a combination of the two. This blended model is true in medical tourism as well, as hospitals, physicians, dentists, and other providers more recently have changed their relationship and amended their contracts with facilitators. They now provide a non-commissioned price to the facilitator, and require that the facilitator act as a consultant and charge a fee for services rendered to the client by the facilitator.

Some agencies are attempting to move from a sales model to a true retail model, whereby the agency determines its own markup and pricing strategies. The retail model is attractive to agents because it allows them to set their own profit margin. However, there are only a few leisure package products on the market today that give agents this freedom. In medical tourism, you may actually design your own package products from a combination of tourism, medical, and other supplier resources. This is limited only by your creativity, contracts you can negotiate for commissions, and wholesale prices from suppliers.

In Thailand and other countries in Southeast Asia, there are an abundance of custom tailors that will provide suits in beautiful fabrics in about a day's time. One creative package that I designed combines an executive checkup with a few rounds of golf, a few custom suits, a massage, and one or two fine-dining experiences with a business class hotel on its concierge floor. This can be marketed to companies that require their executives to have this sort of annual checkup at the company's expense. The savings on the medical services in Southeast Asia more than make up for many of the extras in the package. I offered this package to a company that I knew required these checkups and the entire executive team went as a group. By having a group of 12, I was able to get group fares on business class travel, a great discount on rooms, and three complete teams of four for golf. By giving advance notice to the tailor, who I know well, he was able to rally additional staff to take measurements, assist with fabric selection, and rotate appointments so that everyone was taken care of without delay for fittings, final adjustments, and delivery. The cost of the complete package was so reasonable that many of the executives opted to take spouses along for the shopping, the golf, and the executive checkups. All in all, 20 travelers went as a group, and I joined them to ensure that their trip went well. In addition to the commissions I earned, the cost of my airfare was minimal, I received three suits at no charge, a complimentary hotel room as tour leader, a complimentary dinner, complimentary golf, and 20 new clients who trusted me and will use my services again in the future.

Of note, two of the physical exams identified the need for additional investigation warranted by diagnosed conditions. If those executives need additional medical services, they now know about how medical tourism works, they are familiar with the process, the access, the services abroad, and the quality. They will not hesitate to consider additional services, or to explore how they might expand the option to other employees in the company now that they have been there and experienced the system firsthand.

With the consultant model, the agent acts as a consultant and charges a professional fee for services. As a result, the travel consultant works primarily for the medical traveler. While most major corporate travel management companies follow this model, only a handful of independent travel agents operate their businesses in this manner. This model is likely to become the standard model for medical travel facilitators because of the nature of the services being rendered with the medical providers, and the fact that an unexpected outcome or turn of events that significantly increases the cost of the case may not warrant additional commission on a percentage of charges (POC) basis.

The typical agent earns about $30,000 to $35,000 annually. About 25% receive their compensation as salary, while about 23% are paid by commission only, according to industry surveys by the Travel Institute. The remaining 52% are paid a combination of salary and commission, or bonuses. A manager of an agency with several years of experience earns in the mid-$40,000 range.

Being a travel professional requires extensive knowledge of the travel industry as well as various computer reservation systems, known as Global Distribution Systems (GDS). Even if you are not considering working in a traditional travel agency, I strongly encourage you to enroll in a travel school to receive formal training in the travel industry to ensure success in your career as a medical travel facilitator. If you don't take the training yourself, you could always hire an agent that has credentials so that you are able to provide an ARC number to receive commissions. Attending a travel school is a crucial part if you don't already have this experience and training. There are many options out there, so it is important that you carefully research all the professional travel training possibilities. To find a travel school in your area, visit www.asta.org and select the Education/Careers section. Also check community colleges and community adult education programs. I received my training in a three-month community adult education program at the local vocational education school back in the 1970s.

When you do your due diligence on schools, ask about any approvals, registrations, or licensing by the state's Bureau of Private Postsecondary Education or other recognized accrediting body. Also inquire as to how recent the trainers' industry experience is or if they have obtained their Certified Travel Counselor (CTC) credential. As you review the curriculum, determine if it includes travel courses in geography, fares/ticketing/tariffs, industry forms and procedures, automation, sales, marketing, and travel industry operations. Does the school provide internships? Does the school offer extracurricular activities such as familiarization tours? Also, ask about hands-on training using computerized reservation systems. They should teach both domestic and international reservations as well as accessing airline availability, pricing, selling, creating a passenger name record (PNR), booking a hotel, car rental, and rail reservations. You may also want to ask who is on their advisory board and see how active the members of that advisory board are with the local ASTA chapter. Also, ask local travel agents for recommendations of schools and programs in your area. Be a prudent buyer. The program need not cost a lot of money, and the fee should not include a lot of extras (like placement assistance, etc.), which may not be necessary for your intended purpose as a medical travel professional.

TRAVEL AGENT INDIVIDUAL DESIGNATIONS AND CREDENTIALS

TRAVEL AGENT PROFICIENCY (TAP) TEST

Although it is anticipated that most candidates who take the Travel Agent Proficiency (TAP) Test have completed a travel school program or are already working in the travel industry, the test is not restrictive and has no eligibility requirements. Consequently, anyone may register to take it. Learn more about the test by visiting the Travel Institute (TI) at www.travelinstitute.com.

CERTIFIED TRAVEL ASSOCIATE (CTA) DESIGNATION

The Travel Institute's first level of professional certification focuses on the core knowledge and practical skills required for success. The CTA designation represents 40% of the study required to earn the industry pinnacle, the Certified Travel Counselor (CTC) designation. Topics include communications and technology, geography, sales and service, and the travel industry. TI offers a variety of study methods for the CTA designation. You can choose the home study program, attend one of TI's licensed schools or participate in a local study group.

TRAVEL AGENCY CREDENTIALS

The most widely recognized credential is provided by the International Airlines Travel Agent Network (IATAN). IATAN is an industry association that offers credentialing and endorsement services.

IATA/IATAN ENDORSEMENT

Once you apply for and receive an IATAN number or endorsement, your name and company information (address, phone, fax, e-mail, etc.) will be listed on a central database for suppliers to use. Suppliers can then verify that you are a legitimate travel agent, use the IATAN number to track your consumer bookings, and send you any commissions you have earned.

An IATAN number is extremely helpful in developing relationships with industry suppliers. Once you have this number, airlines, hotels, and cruise lines will allow you to book their product for your clients, as well as your own personal travel. In addition, an IATAN appointed or endorsed agency is authorized to issue airline e-tickets. There are several types of endorsements that have different financial and other business requirements. This information is provided in detail at www.iatan.org.

IATAN CREDENTIALS/ID CARDS

IATAN provides the agency community with the primary personnel registration service for the industry. The personnel list of IATAN-endorsed agencies is the primary record most international airlines will accept before considering granting reduced rate privileges.

In addition, IATAN administers the Travel Agent ID Card Program. This card is useful to both agents and suppliers. In fact, some believe that the significance of this program alone justifies the need for IATAN endorsement for professional U.S.-based travel agencies. To review the eligibility requirements to obtain an IATAN card, visit www.iatan.org.

AGENCY APPOINTMENTS

An agency, by definition, is one who is appointed by a principal. A travel agency may be appointed by many different principals such as airlines, cruise lines, hotels, and other suppliers of travel-related services. In general, there are two ways in which an agency obtains these appointments. These include direct appointment by the supplier and appointment by a coordinating body accepted by the supplier.

If you are appointed directly by a travel supplier, as is typically the case with hotels, car rental companies, and tour operators, you will deal with each supplier directly to work out an agreement as to how bookings will be made and how commissions will be awarded. For this, your attorney will have to develop a contract for you that will protect your interests and spells out the understandings between the parties and providers for international dispute resolution in the event of a disagreement about responsibilities or fees.

The second option is for the agency to be appointed by a coordinating body accepted by the various suppliers. This is a common practice among airlines. The two coordinating bodies for airlines are the Airlines Reporting Corporation (ARC) and the International Airlines Travel Agency Network (IATAN). (Note: If you plan to purchase an existing agency, keep in mind that the agency's appointments do not automatically transfer to the new owner.)

AIRLINES REPORTING CORPORATION (ARC)

The ARC is a coordinating agency that assists travel agencies and airlines in doing business with one another. The ARC provides a mechanism that facilitates carrier appointments with travel agencies and enables agencies to use ARC standard ticket stock for issuing traffic documents (vouchers, tickets, and miscellaneous charge orders [MCOs]) for carriers that participate in the system's Area Settlement Plan (ASP). Once an agency is listed by the ARC, that agency is able to issue airline tickets on the vast majority of domestic and international carriers. More than 100 domestic and international carriers have given ARC their general concurrence. The ARC acts as a clearinghouse to provide weekly reconciliation of sales, refunds, exchanges, and payment of base commissions to travel agents. Each week, agents must submit a single comprehensive report of all sales to the ARC. Then, the ASP enables agencies to report and remit all transactions to all participating carriers and claim base commissions with one weekly report and check draft.

All this terminology can be daunting for a novice and further emphasizes the need for training if you are not sure what these terms and organizations are all about. The purpose of this book is not to train you to be a travel agent. But instead, it is to give you an overview of what the domain of medical travel facilitation involves so that you can become the best professional possible at your chosen avocation.

To become an appointee through the ARC, you must meet the requirements for establishing an ARC-accredited agency. These can be found online at http://accreditation.arccorp.com/. If you decide to become a new ARC-accredited agency, you will first need to order a new application kit from the ARC. The current fee for the kit at this time is $1,500. All new locations are required to obtain and maintain a bond or irrevocable letter of credit as a condition for being appointed or retained as an ARC-listed travel agency. Today, the minimum amount required is $20,000 for the first two years, which can then drop to $10,000. Travel agency bonds or letters of credit do not protect consumers' monies. Agencies' financial security is payable only to the ARC when an agency defaults. The bond ensures that the money collected by the travel agency for tickets sold by the agency will be forwarded to the proper airlines. Remember to add that to your business plan budget if you plan to become a travel agent as part of your business model.

AGENCIES WITHOUT ARC ACCREDITATION OR APPOINTMENTS

If you don't have an ARC number, the Travel Services Intermediary program, administered by IATAN, the Travel Retailers Universal Enumeration (TRUE) program, managed by the Outside Sales Support Network (OSSN) and TravelSellers.com, managed by the National Association of Commissioned Travel Agents, may be helpful.

REGULATORY OVERSIGHT

Many states require registration to regulate how travel is sold by travel sellers. You can obtain additional information at the offices if you will operate your business in the United States in one of the states mentioned in Table 1.1.

Additionally, check with your state's department of regulatory affairs or a similar office to determine if your state has enacted any rules or oversight since the time this book was written. Be prepared to add any required fees into your business plan budget.

COMPUTER SOFTWARE AND PROGRAMS TO SUPPORT YOUR TRAVEL AGENCY BUSINESS

If you are going to operate a travel agency within your medical travel facilitator business, you will need to install a computer reservation system known as a Global Distribution System (GDS). With this system, you can book tickets and sell tickets, make reservations for clients and also book cars, hotels, and cruises, as well as rail passage and tour packages.

There are four major vendors in the United States with different pricing and who offer leases. There are others who provide regional or national coverage, but the following four are the most

TABLE 1.1
State Regulatory Oversight for Travel Sellers

California
Seller of Travel
Program Department of Justice
213-897-8065

Delaware
Division of Revenue
302-577-8200

Florida
Division of Consumer Services
Seller of Travel Programs
850-410-3805

Hawaii
Travel Agency Program
Department of Commerce & Consumer Affairs
808-586-3000

Illinois
Attorney General
217-782-1090

Iowa
Office of the Secretary of State
515-281-5204

Massachusetts
Attorney General
Antitrust and Consumer Protection Division
617-727-2200

Nevada
Department of Business and Industry
Consumer Affairs Division
702-486-7355

New York
Office of the Attorney General
518-474-2121

Pennsylvania
Public Utility Commission
Bureau of Transportation & Safety
717-783-5895

Rhode Island
Department of Business Regulation
State of Rhode Island & Providence Plantation
401-277-2246

Virginia
Consumer Affairs Office
Department of Agriculture & Consumer Service
804-786-2042

Washington
Department of Licensing
Sellers of Travel Licensing Program
360-586-0396

widely recognized in the world. They are Sabre, Amadeus, Worldspan, and Galileo. The others are usually owned by partnerships or airlines and other travel industry companies. Amadeus is the largest GDS in the world and is headquartered in Madrid, Spain, with operations facilities in Germany and other customer support facilities in France and Miami. Much of their customer base was previously identified as "System One" from the 1990s.

The Galileo system was developed originally as Apollo, an internal central reservation system for United Airlines. Their offices are in Rosemont, Illinois, near O'Hare International Airport in the Chicago metro area. It serves users in Canada, Europe, South America, Asia, and Africa.

The Sabre system is actually an acronym for Semi-Automated Business Research Environment, a GDS operated by Sabre Group Holdings, Inc., based at the Dallas/Fort Worth Airport, Texas.

Worldspan is based in Atlanta, Georgia and was formed by the merger of PARS and DATAS II GDS in February 1991. PARS partnership companies were operated by TWA and Northwest Airlines, Inc., and DATA II GDS was operated by Delta Airlines. TWA PARS was the first GDS to be installed in travel agencies back when I was in the business in 1976. It was a tremendous improvement from managing paper tariff manuals that directed agents on ticketing fares and the rules associated with them.

In December 2006, Travelport, the owner of the Galileo GDS, Gullivers Travel Associates (GTA) and a controlling share in Orbitz, agreed to acquire Worldspan. In August 2007, the acquisition was completed for $1.4 billion and Worldspan became a part of Travelport GDS, which also includes Galileo and other related businesses. Later, in September 2008, the Galileo and Apollo

GDS systems were moved from the Travelport datacenter in Denver, Colorado to the Worldspan datacenter in Atlanta, Georgia (although they continue to be run as separate systems from the Worldspan GDS).

You can find them listed in the additional resources section of this chapter or search for them online.

WEB PORTAL (ELECTRONIC MAIL)

A Web portal developer is one who develops a website where others will promote their services on a platform that is tantamount to a virtual shopping mall. The portal generally serves two audiences: consumers and providers. For consumers, it offers a one-stop source of information on doctors, hospitals, treatment packages, and other options. For providers, it serves as an online platform to market their services and products to consumers seeking a convenient "shopping mall" of options in medical tourism.

In the medical tourism world, we often encounter physicians, dentists, and facility providers, as well as medical spa and wellness providers and tour operators that pay a Web portal service a monthly fee or a pay-per-click (PPC) fee to market their services instead of developing and maintaining their own website.

Patients, their case managers, facilitators, and even their personal physicians are able to search and find doctors worldwide, based on location, specialty, procedures, and board certification, as well as treatment packages based on country and procedure. These Web portals establish partnerships with online advertising and social media and Web marketing companies because the portal drives engagement and connectivity that providers and consumers might not otherwise be able to develop and support on their own.

MEDICAL TOURISM CONCIERGE

The destination medical tourism concierge is more often a term used to describe the role of the greeter who receives the traveler at the airport on arrival, assists them to their hotel, coordinates their medical services and appointments, orients them to their agenda, provides language interpretation if necessary, advises them of safety precautions and risk management, and may actually collect payments and arrange local tours and services. They are often responsible for coordinating the patient's agenda from arrival until departure. These concierge specialists may be employed by the hospital, or the medical or dental provider, or work independently under contract. Sometimes, they contract with facilitators who use them to greet the patient and handle arrival details for a fee. Other times, they market their services directly to the medical traveler independent of the hospital or provider, and they either charge a fee for their services or are commissioned on a percentage basis by the providers to which they refer cases.

ADDITIONAL RESOURCES

TRADE AND INDUSTRY ORGANIZATIONS

American Society of Travel Agents

The ASTA has developed a membership specifically designed for individual travel agents, independent contractors and home-based agents, subject to restrictions and minimum guidelines.

For more information on travel agent membership with the ASTA, visit www.astanet.com or e-mail them at consumeraffairs@astahq.com.

ASTA Future Travel Professional (FTP) Club

This club allows one to network with more than 20,000 ASTA members who are leaders in the travel agency industry. The club was created exclusively for travel school students, and provides members access to all of their online educational materials to help prepare them for success. They also have a scholarship program that can be applied for to help pay for travel school. To qualify for membership in FTP, you must be enrolled in a travel school. For additional details, feel free to e-mail ASTA at consumeraffairs@astahq.com.

National Association of Commissioned Travel Agents, Inc.

Another travel association dedicated to outside sales employees and independent contractors is the National Association of Commissioned Travel Agents, Inc. (NACTA). For more information on NACTA, call 703-739-6826 or visit their website at www.nacta.com.

International Airlines Travel Agent Network (IATAN)—www.iatan.org
Airline Reporting Corporation—www.arccorp.com
TRAVEL AGENCY BONDS

You can research more about travel agency bonds at www.arcbonds.com. As part of the process, you will be required to provide information on a lengthy personal financial statement and a credit release form. The business financial statement must include a balance sheet and an income statement, not tax returns.

TRAVEL TRADE PUBLICATIONS

Business Travel News—www.btnonline.com
Travel Weekly—www.travelweekly.com

TRAVEL AGENCY SOFTWARE

Computer Reservation Systems/Global Distribution Systems (CRS/GDS) vendors:
Amadeus—www.us.amadeus.com
Galileo—www.galileo.com
Sabre—www.sabretravelnetwork.com
Worldspan—www.Worldspan.com

2 Business Startup

As a medical travel facilitator, you are establishing a new service business in which you will make services available to others and for which you will be paid a fee. Unlike a durable goods business, you will market other providers of medical and related services in an agency relationship.

To begin, you have to establish the business similar to all other service businesses. You will need to plan for certain contingencies, establish a budget, learn about regulatory compliance and establish compliance plans, policies, and procedures to maintain compliance, including updates to those regulations. It will be necessary to develop a marketing plan including a competitive strategy and a way to differentiate your business from every other startup medical tourism facilitator on the Internet. These are not checklists but explanations and road maps of how you will conduct your business to derive a profit.

If you don't derive a profit after a certain period of time, the tax authorities will assume you are not in a business but instead are a hobbyist. Such a determination could result in a loss of any tax incentives or advantages you assumed and could cost you financially.

You must either hire an accountant and bookkeeper or learn how to keep your own books. If you choose to do this yourself, you might benefit from attending a business startup course by the Small Business Administration's Service Corps of Retired Executives (SCORE) program. Their classes are inexpensive and well worth the investment of time. Software applications such as QuickBooks and its competitors will also help you, if you are so inclined. Keep in mind that the software does not run itself. You will still have to enter the data, and that takes time and discipline.

BUSINESS PLAN

If you intend to start a business, you should always develop a business plan. The plan will help you develop your ideas and your business model. It will be required by your bank and other lenders before they extend you credit, business loans, or overdraft protection. Your business plan should be simple, practical, and uncomplicated without jargon that is undefined or not clearly explained to a reader outside of your business.

Once you complete your plan, you will have a better grasp of whether or not this is a dream or potential reality. You may decide to pursue or delay your idea or refine it after you perform the competitive analysis. Down the road, as you are active in your business, it will serve as a road map for you to stay on track and not deviate from that which your research and investors determined to be the course and model for the business.

Your business plan has to answer a few basic questions:

- What is the nature and purpose of your business? (Keep it succinct and state it in 25 words or less.)
- What benefit are you providing, or what problem are you solving? If you have a strong business purpose, then it often builds into a strong, competitive advantage.
- What values and vision add force and substance to your business?
- What do you intend to do? While this can be harder to achieve in a couple of sentences than a couple of pages, limit this answer to about 100 words if possible.
- What credibility do you have in this industry?
- Why should clients, physicians, dentists, medical spas, hospitals, and travel suppliers trust you?

- How will you convince a naysayer that your business idea is realistic and viable?
- What are the specific strengths you have going for you to start and succeed in this business?

PRESENT STATUS OF THE BUSINESS

- Are you incorporated?
- What business form will you choose?
  - Sole proprietorship
  - Partnership
  - Corporation
  - Limited liability corporation
  - Other
- Why did you choose that particular form of business?
  - Do you plan to do so?
  - How much have you completed to this end?
- What still needs to be done? (Leave lots of room and use a word processing program so you can continue to add items as you read this book.)
- What legal protection will you need? How much will it cost?
- What intellectual property do you own? How will you protect your intellectual property?
- Do you have a logo, slogan, or motto?
- How will you protect these internationally?

DESCRIBE YOUR COMPETITIVE ADVANTAGE

- What differentiates you from every other medical travel facilitator out there on the Internet? Be specific. While it is okay to use descriptive language such as "quality," "service," and "price," these things are not competitive advantages all by themselves. What about your quality differentiates you from others? If the hospitals give the same prices to all facilitators, how will you compete on quality?
- What have you demonstrated that will convince people that you possess enough skills, training, and experience to succeed in your own business?

INDUSTRY OVERVIEW

The medical tourism industry is in a fast-growth cycle. How much do you know about it?

- Don't just echo the most recent Deloitte study on worldwide statistics; do some real research of your own. If you are going to echo a published study, why do you agree or disagree with it?
- Statistics in the markets you will serve, if you will only serve certain service lines, populations, countries, provider types, etc.
- Are you a member of the Council on the Global Integration of Healthcare (CGIH) www.cgih.org?
- Are you a member of the various trade associations involved in your business? How do you keep up-to-date with current events, regulations, and legislation in the industry?
- Outline the established evidence that supports the feasibility of your business idea.
- Can you give citations of published industry market research and overseas trends?
- Have you interviewed potential customers or suppliers you've spoken with? What did you ask them? What were the results of your research?

The questions in Table 2.1 can help you put together some initial research for your medical travel facilitator business.

TABLE 2.1
Market Research Survey

Would you travel out of your hometown for medical care?

Would you travel out of the country for medical care?

If not, why not?

If so, where would you go?

How much would you pay for a service to coordinate all aspects of your travel and medical care?

Would you travel for a physical if it was combined with other tourist and leisure activities?

Do you have a regular travel agent?

Do you have health insurance?

Does it cover care outside your hometown area?

How much is your deductible and co-pay each year?

Can you afford to pay your part of the cost share for your care through your health plan?

How will you access necessary care if you cannot afford it?

Do you know anyone who ever traveled outside their hometown or abroad for medical care?

How did that turn out for them?

What features would you expect to see as part of this service?

What is your gender?

What age group do you belong to?

MARKETING PLAN

You will need to conduct market research to determine if there is a demand for your business, products, or services. This plan also details the resources you will need to make your business a reality and meet your established goals for sales, revenue, and promotion. Without this, you risk business failure because of inadequate preparation and research, vagueness on how you will roll out your plan, and engaging in dreams and fantasies that are not supported by realistic facts that prove that your business is viable.

Here are some key questions to start thinking about for your marketing plan:

- Who is your target market? Why?
  - What age brackets are likely to use your services?
  - Do they use the Internet to shop for health services and health information?
  - Do they travel to foreign countries?
  - How do they travel? (purpose, budget, class of service, etc.)
- Where are your customers?
  - Where do they reside?
- From where will future growth come?
- With what business might you ally yourself?
- Who are your five direct competitors?
  - How long have they been established in business?
  - Will they continue to compete? If not, why?
- How is your business model different? Why do you believe it is better?
- Have others tried and failed? Why did they fail?
- Name five key threats presented by the competition.
  - How will you address them or prevent them from causing problems?
- Name five key threats presented by changes in the market or laws and regulations that could occur.
  - How will you address them or prevent them from causing problems?

- How will you promote your business?
  - How will you promote your business to those who are not Internet savvy?
  - Will you operate a website? Purchase magazine or print advertising? Develop and distribute flyers?
- How will customers buy from you? Is it easy to buy from you?

CUSTOMER SERVICE PLAN

The old saying goes, "When one customer is happy, they tell one other; when one customer is unhappy, they tell 10." That was before the Internet and social networking! What will you do to build your client list? How will you measure customer/client satisfaction? How will you measure provider satisfaction?

When you first start out, it is unlikely that you will have testimonials from satisfied clients. In health care, this is tricky because of privacy laws and confidentiality. You will need a release form in order to include customer references and testimonials for use in your marketing plan.

Before you leave this section, consider how you will integrate the following action items into your plan:

- Will you develop a customer newsletter that highlights recent new business arrangements, features packages, services, or providers?
- Will you use photographs of clients or providers?
- Will you need a model's release for each identifiable person? If yes, who will develop it for you?
- Will you post and publish prices in your marketing and promotional materials?
- How will you measure client satisfaction?
- How will you measure provider satisfaction?
- How will you implement corrective actions if warranted?
- How will you measure patient perceived clinical outcomes?
- How will you measure medical outcomes?
- What if something goes wrong? How will the situation be mitigated?
- What if there is an allegation of malpractice?
- What if there is a confirmation of negligence noticed after the client returns home?

All of these things must be addressed before you activate your business. The last thing you want is to start out with a complaint that is not mitigated and dealt with to the satisfaction of the customer (within reason, of course) and have it end up on a comment board on the Internet.

TECHNOLOGY PLAN

Think about e-mail, cell phones, computers, laptops, desktops, databases, software, e-commerce applications, websites, data, and medical records transfers to and from providers.

How will you utilize technology?

- How will you use each of these for increased efficiency and convenience?
- How much will it cost to keep up-to-date and current on software releases, equipment, and hardware?
- Will you own or lease your technology?
- Who will maintain it?
- How will you back it up and how often?
- Address technology failures and disaster recovery in your plan.
- Technology exists that helps you learn anatomy and physiology.

The Blausen Human Atlas iPhone application provides point-of-care access to 3-D animations of common medical treatments and conditions (approximately 1 to 2 minutes in length) with accompanying narration. Derived from the world's largest award-winning medical animation library, this digital resource tool has no equal in quality/quantity of animation, scientific accuracy, and ease of use. The Blausen Human Atlas iPhone digital resource tool is derived from Blausen's proprietary medical animation library, containing over 7,000 individual animations and 13,000 illustrations. The atlas is available in 10 languages and is internationally recognized as unequaled in the field of medical illustration.

The Human Atlas covers 15 general medical topics including cancer, the circulatory system, the digestive system, the ear, the endocrine system, the eye, the immune system, musculature, the central nervous system, pediatrics, reproductive systems, respiration, the skeletal system, skin, and the urinary tract, each with an average of 10 animations.

Developed on a sixth- to seventh-grade reading level, the Human Atlas provides readily accessible and understandable educational content. It is an excellent point-of-care digital tool for patients, health care professionals, students, and consumers. At the time of this writing, investing in the application if you already have an iPhone 3G takes only $20.

Personnel

- What experience, training, and skills will you need to start, operate, and grow your business?
- Will you be able to do it all yourself?
- If not, who will help and what will it cost to hire them?
- What skills will they need?
- Will you ask them to sign a noncompete and an anticircumvention agreement?
- Will they be employees or contractors?
- Who will draw up the employment agreement or independent contractor agreement?
- What benefits will you provide, if any?
- Where will they work?
- What equipment will they need?
- Will they need certifications and licenses? Will you be expected to pay for those renewals?
- Will they need professional liability insurance? Will you be expected to cover those premiums?

CONSULTANTS FOR YOUR BUSINESS

What other business associates, partners, affiliates, advisors, or consultants will you require to assist you?

To manage these relationships and get the most for your money, consider writing a request for qualifications (RFQ) and a request for proposals (RFP) that will enable you to distill exactly what services or information you want to buy from them and manage the scope of their engagement, rather than be "sold" what they have to sell. For some of the key elements for these, review the lists of elements in Tables 2.2 and 2.3.

COMPLIANCE PLAN

If there is any single body of knowledge necessary for professional advancement within the medical community, it would be a basic knowledge of the laws, rules, and regulations that affect the daily operation of a medical services business. Without this basic knowledge, it can be impossible to make critical decisions, or in some cases even realize a decision needs to be made. As a medical

TABLE 2.2
Elements for a Request for Qualifications

- Project background and current status
  - Who will be assigned to be the contact person for the project from the client?
- Scope of work
  - What will the project deliver as a final deliverable?
  - An analysis? Guidelines? Customized policies and procedures?
  - Future goals, targets, and objectives for use of the deliverable?
  - Incorporate regulations, laws, options, compliance plans, etc.
  - How long should the deliverable be useful?
- Funding
  - Where will the money come from to pay for the services?
  - Is there a budget?
- Duties
  - The consultant will be expected to …
  - The client [you] will be expected to …
- Project schedule
  - Advertise RFQ
  - Evaluate responses/reference checks/interviews/short list development
  - Letter to selected consultants and issue RFP
  - Select consultant and begin fee negotiations
  - Award contract
  - Client/consultant work
  - Project completion
- Qualification format

The qualification submitted must address the following major topics in the following order:

- **Approach.** Include a general statement of the firm's approach with particular focus on distinguishing characteristics or services.
- **Work proposed to be performed.** A discussion of the consultant's general understanding of the scope of services to be provided and the major work tasks to be performed.
- **Project schedule.** Request that the consultant include a Gantt or other graphic chart schedule indicating the anticipated duration, start, and completion dates for tasks, keyed to the scope of work, and integrating critical elements of the client's approval process. The schedule should also show consultant payments by percentage of total.
- **Key personnel.** The proposal must include information about the firm's personnel, stating their proposed role in this project, education, title, related qualifications, past relevant experience, and the date in which that person joined the firm. The qualifications package shall specifically identify the personnel assigned. Submit a statement of qualifications, demonstrating experience and previous projects successfully completed.
- **Writing sample.** Please include a minimum of one sample document prepared by or under the guidance of the proposed project manager. This sample should be illustrative of the project manager's writing skills as well as management capabilities.
- **Relevant experience.** A statement of the firm's past appropriate experience, including a brief description of the project and the client's name, address, and telephone number. Also provide a description of the consultant's exact responsibilities on the project, and clarify whether this project is an example of the firm's experience or an individual's experience.
- **References.** Request the inclusion of three professional references in the proposal. This information should include the person's name, title, address, and telephone number.
- **Additional information.** The consultant may include any other information in the proposal that will assist you in the selection process.
- **Professional service agreement.** Note any exceptions to the enclosed agreement that would prevent your firm from executing the agreement. Do not accept any request to include language to limit liability with regard to insurance and/or modification of the indemnification clauses. Proposal submittals should include a separate letter affirming the intent of the proposer's acceptance of terms and conditions contained in the agreement.
- **Certificate of insurance.** Note any exception to the certificate requirements and provisions that would prevent your firm from executing an agreement. Qualification submittals shall include a separate letter affirming the intent of the proposer's acceptance of terms and conditions contained in the certificate of insurance.
- **Instruction to applicants.** Consultant teams with qualifications that include experience in the design of projects similar in scale and scope are encouraged to respond to [where should they send this, deadlines, and how the documents should be submitted].

TABLE 2.2 *(Continued)*
Elements for a Request for Qualifications

- Selection criteria.
  - Subject matter expertise
  - Program responsiveness
  - Evaluation of consultants proposed to be engaged
  - Production capability
  - Coordination and supervision
  - Proximity
  - Client relationships and references
- Equal opportunity, if applicable

TABLE 2.3
Elements for a Request for Proposal

A request for proposal (RFP) is the primary document that is sent to suppliers that invites them to submit a proposal to provide goods or services. Internally, an RFP can also be referred to as a sourcing project, a document, or an associated event (competitive bidding). Unlike a request for information (RFI) or a request for quotation (RFQ), an RFP is designed to get suppliers to provide a creative solution to a business problem or issue. RFPs should be used carefully since they can take a lot of time for both the organization and its suppliers. However, for more complex projects, an RFP may be the most effective way to source the goods or services required.

Key elements of a request for proposal (RFP):

An overview of the business issue (why you need help or service)

Description of products or services

Detailed business requirements

Other information needed for proposal

Approach suggestions

Performance metrics

Proposal format

Due date

Selection criteria

Questions

Timeline

Point of contact

Cost breakdown (optional)

Other documents

How to respond

industry professional, you will be expected to design your compliance efforts to establish a culture within your company. You will also be tasked with assisting your clients and providers in promoting prevention, detection, and resolution of instances of conduct that do not conform to national, federal, and state laws as well as conforming to private payer health care program requirements and exemplary ethical and business policies.

To begin, you will need to research all relevant laws to ensure you meet all laws applicable to your business. Not every attorney will be knowledgeable about this, especially when you mention "medical tourism." Still, if they are a health law specialist, they may be able to guide you in regard to medical records confidentiality, privacy, the Health Insurance Portability and Accountability Act (HIPAA), and other related laws, fraud, abuse laws, anti-kickback laws, and other compliance issues that may affect you, depending on where your providers are and the relationships you establish with them for referrals and payment for your services.

Also note that in some countries it is illegal for a physician or a dentist to market their services, directly or through an agent. It will be your responsibility to know what laws apply before engaging in these relationships, or you might find yourself at the center of a major legal compliance incident.

As we discussed earlier, you may wish to prepare an RFQ and RFP for a law firm specializing in health care law to clearly define and explain the guidelines, regulations, and statutes associated with the implementation of a comprehensive compliance program for your medical travel facilitation business. The deliverable should include a manual or guide for all the knowledge, tools, and forms necessary to design, develop, and implement a compliance program for all of your medical tourism business operations. It should provide organizational tools and templates such as forms, compliance project checklists, flowcharts, and worksheets necessary to develop, implement, and maintain a compliance program for the life cycle of the business.

The deliverable may also include additional language snippets for you to integrate into your agency agreements in regard to fraud, abuse, false claims, patient confidentiality, data privacy, and security that you will need if you are based in the United States, or other countries where such laws are applicable.

If you decide to undertake this yourself and miss something, I suggest you shop around for a good professional liability insurance policy for errors and omissions, as well as coverage for officers and directors. If you do something that is punishable by a fine, your policy may cover you. If, on the other hand, you do something criminal, the policy should provide you with an attorney to defend you. Make sure that the defense is covered for any country, not just your home country.

In the event you become involved with third-party insurance reimbursement for services you or your represented providers have rendered, your compliance plan will escalate to the same responsibilities that any hospital or other medical provider has as their clearinghouse. These policies and procedures will need to be implemented into a compliance program to establish effective internal controls that promote adherence to applicable federal, national, state, and international laws, treaties, and program requirements for all applicable private and public health plans. In the United States, your business compliance program guidelines will need to be established in accordance with the Office of Inspector General (OIG) of the U.S. Department of Health and Human Services.

There are numerous websites that advertise that they sell fully customizable templates for compliance plans, but of those that I reviewed, none were particularly customized to a medical travel facilitator business. Few had any mention of international resources that would be useful, and your business activities will likely be both domestic and international. Finally, check that your business activities are legal from your home or place of business.

BASIC PRIVACY LAWS

In the United States, we all have a right to expect privacy. As such, if our privacy is invaded, the law allows a client or other aggrieved party to bring a lawsuit against an individual or company that unlawfully intrudes into his or her private affairs, discloses his or her private information, publicizes him or her in a false light, or appropriates his or her name for personal gain. This could have several implications in a business such as a medical travel facilitator company.

Modern tort law includes four categories of invasion of privacy, the two most relevant being the public disclosure of private facts, where there is dissemination of truthful private information such as medical records that are not of public concern and may be found objectionable by a reasonable person, and appropriation, which involves using the patient's name or likeness in marketing, unauthorized testimonials, etc., to obtain some sort of benefit.

In determining whether intrusion has occurred, one of three main considerations may be involved: expectation of privacy; whether there was an intrusion, invitation, or exceedance of invitation; or deception, misrepresentation, or fraud to gain admission. Intrusion is the gathering of information and not a publication tort where a legal wrong occurs at the time of the intrusion. In this case, no publication is necessary.

There was a recent case where a medical travel facilitator was not paid for services rendered to a client and, in retaliation, published the client's medical records and name on the Internet out of spite. The facilitator was located in a foreign country. While you might think that is unconscionable, it is not the only time this has happened.

DEVELOPING A MEDICAL RECORDS AND ELECTRONIC DATA PRIVACY AND SECURITY PLAN

In order to operate a medical travel facilitator business, you will have to include several safeguards to protect medical records and other electronic data entrusted to you. You will need to become familiar with several specific regulations and laws, and you might be held accountable criminally and civilly in perhaps more than one country where records and data are exchanged with providers with which you do business.

You will need to establish a structured and programmatic approach that is practicable and not so difficult that once you write the plan and the process, you shelve it and never operationalize it or monitor its effectiveness. If you are called upon to defend that you didn't let something slip through the cracks, those audits and processes will be crucial in your defense.

To develop your plan, you will need to establish some priorities to mitigate risk exposures and eliminate the ones you can, while controlling others to the extent that you can. No one expects you to become the chief information security officer (CISO), but you will not be exonerated from the responsibility of meeting compliance standards, whether it is you personally or someone contracted to handle this on your behalf.

To narrow down priorities, if you build your business plan and explain your model in writing, you can approach one of many available certified information systems security professionals (CISSP) to assist you and your attorney in focusing on what you need to do before you activate your business and put the first client's information into your computer. Have them assist you in determining what is critical to your business operations and which business processes, if affected, would cost them their credentials or their license if something went wrong.

Establish a set of objectives that describe how your data and information security plan will function in a perfect world, with special attention paid to all compliance regulations for which you are connected or responsible. This is where the technology risk assessment comes in, and your trusted advisors will earn their keep in establishing the objectives, the plan, and the budget. If you need help, contact the Healthcare Information Management Systems Society (www.himss.org) for some leads to expertise with this type of a project.

Second, do a penetration test or a risk assessment. This is a job for the CISSP. Create a dummy record set that mimics the record set you will receive from clients and transmit to providers. You will need to identify holes in your security systems, processes, and data handling in the form of a gap analysis. Then, use the findings as a baseline to measure your progress and process improvement.

While you are at it, immediately fix any gaping holes. Don't wait for problems to arise in which a client is actually involved. Make sure you keep a record of all the steps you took to mitigate and correct a situation in a log book that is part of your official corporate records.

Next, operate in your environment to determine if it is really secure. Be vigilant to determine and record how you identify things that go wrong and record what action steps you took to correct any identified problems. You have to be able to react quickly if there is a security breach.

If you have excellent records of security controls and processes that you have in place and that you regularly test for penetration and risk, you will be able to demonstrate due diligence and best efforts to control and monitor your operations and handle any issues that may arise. If an auditor wants to inspect your operations, this will serve you well.

There are some very broad and extensive frameworks that address data and electronic security. Two of the most popular are ISO 27001 and Control Objectives for Information and Related Technology (COBIT). No doubt your CISSP consultant will be familiar with both and direct you as to how each is involved in standardizing your plan to meet regulatory requirements and best practices.

ISO 27001 was formerly known as ISO 17799, which provides a "model for establishing, implementing, operating, monitoring, reviewing, maintaining, and improving an Information Security Management System." Published in 2005, it is the specification for an Information Security Management System (ISMS). "The design implementation of an organization's ISMS is influenced by their needs, objectives, security requirements, the process employed, and the size and structure of the organization." It uses the plan-do-check-act (PDCA) cycle as a model. This information will be invaluable for you to have as you plan and publish a request for qualifications and a request for proposals from your vendors specifying what exactly you require for your business.

As the industry matures, it may prove beneficial for you to seek ISO 27001 certification if your business and, consequently, concerns over risks grow. More information on the information security management system (ISMS) certification process can be found at www.27000.org/ismsprocess.htm.

COBIT is an international open standard that defines requirements for the control and security of sensitive data and provides a reference framework. COBIT was introduced in the 1990s by the IT Governance Institute and is a set of best practices, measures, and other methods for information security, as defined by the IT Governance Institute and the Information Systems and Audit Control Association. COBIT consists of an executive summary, management guidelines, frameworks, control objectives, an implementation toolset, and audit guidelines. Extensive support is provided, including a list of critical success factors for measuring security program effectiveness and benchmarks for auditing purposes. COBIT has been revised several times since its inception, and its upgrades are published at regular intervals. Currently, the standards for Version 4.1 are available. Find out more about COBIT at www.isaca.org.

THE RED FLAGS RULES: FAIR AND ACCURATE CREDIT TRANSACTIONS ACT (FACTA) COMPLIANCE

Medical travel facilitators accept payments from individuals who have to pay for services rendered. Accepting credit cards as a form of payment does not, in and of itself, make an entity a creditor. First, you must examine some of the official terminology from the "Red Flags Rules." The Federal Trade Commission (FTC), the federal bank regulatory agencies, and the National Credit Union Administration (NCUA) have issued regulations (the Red Flags Rules) requiring financial institutions and creditors to develop and implement written identity theft prevention programs as part of the Fair and Accurate Credit Transactions (FACT) Act of 2003.

A **transaction account** is a deposit or other account from which the owner makes payments or transfers. Transaction accounts include checking accounts, negotiable order of withdrawal accounts, savings deposits subject to automatic transfers, and share draft accounts.

A **creditor** is any entity that regularly extends, renews, or continues credit; any entity that regularly arranges for the extension, renewal, or continuation of credit; or any assignee of an original creditor who is involved in the decision to extend, renew, or continue credit. Creditors include, but are not limited to, finance companies, automobile dealers, mortgage brokers, utility companies, and telecommunications companies. Where nonprofit and government entities defer payment for goods or services, they, too, are to be considered creditors. Most creditors, except for those regulated by the Federal Reserve Bank regulatory agencies and the National Credit Union Administration (NCUA), come under the jurisdiction of the Federal Trade Commission (FTC).

A covered account is an account used mostly for personal, family, or household purposes, and that involves multiple payments or transactions. Covered accounts include credit card accounts, mortgage loans, automobile loans, margin accounts, cell phone accounts, utility accounts, checking accounts, and savings accounts. A covered account is also an account for which there is a foreseeable risk of identity theft—for example, small business or sole proprietorship accounts.

The Red Flags Rule was developed pursuant to the Fair and Accurate Credit Transactions Act of 2003. Under the rule, financial institutions and creditors with covered accounts must have identity theft prevention programs to identify, detect, and respond to patterns, practices, or specific activities that could indicate identity theft.

Guidelines issued by the FTC, the Federal Reserve banking agencies, and the NCUA (ftc.gov/opa/2007/10/redflag.shtm) should be helpful in assisting covered entities in designing their programs. A supplement to the guidelines identifies twenty-six possible "red flags." These red flags are not a checklist, but rather, examples that financial institutions and creditors may want to use as a starting point.

The red flags fall into five categories:

- Alerts, notifications, or warnings from a consumer reporting agency
- Suspicious documents
- Suspicious, personally identifying information, such as a suspicious address
- Unusual use of—or suspicious activity relating to—a covered account
- Notices from customers, victims of identity theft, law enforcement authorities, or other businesses about possible identity theft in connection with covered accounts

Depending on how you operate and structure your business model, if you are going to handle credit accounts or be involved in a process of securing credit for the payment of health care services through a medical finance company, you may fall under the purview of this rule. Ask a qualified attorney for guidance before making assumptions that you are excused from compliance.

HEALTH INSURANCE PORTABILITY AND ACCOUNTABILITY ACT (HIPAA) PRIVACY AND SECURITY COMPLIANCE

Among the questions regarding legal matters rarely considered by most startup medical travel facilitators without experience in the health care industry in the United States are to what extent are they governed by the Health Insurance Portability and Accountability Act (HIPAA) of 1996 and what are their obligations under HIPAA with respect to patient privacy? HIPAA applies to intermediaries and facilitators in the United States who facilitate medical tourism abroad in most medical tourism and global health care arrangements.

HIPAA is a United States federal statute that includes several sections intended to protect the privacy and security of an individual's personal health information (PHI). This PHI includes information created or received by a health care provider, health plan, insurance plan, employer, or health care clearinghouse that relates to the past, present, or future physical and/or mental health condition or provision of health care to an individual. It is also the past, present, or future payment for the provision of health care to an individual that identifies or provides a way to identify that individual.

"Covered entities" are health care providers and others who translate data into required formats, including but not limited to:

- Physicians
- Hospitals
- Health plans
- Health insurance and managed care companies
- Employer-sponsored benefit plans
- Health care clearinghouses
- Web portals
- Intermediaries between providers and payers

HIPAA security rules are applicable to covered entities that transmit, create, or receive PHI in electronic form, and these rules require reasonable physical, technical, and administrative safeguards to protect the security of PHI. While you may not exactly be a "covered entity," and therefore feel as though you may be excused from requirements of compliance, this last application would clearly implicate you as a medical travel facilitator if you become a "business associate" of a covered entity.

If your client will receive medical care abroad or aftercare in the states, and you facilitate any part of that episode of care, you may or may not be liable for compliance under HIPAA with respect to the use and disclosure of the PHI of the patient, but the overseas hospital or treating physician or dentist may still be held liable if the violation of any applicable privacy laws of the local country where the treatment was provided occur. Both the facilitator and/or the foreign provider may also be held liable if they violate any agreement they entered into with the client, or any policy to which they have adopted that the patient relied upon, governing the use and disclosure of the medical information of the client.

As a facilitator, keep in mind that while HIPAA preempted all less stringent state privacy laws, to the extent a state's privacy laws are more stringent, they remain in effect and are applicable in addition to the requirements of HIPAA. Therefore, whether or not you are a business associate of a covered entity under HIPAA, you should ask a competent health law attorney for advice as to whether any state laws would be applicable in the state in which it is located and in which the clients you serve reside. California is one of the states to which this applies.

While it may not be the case at the present time, this book's usefulness will last beyond the present-day adoption of medical tourism and globally integrated care by employers and health plans. For these clearly implicated covered entities, if they are going to offer access to care received abroad by means of medical travel, they will have to bring all their providers into compliance and require compliance and performance by contract in their provider network participation agreements. Since the health plan in the United States is a covered entity, it is not, in many instances, allowed to disclose protected health information to third parties unless the third party enters into an agreement to become a "business associate" of the health plan.

As a "business associate," any intermediary or facilitator is required to use appropriate safeguards to prevent use or disclosure of the PHI, other than as provided for by its contract with the health plan; report to the health plan any use or disclosure of the information not provided for by its contract of which it becomes aware; and ensure that any subcontractor to whom it provides PHI agrees to the same restrictions and conditions that apply to the business associate. Since your role will fall under this definition of business associate, you will likely see an appendix to contracts from providers, health plans, or employers if they have a nexus in the United States. This addendum, or appendix, will require that you accept responsibility as a "business associate" as defined by HIPAA. As such, you will be required to satisfy individual rights requirements pertaining to access, amendment, and accounting on behalf of the health plan; make internal practices, books, and records relating to the use and disclosure of PHI available to the U.S. Secretary of Health and Human Services; and return or use reasonable care to destroy all PHI at the termination of the agreement.

If you violate HIPAA, the penalties are quite stiff. "Covered entities" can be subject to both civil and monetary penalties as well as imprisonment. The fines can be as high as $50,000, and if the offense was with intent to sell, transfer, or use individually identifiable health information (IIHI) for commercial advantage, personal gain, or malicious harm, the fines can escalate up to $250,000. While the business associate may not be directly liable to the government or individual patients, the business associate agreement will likely require that the business associate indemnify the covered entity for damages incurred by the covered entity that arise out of violations by the facilitator as a business associate. The covered entity may also add a provision in their contract regarding your duty for compliance, from which they will not excuse you, no matter how much you attempt to negotiate it away.

The provision typically looks like this:

To the extent and so long as, required by applicable law (whether the destination country, United States, or any other jurisdiction), the Facilitator does hereby agree it will appropriately safeguard Patients' personal health information (PHI) made available to or obtained by the Facilitator in accordance with the provisions set forth in the "Health Care Business Associate Agreement" enclosed hereto as Exhibit G. In implementation of such assurance and without limiting the obligations of the Facilitator otherwise set forth in this Agreement or imposed by applicable law, the Facilitator hereby agrees to comply with applicable requirements of law relating to PHI, to the extent that the Hospital would be required to comply with such requirements.

The Facilitator agrees that it will:

a) Not use or further disclose such PHI other than as permitted or required by this Agreement;
b) Not use or further disclose the information in a manner that would violate the requirements of applicable law;
c) Use appropriate safeguards to prevent use or disclosure of such information other than as provided for by this Agreement.

Whether or not the Facilitator or Hospital is now, or may become, subject to the U.S. Health Insurance Portability and Accountability Act (HIPPA) of 1996 and the regulations promulgated thereunder, the Parties will store, transmit, and use patient medical information according to standards and policies no less stringent than those set forth by HIPAA and the regulations promulgated thereunder from time to time.

The word "indemnify" as used above means you will make them whole and restore them back to the financial position they were in prior to the incident. The language used in the contract typically includes the following indemnification provision:

Indemnification

The Facilitator will hold harmless and will indemnify the Hospital from any and all liability, loss, damage, claim, or expense of any kind, including costs and attorneys' fees which result from negligent, reckless, or willful acts or omissions by the Facilitator, regarding the duties and obligations of the Facilitator under this Agreement to Participants, based on any laws that are applicable to the Facilitator rendering its services to Participants.

In plain language, it means that they will come to the facilitator who caused the violation and seek, not just the fine, but all the legal and defense costs associated with the violation. Worse, even if you carry a professional liability policy, if it does not cover you for liability by contract (ask your agent and read the policy yourself), you may be exposed to cover the expense without insurance.

As a business associate, there are many practices that you should research and implement. A sample manual of policies, procedures, and monitoring mechanisms that can be used by a medical group or facilitator is available for purchase on CD-ROM at www.askmariatodd.com, or by contacting me directly at maria@mariatodd.com. It includes many of the forms, policies, and procedures you will need to establish your compliance program under the requirements of HIPAA. All the documents may be edited to customize your compliance plan. It is available for purchase and may also be delivered to you electronically. The manual contains over 300 pages of forms, policies, and procedures that will save you the hundreds of hours that it takes to develop such a document set.

In order to familiarize you with what the business associate contract addendum looks like, I have included a model in Figure 2.1 for your review. It is a lengthy and important document, one that will no doubt add costs to your startup as a facilitator as well as ongoing expenses to comply and keep detailed records. It will also demonstrate the need for transmitting medical records to providers abroad using secure, encrypted transmissions and chain-of-custody measures to defend your policies and practices in the event of an allegation of wrongdoing. One such service for accomplishing this is available for a nominal fee through the Council on the Global Integration of Health Care (CGIH), a nonprofit association. For more information about that service, visit www.cgih.org.

HEALTH CARE BUSINESS ASSOCIATE AGREEMENT

[Name of the Facilitator] ("Business Associate")_____ and [Name of the Hospital] (the "Covered Entity") wish to enter into this Health Care Business Associate Agreement (the "Agreement") this _____ day of _____, 20_____.

RECITALS

WHEREAS, _____, is a covered entity under the Health Insurance Portability and Accountability Act ("HIPAA") of 1996 and, as such, must comply with the Administrative Simplification Provisions of HIPAA, including the Privacy Standards, as of the dates indicated by relevant governmental agencies.

WHEREAS, Covered Entity, is interested in Business Associate furnishing _____ services to Covered Entity, and Business Associate has expertise necessary to provide such services. In order for Business Associate to furnish such services to Covered Entity, Covered Entity must furnish reasonable and necessary Protected Health Information (PHI) to Business Associate and Business Associate may use such information to perform its obligations to Covered Entity.

DEFINITIONS

Terms used, but not otherwise defined, in this Agreement shall have the same meanings as those terms in 45 CFR 160.103 and 164.501.

Specific Definitions

(a) *Business Associate. "Business Associate" shall mean _____;*
(b) *Covered Entity. "Covered Entity" shall mean _____;*
(c) *Individual. "Individual" shall have the same meaning as the term "individual" in 45 CFR 164.501 and shall include a person who qualifies as a personal representative in accordance with 45 CFR 164.502(g);*
(d) *Payment. "Payment" shall have the same meaning as the term "payment" in 45 CFR 164.501, which includes billing, collection activities, review of medical services with respect to medical necessity, appropriateness of care, or justification of charges, and disclosure to consumer reporting agencies the name, address, date of birth, social security number, payment history, account number, and name and address of the health care provider;*
(e) *Privacy Rule. "Privacy Rule" shall mean the Standards for Privacy of Individually Identifiable Health Information in 45 CFR part 160 and part 164, subparts A and E;*
(f) *Protected Health Information. "Protected Health Information" shall have the same meaning as the term "protected health information" in 45 CFR 164.501, limited to the information created or received by Business Associate from or on behalf of Covered Entity;*
(g) *Required by Law. "Required by Law" shall have the same meaning as the term "required by law" in 45 CFR 164.501; and*
(h) *Secretary. "Secretary" shall mean the U.S. Secretary of Health and Human Services or his/her designee.*

Obligations and Activities of Business Associate

(a) *Business Associate agrees to not use or disclose Protected Health Information other than as permitted or required by the Agreement or as Required by Law;*

FIGURE 2.1   Model HIPAA Business Associate Addendum.

(b) *Business Associate agrees to use appropriate safeguards to prevent use or disclosure of Protected Health Information other than as provided for by this Agreement;*

(c) *Business Associate agrees to mitigate, to the extent practicable, any harmful effect that is known to Business Associate of a use or disclosure of Protected Health Information by Business Associate in violation of the requirements of this Agreement or applicable law, to include any potential harmful effects due to amendments in applicable law;*

(d) *Business Associate agrees to report to Covered Entity any use or disclosure of Protected Health Information not provided for by this Agreement of which it becomes aware;*

(e) *Business Associate agrees to ensure that any agent, including a subcontractor, to whom it provides Protected Health Information received from, or created or received by Business Associate on behalf of Covered Entity, agrees to the same restrictions and conditions that apply through this Agreement to Business Associate with respect to such information;*

(f) *Business Associate agrees to provide access, at the request of Covered Entity, and in a reasonable time and manner, to Protected Health Information in a Designated Record Set to Covered Entity or as directed by Covered Entity, to an Individual in order to meet the requirements under 45 CFR 164.524;*

(g) *Business Associate agrees to make any amendments(s) to Protected Health Information in a Designated Record Set that the Covered Entity directs or agrees to pursuant to 45 CFR 164.526 at the request of Covered Entity or an Individual, and in a reasonable time and manner; and*

(h) *Business Associate agrees to provide to Covered Entity, or an Individual, in a reasonable time and manner, information to permit Covered Entity to respond to a request by an Individual for an accounting of disclosures of Protected Health Information in accordance with 45 CFR 164.528.*

Permitted Uses and Disclosures by Business Associate

(a) *Except as otherwise limited in this Agreement, Business Associate may use Protected Health Information for health services payment, proper management and administration of the Business Associate, or to carry out legal responsibilities of the Business Associate, to include payment services for medical service accounts;*

(b) *Except as otherwise limited in this Agreement, Business Associate may disclose Protected Health Information that is permitted or Required by Law, and/or if Business Associate obtains reasonable assurances from the person to whom the information is disclosed that it will remain confidential and used or further disclosed only as permitted or Required by Law or for the purpose for which it was disclosed to the person, and the person notifies the Business Associate of any instances of which it is aware in which the confidentiality of the information has been breached;*

(c) *Business Associate may use Protected Health Information for payment of health care service accounts, as reasonably necessary to secure payment on such accounts; and*

(d) *Business Associate may use Protected Health Information to report violations of law to appropriate Federal and State authorities, consistent with 45 CFR 164.502(j)(1).*

Obligations of Covered Entity

(a) *Covered Entity shall notify Business Associate of any limitation(s) in its notice of privacy practices of Covered Entity in accordance with 45 CFR 164.520, to the extent that such limitation may affect Business Associate's use or disclosure of Protected Health Information;*

FIGURE 2.1 *(Continued)*   Model HIPAA Business Associate Addendum.

(b) *Covered Entity shall notify Business Associate of any changes in, or revocation of, permission by Individual to use or disclose Protected Health Information, to the extent that such changes may affect Business Associate's use or disclosure of Protected Health Information;*

(c) *Covered Entity shall notify Business Associate of any restriction to the use or disclosure of Protected Health Information that Covered Entity has agreed to in accordance with 45 CFR 164.522, to the extent that such restriction may affect Business Associate's use or disclosure of Protected Health Information; and*

(d) *Covered Entity shall provide Business Associate with reasonably necessary Protected Health Information so that Business Associate is able to carry out its assigned duties with respect to billing and collection of health care services.*

Permissible Requests by Covered Entity

Covered Entity shall not request Business Associate to use or disclose Protected Health Information in any manner that would not be permissible under the Privacy Rule if done by Covered Entity. Covered Entity may use or disclose Protected Health Information for management and administrative activities of Business Associate.

Term and Termination

(a) *Term. The Term of this Agreement shall be effective as of _____, and shall terminate when all the Protected Health Information provided by Covered Entity to Business Associate, or created or received by Business Associate on behalf of Covered Entity, is destroyed or returned to Covered Entity, or, if it is infeasible to return or destroy Protected Health Information, protections are extended to such information, in accordance with the termination provisions in this Section;*

(b) *Termination for Cause. Upon either party's knowledge of a material breach by the other party, the party shall give written notice of the breach, and:*

   (1) *Provide a reasonable opportunity for the other party to cure the breach and end the violation and terminate this Agreement if that party does not cure the breach and end the violation within a reasonable time, as specified in the written notice; and*

   (2) *Immediately terminate this Agreement if the other party has breached a material term of this Agreement and a cure is not possible.*

(c) *Effect of Termination.*

   (1) *Except as provided in paragraph (2) of this section, upon termination of this Agreement, for any reason, Business Associate shall return or destroy all Protected Health Information received from Covered Entity, or created or received by Business Associate on behalf of Covered Entity. This provision shall apply to Protected Health Information that is in the possession of subcontractors or agents of Business Associate. Business Associate shall retain no copies of the Protected Health Information; and*

   (2) *In the event that Business Associate determines that returning of destroying the Protected Health Information is infeasible, Business Associate shall provide to Covered Entity notification of the conditions that make return or destruction infeasible. Upon written notice that return or destruction of Protected Health*

FIGURE 2.1 *(Continued)*   Model HIPAA Business Associate Addendum.

Information is infeasible, Business Associate shall extend the protections of this Agreement to such Protected Health Information and limit further uses and disclosures of such Protected Health Information to those purposes that make the return or destruction infeasible, for so long as Business Associate maintains such Protected Health Information.

Miscellaneous

(a) *Regulatory References. A reference in this Agreement to a section in the Privacy Rule means the section as in effect or as amended;*

(b) *Amendment. The Parties agree to take such action as is necessary to amend this Agreement as is necessary for Covered Entity to comply with the requirements of the Privacy Rule and the Health Insurance Portability and Accountability Act (HIPAA) of 1996, Pub. L. No. 104-191;*

(c) *Survival. The respective rights and obligations of Business Associate to not disclose and/or safeguard Protected Health Information shall survive the termination of this Agreement;*

(d) *Interpretation. Any ambiguity in this Agreement shall be resolved to permit Covered Entity to comply with the Privacy Rule;*

(e) *Complete Agreement. This Agreement, including any exhibits or attachments attached hereto, constitutes the entire agreement among the parties with respect to this subject matter, and supersedes any and all prior agreements or statements among the parties relating to the same subject matter. This agreement may not be amended, modified, or terminated except by a writing signed by both parties; and*

(f) *If any provision of this Agreement shall be found or determined to be invalid or unenforceable, such invalidity or unenforceability shall attach only to the specific provision and shall not in any way affect or render invalid or unenforceable any other provision of this Agreement.*

Please confirm that the foregoing is in accordance with your understanding of our agreement by signing and returning to us a copy of this letter.

[Business Associate Name]

By: _____

Name: _____

Title: _____

Date: _____

Hospital Name

By: _____

Name: _____

Title: _____

Date:_____

FIGURE 2.1 *(Continued)*   Model HIPAA Business Associate Addendum.

In a nutshell, HIPAA's standards require that all health care providers in the United States or their business associates apply and enforce certain protections. The implementation process will be different for every organization depending on its size, budget, risks, and infrastructure complexity. But, regardless of each organization's different needs in terms of HIPAA implementation, the general HIPAA requirements stay the same:

- Organizations must have an administrative authority, or "Privacy Officer," in charge of managing and enforcing HIPAA compliance rules, regulations, and efforts. There should be a clear set of guidelines in place regulating who is and isn't permitted to access patient information. All access to sensitive data and systems should be monitored.
- Documentation should be provided to patients informing them of their rights.
- All corporate systems, machines, and buildings must have physical and technical data and intrusion protection controls to prevent malicious hacking and other unauthorized access.
- There must be a traffic-monitoring device, such as a firewall, in place to examine activity coming into and leaving the organization's network.
- Management should practice risk assessments, data-handling policies, data loss prevention (DLP), and record all security policies and procedures.
- All organizations affected by HIPAA should ask employees to undergo some form of HIPAA training to make sure the rules and regulations are clear and everyone is on the same page. It should be clearly identified in the training sessions what constitutes sensitive patient information, how it should be protected, and who is allowed to access that information. This will avoid an incident down the road in which an employee claims that he or she was unaware that a patient's name is considered "sensitive" data.

As a professional medical travel facilitator, take the time to learn how to be compliant and establish your business practices in a compliant manner. Please obtain appropriate legal counsel to ensure that you took all the necessary steps to give your business every opportunity to succeed.

HEALTH INFORMATION TECHNOLOGY FOR ECONOMIC AND CLINICAL HEALTH (HITECH)

A portion of the new economic stimulus bill, called the Health Information Technology for Economic and Clinical Health (HITECH) Act, will have a significant impact on employers that sponsor group health plans. The HITECH Act effectively mandates that group health plans secure the protected health information (PHI) of plan participants by using a technology or methodology to be specified by guidelines that are not yet finalized at the time this was written. I expect that it will carry through to fruition, so it is imperative that you research your role and responsibilities for compliance. Plan sponsors that fail to bring their group health plans into compliance are at risk for enforcement actions, large penalties, class action lawsuits, and injuries to reputation. By any measure, this is the toughest federal law ever enacted to regulate employee benefit plans. If you will facilitate medical travel for employers or insurers, this will undoubtedly affect you. While you may not be involved in this now, keep this handy for future reference in the event that your business model includes clients from these organizations.

The HITECH Act, which amends the privacy and security regulations promulgated under the Health Insurance Portability and Accountability Act (HIPAA) of 1996, creates the following new risks and penalties:

- **Notice to individuals and media outlets.** If unsecured PHI is "accessed, acquired, or disclosed" by or to an unauthorized person, a detailed notification of the breach must be provided to each affected individual and to the Department of Health and Human

Services (HHS). If the breach affects more than 500 residents of the same state, notice must be published in prominent media outlets serving that state. If the breach affects smaller numbers of individuals, and ten or more of those individuals cannot be located, then, in most cases, notice must be posted in major print media. Such notifications may increase the risk of class action lawsuits under state privacy laws. Plans can avoid these breach notification requirements by securing PHI using a technology or methodology to be specified by HHS guidance.

- **Penalties for violations.** If HIPAA or the HITECH Act is violated due to willful neglect, HHS may be required to assess a penalty in the amount of $50,000 per violation, with no maximum penalty for multiple violations. The term "willful neglect" is not defined, but arguably that standard will apply whenever there is a failure to adopt safeguards and procedures required by law. Lesser penalties may be imposed where the violation does not result from willful neglect, or is corrected within 30 days of the date it is discovered (or should have been discovered).
- **Enforcement.** The Secretary of HHS is required to fully investigate cases if an initial investigation of a complaint indicates possible willful neglect. Regulations issued within three years will allow harmed individuals to share in penalties collected under the Act, which should increase the likelihood and frequency of complaints. State Attorney Generals may also sue under the HITECH Act to obtain an injunction or damages of up to $25,000, increasing the likelihood of uneven interpretation of the law.

Plan sponsors should act quickly to limit their exposure under the HITECH Act. While many of the provisions are subject to guidance that will be issued over the next 3 years, there are steps that can and should be taken now. These are listed in Figure 2.2 for your convenience. After the dates indicated, the list will still be valid. You will simply have to be compliant prior to activating your business.

- Review HHS guidelines, expected by mid-April 2009, on the technologies or methodologies that make PHI unusable, unreadable, or indecipherable to unauthorized individuals (so that it is no longer "unsecured" PHI) and consider implementing.
- This is particularly relevant to professional medical travel facilitators that receive and transmit records to hospitals, clinicians, and others via unsecured means such as AOL, Gmail, and Yahoo! e-mail accounts.
- If you do not adopt the technologies or methodologies that make PHI unusable, unreadable, or indecipherable to unauthorized individuals, you must comply with new notification rules for any breach of such "unsecured PHI" effective 30 days after notification regulations are issued. (Regulations are due by August 16, 2009, so notification requirements will apply no later than September 15, 2009.)
- Review HHS guidelines, expected by January 1, 2010 (and to be updated annually), on the most effective and appropriate technical safeguards for protecting electronic PHI and consider implementing. Bring this to the attention of your chief technology or information officer, or a carefully selected external consultant with valid and current certified information systems security professional (CISSP) credentials.
- Comply with new HITECH requirements regarding the minimum necessary PHI that may be used and disclosed (including disclosure to the plan's business associates) effective February 17, 2010. (Further HHS guidelines are expected by August 17, 2010.)
- Effective February 17, 2010, agree to individual requests for restrictions on disclosure of PHI to the plan for purposes of payment or health care operations if the PHI relates to an item or service for which the individual paid in full, out-of-pocket.
- Comply with new marketing restrictions effective February 17, 2010.
- Abide by new rules restricting the sale of PHI beginning no later than February 17, 2011, depending on when regulations are issued.
- Review future HHS guidelines on applicability of new requirements to log disclosures of PHI made for treatment, payment, and health care operations through an electronic health record effective January 1, 2011 or January 1, 2014 (depending on when the records were acquired).
- If you use a system that stores electronic health records, individuals must be permitted to receive access to PHI in an electronic format and to direct it to be sent to another person or entity effective February 17, 2010.
- Anticipate a request for due diligence by "covered entities" that will be required to conduct an inventory of business associates. HITECH specifically provides that business associates include data transmission service providers.
- Amend business associate agreements by February 17, 2010 to reflect the new privacy and security requirements.
- Amend HIPAA privacy and security amendment to each group health plan to reflect the new requirements (e.g., minimum necessary disclosure to the plan sponsor).
- Update HIPAA privacy policies and procedures to reflect the new privacy requirements (recommended by February 17, 2010 and as needed as additional guidelines are issued).
- Update HIPAA security policies and procedures to reflect the new security requirements (recommended by February 17, 2010 and as needed as additional guidelines are issued).
- Update HIPAA privacy notice to reflect new privacy requirements (recommended by February 17, 2010).
- Update HIPAA authorization if PHI will be disclosed for marketing purposes (by February 17, 2010) or sold for certain purposes (beginning no later than February 17, 2011, depending on when regulations are issued).
- Conduct privacy and security workforce training as new guidelines are issued.

FIGURE 2.2   HITECH compliance checklist and work plan for medical travel facilitators.

3 Developing a Business Startup Budget

In order to avoid surprises, once you develop your requests for qualifications and requests for proposals, you may wish to start developing a budget and find out what these services will cost you to activate your business. Start off by completing the chart below in Figure 3.1 with a best "guesstimate" of expenses for the items listed. Then, do some research and see how close you were to reality.

FINANCIAL PROJECTIONS

How much can you make as a professional medical travel facilitator? Will your business have the potential to pay you a reasonable salary and also have funds left over for further expenses and development? For your profit forecast, Table 3.1 is a worksheet you can use to begin your rough estimations.

In addition to a profit forecast, you also have to develop a formula to describe your charge-out price for your time. How much do you need to make to cover your time and expenses in addition to an expected profit? To help you calculate this, use the worksheet in Figure 3.2.

CASH MANAGEMENT PLAN

What happens if you are not paid by a client or their check bounces? What happens if a provider that owes you a commission fee pays slowly, late, or not at all? What happens if your customer expresses dissatisfaction with your service and requests a refund for services rendered after you have done your best but it truly wasn't enough?

You may have to advance ongoing fees for utilities, cell phone service, secure data transmission services to transfer medical records to and from providers, and to pay for your website hosting and insurance premiums for professional liability. You will need to establish a cash reserve to be able to pay your bills and keep your business in operation, as these things will happen sooner or later. Good cash flow is not just a spreadsheet of numbers. This is where anyone examining your business for investment potential or evaluating your ability to repay loans will focus intently. This forecast will include examples of how you projected your sales and how you priced your product and estimated your costs. You should probably outline how you arrived at your assumptions and anticipate a good grilling, even if only from your accountant if you decide to bootstrap your business.

To help you get started, you will need to develop a cash flow forecast. The example in Figure 3.3 will help you get started. Keep in mind that not every commission payment comes in on time, and, sometimes, checks for payment for your services bounce. Decide on a realistic factor for this and work it into the formula and cash management strategy. In every business I have ever started, I always added a contingency fund contribution to my plan. If I didn't need it, I saved it for a rainy day. Sometimes it rained in buckets and I was glad I had it stashed. Leave it there and pretend it is not there when you don't absolutely have to tap into it. The minute we feel cash crunched, we have a tendency to allow our creativity to wane and divert energy to depression and fear, and business is impeded. Prepare at least 2 years of cash flow so you can see what might happen in the second year of business. Don't look too far ahead because longer predictions are unlikely to be accurate.

Once you have completed your cash flow forecast, be prepared to defend your assumptions and estimates. For example:

```
Expense:
    Guesstimate
    Actual

Accountant fees
Advertising and promotion
Attorney fees
Bank fees
Business expertise consultants
Business startup capital
Cell phone service
Registration and licensing fees
Computer and technology equipment
Consultation with professional advisors
Incorporation fees
Insurance/professional liability
Internet URL
Long distance and telephone service
Policies and procedures templates
Touring facilities and meeting providers
Website development and maintenance
```

FIGURE 3.1   Business startup—rough budget estimate.

```
Desired income
Wages
Total annual overhead
Working hours in a year
Working hours in a day
Nonchargeable days
Statutory holidays
Annual leave
Other
Working hours per annum
Other nonchargeable hours per week
Quoting for work
Administrative paperwork
Other
Total nonchargeable hours per week _____
Chargeable time in hours per year _____
Charge-out rate for direct labor _____
```

FIGURE 3.2   Charge-out rate calculation.

- How did you work out your monthly sales estimate? Are some months going to be more profitable than others? If so, why?
- Will your salary fluctuate throughout the year? Why?
- How did you calculate wages for yourself and employees or contract labor?
- How will you spend money on marketing and promotion?
- Did you classify a lot of little expenses into "other?" What are they? Are they needs or wants?

TABLE 3.1
Profit Forecast
(replicate for each month in business)

Sales revenue

This month
Previous month
Year-to-date

Fee for service

Commissions
Miscellaneous income

Total income

Cost of sales

Direct wages
Commissions paid
Other direct costs

Gross profit

Overhead expenses

Accounting
Advertising
Bank charges
General expenses
Insurance premiums
Interest paid
Legal fees
Consulting services
Motor vehicle expenses
Postage
Power
Printing and stationery
Rent
Repairs and maintenance
Technology equipment
Equipment leases
Software licenses
Staff wages and salaries
Workers' compensation and benefits
Memberships, education, and seminars
Telecommunications
Travel and accommodation
Travel for inspections of facilities, etc.

Total overhead

Operating profit

Bad debts
Refunds
Depreciation
Net profit before tax
Tax on net profit

Net profit after tax

```
Month
Receipts
Sales
Other revenue
                                        (a) Total receipts

Less payments
Wages
Draws against commissions
Overhead
Marketing
Loan repayments
Tax payments
Income tax payments
Client refunds
Transaction fees (credit cards, etc.)
                                        (b) Total expenses
                                        (c) Net cash flow (a–b)
                                        (d) Opening bank balance
                                        Closing bank balance (c–d)
```

FIGURE 3.3   Cash flow forecast (monthly).

- Will a reader need to have any other information to validate your assumptions as reasonable and realistic in their own mind?
- How many conversions from inquires to sales must you have each week on average?
- How many active clients/accounts can you handle at one time?
- Will you need to ramp up help if you get busy very quickly?
- If yes, where will this specialized help come from?

COSTLY CONTINGENCIES, REFUNDS, AND LIABILITIES

Your service agreement should spell out specifically how and when refunds will be considered for your services and how liability for refunds from other providers will be handled. Be sure to develop terms of trade that reduce the chance of bad debt and keep tight control over your receivables.

NONREFUNDABLE AND PARTIALLY REFUNDABLE DEPOSITS

While you may have a contract that clearly spells out how refunds are handled, and if they will be entertained, your client can file a small claims petition and let the judge decide. Even though, in some cases, nonrefundable deposits are enforceable, there may be sufficient grounds for a refund. To avoid problems and mitigate your exposure to recuperation of any fees for which you rendered services and/or incurred costs, document all your activity and time on a client's behalf so that if they take this action you will have a defense against the cause of action, if you feel it is worth defending. Obtain expert guidance from qualified legal counsel and have them draft your business transaction documents for use with both suppliers and clients.

OSTENSIBLE AGENCY LIABILITY

This concept of liability refers to certain powers granted to an agent, even if a principal (a hospital, physician, or other medical or dental services provider, hotel, limousine service, etc.) has not actually granted such powers. In a medical professional liability context, the ostensible agency liability doctrine is often used to hold hospitals liable for the acts of independent contractor physicians who work in emergency and operating rooms. This could also apply to medical travel facilitators, where the public will look to the facilitator and assume that they did their due diligence in reviewing credentials and privileging before agreeing to offer them as a part of the facilitator's product or network of providers. If you have no policy or standard procedure for reviewing provider credentials, and are relying upon accreditation performed by another party, that party needs to indemnify you and hold you harmless in the event of a lawsuit, or you could find yourself liable for negligence under this theory of liability. If you discover a problem with a physician, choose to ignore the situation, and anyone can track it down and associate you with the problem, your risk greatly increases. Speak with your professional liability carrier and your hospital suppliers if they are the ones that vet the credentials and grant privileges to medical and dental providers. As for chauffeurs, limousines, hoteliers, and other suppliers, the same responsibility applies. If the fire exits are blocked, the limousine has no insurance, or the driver is drunk, who is responsible in the event of an adverse situation? Ensure that your supplier agreements provide you both the right of review upon request for production of documents and certifications, as well as indemnification against any fines, damages, or costs associated with a liability case that might be brought against you.

FAILURE TO PERFORM DUE DILIGENCE

While you may disclaim liability for professional services rendered by doctors, dentists, nurses, therapists, hospitals, clinics, and others, how much protection does that disclaimer provide? So many medical travel facilitators put forward the assertion that the hospital is accredited, so they must be in compliance. Do not be one of those who would entrust the success and survival of their business to such a cavalier dismissal. Also, remember that the hospital and the physicians are not your only network suppliers. How will you perform due diligence on your other nonmedical suppliers that will be charged with the responsibility of caring for and serving to your clients?

PRIVITY OF CONTRACT

Privity of contract is another key issue that may arise in your negotiated supplier and provider agreements as well as your client agreements. For example: If you contract with a hospital and the hospital contracts with a local independent physician who is not employed by or controlled by the hospital, but promises to pay that physician for their services from the proceeds of the case paid in full to the hospital, can the physician look to you for payment for services rendered?

If the case was anticipated as a routine case with a 90-minute block of time set aside and the case ends up taking the physician 5 hours in the operating room and he misses his following cases scheduled at another hospital in town, if the hospital fails to seek additional payment from your client or, indeed, seeks and is paid the additional surcharge but then fails to pay the physician his or her rightful share, can the physician come to you or your client for the additional reasonable payment due to them?

In the doctrine of privity of contract, third parties might be entitled to money, services, or goods. The medical travel facilitator agrees to purchase services from the City Memorial Hospital and instructs City Memorial that the client would like Dr. Jones to perform the surgery on the facilitator's client. The client travels internationally to have the surgery in another country. If City Memorial does not secure the appointment and agreement with Dr. Jones to provide the surgery, then, under the third-party beneficiary rule, the client, as a third party to the facilitator's contract with City Memorial Hospital, has no right to sue City Memorial Hospital. Furthermore, the facilitator may also lack viable legal recourse against City Memorial if the doctor doesn't show up and perform the surgery as expected. The facilitator may have lost nothing due to City Memorial's failure to schedule the surgeon. If he sued City Memorial, the facilitator might be entitled only to nominal damages. In this scenario, the client would wish to assert an affirmative right of action in the contract between the facilitator and City Memorial.

Second, employees or subcontractors, who are deemed to be third parties for the purposes of the rule, might be entitled to a limitation of liability or other contractual defense to a lawsuit. For example, a facilitator contracts with Premier Limousine Service to a client from the airport to the hospital. The contract between the facilitator and the limousine service limits the limousine service's liability for negligently inflicted damage, which would be a taxi fare to the hospital. What about the good name and professional reputation of the facilitator? As you read through your vendor and provider agreements, and even your client agreements, obtain competent legal counsel to guide you through the navigation of all these exposures. Each, when compounded with another, could cause you to incur damages or liability that far exceeds the policy limits of your professional liability coverage.

JOINT AND SEVERAL LIABILITY

When two or more parties are liable in respect to the same liability, most common law systems allow for joint liability, several liability, or joint and several liability. This term is used in contrast to proportionate liability, where a party is only responsible for the damages caused by their own actions.

Under joint and several liability, a claimant may pursue an obligation against any one party as if they were jointly liable, and it becomes the responsibility of the defendants to sort out their respective proportions of liability and payment. This means that if your client pursues a hospital, physician, or tourism supplier and receives payment, that defendant must then pursue the other obligors for a contribution to their share of the liability. That might include you.

For example, the Wisconsin case of *Zimmer vs. the City of Milwaukee* illustrates the rule's unfairness. An uninsured driver of a car with faulty brakes struck and killed a 6-year-old boy at a school crossing, despite a stop sign and a crossing guard. The plaintiff argued that the accident might have been avoided if the crossing guard, instead of signaling the car to stop, had attempted to get the child out of the car's path. The city, as the crossing guard's employer, was found to be simply 1% at fault. Yet, because it was the only solvent party, the city had to pay 100% of the damages.

Many of the countries in which medical tourism services are rendered provide for limited or no professional liability for noneconomic damages. Further, the case has to be tried in that country, in a tribunal specified in the contract for service (often binding arbitration) and possibly in a language other than the native language of the client or the facilitator. A facilitator that has not incorporated and owns a home, a car, a boat, and some nice antiques, art, or other assets could be much more attractive to a tort lawyer than a doctor or hospital in a faraway land.

Joint and several liability is most relevant in tort claims, whereby a plaintiff may recover all the damages from any of the defendants regardless of their individual share of the liability. The rule is often applied in negligence cases, though it is sometimes invoked in other areas of law. As it may be difficult to pursue a hospital, physician, or other supplier abroad, they may come after you because you are more accessible. Where a party with assets can be joined as a defendant, a plaintiff has a greater chance of recovering damages than when the defendants are financially insolvent, judgment-proof, or difficult to bring to trial to be held accountable for their actions.

In the United States, 46 of the 50 states have a rule of joint and several liability, although in response to "tort reform" efforts, some have limited the applicability of the rule. The states of Alabama, Indiana, Kansas, and Oklahoma have never applied the joint and several liability doctrine. Table 3.2 provides a comparative overview of these rules. Pure joint and several liability refers to liability where a defendant as little as 1% at fault could have been responsible for all of the plaintiff's damages.

LIQUIDATED DAMAGES

Liquidated damages (also referred to as liquidated and ascertained damages) are damages whose amount the parties designated during the formation of a contract for the injured party to collect as compensation upon a specific breach (e.g., late performance).

TABLE 3.2
Joint and Several Liability by State

Authority

Alabama
Pure several liability
General Motors Corporation vs. Edwards, 482 So. 2d 1176
(Ala. 1985); Matkin vs. Smith, 643 So. 2d 949 (Ala. 1994)

Alaska
Pure several liability
Alaska Stat. § 09.17.080(d)

Arizona
Pure several liability
Ariz. Rev. Stat. § 12-2506

Arkansas
Modified joint and several liability
Ark. Code Ann. § 16-55-201

California
Modified joint and several liability
Cal. Civ. Code Ann. § 1431.2

Colorado
Pure several liability
Colo. Rev. Stat. § 13-21-111.5

Connecticut
Pure joint and several liability
Conn. Gen. Stat. Ch. 925 § 52-572(h)

Delaware
Pure several liability
Sears Roebuck & Co. vs. Huang, 652 A. 2d 568 (Del.
1995); 1 Del. C. Ann. Title 10 §§ 6301, 8132

Florida
Pure several liability
Fla. Stat. § 768.81(3)

Georgia
Modified joint and several liability
Ga. Code Ann. § 51-12-33

Hawaii
Modified joint and several liability
Haw. Rev. Stat. § 663-10.9

Idaho
Modified joint and several liability
Idaho Code § 6-803

Illinois
Pure several liability
Ill. Comp. Stat. § 735 ILCS 5/2-1117 (from Ch. 110)

Indiana
Modified joint and several liability
Ind. Code § 34-51-2-8

Iowa
Pure several liability
Iowa Code § 668.4

Kansas
Pure several liability
Kan. Stat. Ann. § 60-258a

Kentucky
Modified joint and several liability
Ky. Rev. Stat. Ann. § 411.182

Louisiana
Modified joint and several liability
La. Civ. Code Ann. Art. 2324

Maine
Pure joint and several liability
14 Me. Rev. Stat. Ann. § 156-A

Maryland
Pure joint and several liability
Consumer Prot. Div. vs. Morgan, 874 A.2d 919 (Md. 2005)

Massachusetts
Pure several liability
Shantigar Found. vs. Bear Mountain Builders, 804 N.E. 2d
324 (Mass. 2004); Mass. Gen. Laws Ch. 231B, §1

Michigan
Modified joint and several liability
Mich. Comp. Laws § 600.6304

Minnesota
Modified joint and several liability
Minn. Stat. § 604.02

Mississippi
Modified joint and several liability
Miss. Code Ann. § 85-5-7

Missouri
Modified joint and several liability
Mo. Ann. Stat §537.067

Montana
Modified joint and several liability
Mont. Code Ann. § 27-1-703

TABLE 3.2 *(Continued)*
Joint and Several Liability by State

Authority

Nebraska
Modified joint and several liability
Neb. Rev. Stat. § 25-21, 185.10

Nevada
Modified joint and several liability
Nev. Rev. Stat. § 41-141

New Hampshire
Modified joint and several liability
N.H. Rev. Stat. Ann. § 507:7-e

New Jersey
Modified joint and several liability
N.J.S.A. 2A:15-5.3

New Mexico
Modified joint and several liability
N.M. Stat. Ann. § 41-3A-1

New York
Pure joint and several liability
N.Y.C.P.L.R. 1601

North Carolina
Modified joint and several liability
*Fulk vs. Piedmont Music Ctr., 531 S.E. 2d 476
(N.C. Ct. App. 2000); Charnock vs. Taylor, 26 S.E. 2d 911
(N.C. 1943)*

North Dakota
Modified joint and several liability
N.D. Cent. Code § 32-03.2-02

Ohio
Modified joint and several liability
Ohio Rev. Code § 2307.22

Oklahoma
Modified joint and several liability
23 Okla. Stat. Ann. § 15

Oregon
Modified joint and several liability
Or. Rev. Stat. § 31.610

Pennsylvania
Pure joint and several liability
42 Pa. Cons. Stat. Ann. § 7102

Rhode Island
Pure joint and several liability
R.I. Gen. Laws § 9-20-4

South Carolina
Modified joint and several liability
*Travelers Ins. Co. v. Allstate Ins. Co., 155 S.E.2d 591
(S.C. 1967); S.C. Code Ann. §15-38-20*

South Dakota
Pure several liability
S.D. Codified Laws § 15-8-15.1

Tennessee
Modified joint and several liability
McIntyre vs. Balentine, 833 S.W.2d 52 (Tenn. 1992)

Texas
Pure several liability
Tex. Civ. Prac. Rem. Code § 33.013

Utah
Pure several liability
Utah Code Ann. § 78-27-40

Vermont
Pure joint and several liability
12 Vt. Stat. Ann. § 1036

Virginia
Modified joint and several liability
*Maroulis vs. Elliot, 207 S.E.2d 339 (Va. 1966);
Va. Code Ann. §8.01-443*

Washington
Modified joint and several liability
Wash. Rev. Code §§ 4.22.070

West Virginia
Modified joint and several liability
W. Va. Code Ann. § 55-7-13

Wisconsin
Pure several liability
Wis. Stat. § 895.045

Wyoming
Wyo. Stat. § 1-1-109

When damages are not predetermined/assessed in advance, the amount recoverable is said to be "at large" (to be agreed or determined by a court or tribunal in the event of breach). As a medical travel facilitator, why should you care about this? Let us examine a practical example. You might be due, or worse you might owe monetary compensation for a loss, detriment, or injury to a person or a person's rights or property, awarded by a court judgment or by a contract stipulation regarding breach of contract. This may be in addition to a penalty, which is an amount that is disproportionate to the actual harm in the matter. So, what kinds of losses might you sustain or incur? Here is a short list:

- Damage to brand or reputation
- Failure to "pay timely," causing other debts to fall behind or interest to be incurred or accrue (the time value of money)
- Failure to pay timely, causing a loss of anticipated interest to the benefit of the creditor
- Termination of a contract because of a breach and the associated loss of opportunity
- Backing out of a contract by a client who scheduled time and incurred actual expenses advanced by the facilitator
- Failure by a travel supplier to render prepaid services to your client

The list can continue as long as your imagination and experience will allow.

In order for a liquidated damages clause to be upheld, two conditions must be met. First, the amount of the damages identified must roughly approximate the damages likely to fall upon the party seeking the benefit of the term. Second, the damages must be sufficiently uncertain at the time the contract is made. Such a clause will likely save both parties the future difficulty of estimating damages.

Liquidated damages provisions serve as a source of limited insurance for both parties so that the parties can balance the cost of anticipated performance against the cost of an intentional breach. Other times, the provision in the contract can give guidance to an arbiter to reach resolution on an amount that is mutually agreeable to settle a dispute. Damages that are sufficiently uncertain may be referred to as unliquidated damages, and may be so categorized because they are not mathematically calculable or are subject to a contingency that makes the amount of damages uncertain.

Before you sign any contracts or offer any contracts with suppliers, vendors, providers, or even lease agreements for equipment, be sure that you understand all the terms and conditions of the contract as they apply to you, your punctual and complete performance, and the punctual and complete performance of others. It is worth repeating: Have a qualified attorney on call to advise you before you proceed.

SLOW PAY

In the medical travel facilitator business, there are many professional services fee strategies. Some require that the facilitator collect fees and pay the provider from those fees. Others pay a commission to the facilitator from the proceeds of payment for services and supplies rendered. Similar to a real estate agent, your contract has to have a formula spelled out that can be modeled by a third party. This is critical in the event of a dispute. Without such a formula stated in the contract, it is impossible to defend your claim to the amount that is due to you as compensation for your services as a facilitator, and to indemnify ("make you whole") for any expenses you many have incurred out of pocket, specifically for a particular client for a particular case.

If you are in jeopardy of slow pay by a provider for commission and expenses, you should consider the addition of a provision to your service agreement to address timely payment and penalties for late payments. These penalties should be sufficient both to deter and create a disincentive for slow payment and also to cover you for actual damages experienced because of the lost opportunity based on the time value of money caused by the absence of their cash in your bank account. It should also address repeated offenses by the same payer.

4 Understanding Managed Care and Health Care Reimbursement

HEALTH PLANS IN THE UNITED STATES

Managed care is usually delivered through health care organizations of various shapes and structures that, on the surface, appear very similar. The truth is that they are very different, although most resemble a blended entity capable of providing care and the insurance component to protect the enrollee from financial exposure for claims arising from incurred, covered expenses. It's no surprise to the intended audience of this book that most Americans have little to no understanding of what kind of coverage they have, and don't think of taking the time to understand the nature of their coverage until they have to use it.

True managed care organizations limit the access enrollees have to designated, participating providers within the system, other than primary care physicians (PCPs) and OB-GYNs, in many cases. These limitations were the subject of much backlash in the 1990s, which brought about the change to permit direct access to OB-GYNs as PCPs for women and for access by annual standing referrals to specialists for certain patients with particular diseases as part of the Patient Protection Act in many states. These systems often also limit the ability to self-refer throughout the system of fixed panels of physicians, facilities, and other contracted providers, a methodology known as the "gatekeeper" approach.

The managed care delivery system usually emphasizes preventive care and is often associated with alternative delivery systems such as health maintenance organizations (HMOs), administrative services organizations (ASOs), preferred provider organizations (PPOs), and exclusive provider organizations (EPOs), utilizing a capitated or discounted fee-for-service reimbursement system. In this chapter, we will study the structure and functional differences of each system.

HEALTH MAINTENANCE ORGANIZATIONS (HMOs)

Originally, these were the fastest-growing type of managed care plan as far as the number of covered enrollees. This trend has not continued in the advent of the consumer-driven health plan movement. But the jury is still out as far as if the trend for HMO replacement will continue.

The health maintenance organization is a health plan that may be for-profit or not-for-profit. HMOs may seek federal qualification on a voluntary basis by the Centers for Medicare & Medicaid Services (CMS) in accordance with the HMO Act of 1973, as amended in 1988. Federal qualification status may be designated by the CMS after conducting an extensive evaluation of an HMO's organization and operations. An organization must be federally qualified or be designated as a competitive medical plan (CMP) to be eligible to participate in Medicare and cost and risk contracts, including Medicare Advantage. A federally qualified HMO is also eligible for loans and loan guarantees not available to nonqualified plans. Additionally, HMOs must pass state licensure requirements, which vary state-by-state. The basic regulatory model is that a state insurance department or a corporation's insurance department reviews rates, policy documents, and compliance with state financial reserve and surplus requirements in the amount necessary to cover all covered expenses up to the minute that they are incurred. They may also receive a Certificate of Authority for each county in which they are permitted to sell their product.

While HMOs may be identified in the news media as moving toward acceptance of medical tourism products into their network offerings, several regulatory, accreditation, contracting, actuarial, and premium rate setting and liability issues must first be resolved before this can happen on the part of the HMO.

ADMINISTRATIVE SERVICES ORGANIZATIONS (ASOs)

Few employers possess the health care benefits management and contracting infrastructure that is necessary to administer a health plan for their employees. Therefore, they require a vendor to do this for them that may already have the means and infrastructure available on a time and materials basis, even if the entity does not accept claims risk. While this type of company or vendor is commonly referred to as an administrative services organization (ASO), they can also be referred to as a third-party administrator (TPA).

These companies are capable of applying all their proprietary clinical management tools used for their existing HMO or other managed care operations, including care coordination, case management, disease state management, health plan benefit administration, utilization review, nurse triage call centers, physician credentialing and privileging, and other services to administer and manage their other programs—and they sell their excess capacity to employers and others on a time and usage basis. Often, the clients of these ASO plans include union health and welfare benefit plans, and self-funded employer health benefit programs operated under the rules of the Employee Retirement Income Security Act (ERISA) of 1974 with their own benefit design published in a summary benefit description (SBD). As such, the identification card carried by the employee or union member may display the logo of a recognized HMO or insurance company, but the benefit design is dictated by the employer and not the HMO or insurance company. In this situation, you may encounter a plan member with benefits for medical care accessed from abroad, but this plan member is not an HMO beneficiary.

PREFERRED PROVIDER ORGANIZATIONS (PPOs)

PPOs are networks of providers brought together by some sort of corporation, group, or marketer to contract with providers at a discount for health care services. A PPO is usually a nonrisk-bearing marketing entity that markets itself to insurance companies and self-funded ERISA plans via an access fee. The network is actually rented or leased to the payer(s).

PPOs now expand their presence beyond health plan coverage purchased by individuals and employers to workers' compensation products, motor vehicle accident reparations coverage, and unaffiliated employers involved in health care purchasing coalitions. The panel is often limited in size and may have some utilization review system associated with it. The benefit design of PPOs encourages the covered individual to choose a contracted provider to access the discounted fee-for-service reimbursement system. Typical out-of-pocket expenses, such as coinsurance and deductibles, are less expensive to the member when they utilize "in-network" preferred providers compared to out-of-network providers. Health care providers usually agree to accept payments below their full charges, in accordance with a contractual negotiation that pays the lesser of the provider's actual billed charges or the network's negotiated fee schedule. The provider also usually agrees not to balance-bill the patient, with the exception of deductibles, coinsurance, and noncovered services.

Risk-sharing arrangements, such as capitation, are not encountered in PPO plans because most PPOs are not regulated and do not have a license to engage in the business of "insurance." (At the time of this writing, only a few states regulate and license PPOs to do business.) As such, they cannot transfer the risk of the cost of claims to the providers in the form of capitation. Instead, many times providers are offered a chance to participate in the network if they are willing to negotiate per diem or case rates with the hospital, and ancillary levels and discounted fees-for-service with the physician. Per diem and case rates are flat fees for a daily package of services or an episode of care from beginning to end, with specific inclusions and exclusions concerning payment. Most PPOs reimburse participating physicians under a contract, using a maximum allowable fee, or fee cap. Services provided by PPOs vary greatly from plan to plan. Almost all PPOs contract with managed pharmacy plans, catastrophic case management firms, wellness firms, and long-term care providers.

Many PPO plans charge prospective provider applicants a credentialing fee and retain or withhold a portion of the net payment as a marketing fee. A provider who agrees to withhold with no hope of reclaiming the payment at some later date should more appropriately call it a "discount." Many providers join PPOs in the hope that they will be sent patients to care for in exchange for negotiating the discount. Providers must remember that PPO participation merely makes one accessible to the stream of patients in the system. The PPO does not "send" or steer patients to any provider with any measurable significance. The essential marketing that takes place is the inclusion of the providers' names in a directory.

THIRD-PARTY ADMINISTRATORS (TPAs)

In most cases, PPOs utilize third-party-administrators (TPAs) to process claims. TPAs are organizations outside an insuring organization that handle administrative duties and sometimes utilization review. TPAs are used by organizations that actually fund the health care benefits but do not find it cost-effective to administer the plan themselves. Usually, when a TPA performs the utilization review and management function for a payer, the TPA is accredited through the Utilization Review Accreditation Commission (URAC). In the event that the payer is a self-funded ERISA plan, coverage decisions and utilization management may be outsourced to one of these agencies. But the self-funded plan is still held liable for the utilization and payment actions and decisions of the TPA.

As the PPO may rent or lease the network to a myriad of payers, those self-insured, and to other sources of funding, the number of fee schedules, re-pricing schedules, and TPAs multiply. In essence, one PPO could have this scenario replicated hundreds of times, with claims going in hundreds of different directions at the same time. This brokering and marketing has led to a new phenomenon called the silent PPO.

EXCLUSIVE PROVIDER ORGANIZATIONS (EPOs)

Exclusive provider organizations (EPOs) are similar in purpose and organization to PPOs, but many have the lock-in feature of HMOs. EPOs allow members to go outside the network, but the member must pay the full cost of the services. An EPO is similar to the HMO in that it uses a PCP as a gatekeeper, has a limited provider panel, uses an authorization system, and so forth. The main difference between an EPO and an HMO is that EPOs are generally nonregulated. EPOs are not allowed in some states because they too closely resemble HMOs, but they do not have to obtain and maintain a state HMO license and demonstrate fiscal soundness.

CONSUMER-DRIVEN HEALTH PLANS (CDHPs)

Consumer-driven health plan arrangements (also called consumer-directed or self-directed health plans) involve a combination of an employer-funded spending or savings account with a high-deductible insurance policy, where the deductible amount equals or exceeds the annual funding of the savings or spending accounts.

Consumer-driven health plan design focuses on the following factors:

- The provisions and funding level of the employees' savings and spending accounts
- The amount of the insurance plan primary deductible requirement

- The gap (if any) between the funded level of the employees' savings and spending accounts and the insurance deductible requirement and/or imposition of an upfront employee deductible requirement before funding from the accounts
- The benefit provisions of the insurance plan
- The carve-out of any insurance benefit to be excluded from being subject to a primary deductible requirement
- The relationships between the savings and spending accounts, the gap and/or upfront deductible, the primary insurance plan benefits, and any carved-out benefits

Payments for health care services are made directly from the spending or savings accounts until the account is exhausted and/or the insurance deductible requirement is met. If the deducible exceeds the annual spending or savings accounts' funding (as is usually the case) the employee is responsible for payment of this gap before insurance coverage is applied. The insurance policies in consumer-driven health plans vary greatly in nature in respect to benefit provisions and if managed care features and other components are involved.

There are four types of employee spending or savings accounts that are designated for pretax treatment if properly qualified:

1. *Flexible Spending Accounts (FSAs):* Employer FSAs, when qualified under the tax code regarding "cafeteria plans" for employees, predate the consumer-driven health plan movement. They involve an employer pretax contribution that employees may spend on qualified medical expenses. However, there is a "use it or lose it" provision so that unspent funds can't carry over from year to year, other than for a grace period extending 2.5 months after the close of a plan year for FSA claims to be filed.

2. *Health Reimbursement Arrangements (HRAs):* HRAs refer to an employer-funded health care spending account defined by the IRS in 2002 that allows for eligible funds unspent in a given plan year to be rolled over from year to year on a pretax basis (as opposed to the "use it or lose it" provisions of an FSA). Numerous provisions apply according to the IRS revenue ruling regarding requirements for eligibility under such arrangements. The revenue ruling addresses such situations as recognizing and allowing for spending accounts to occur in combination with a high-deductible insurance policy such as the consumer-driven plans now in the marketplace, or for the spending accounts to pay for insurance premiums. Furthermore, the ruling allows for group retiree plans to use such arrangements.

3. *Medical Savings Accounts (MSAs):* MSAs are tax-advantaged savings accounts that include a number of qualifying provisions that limit the growth and desirability of these accounts. The Health Insurance Portability and Accountability Act (HIPAA) of 1996 included provisions creating MSAs (also sometimes called Archer MSAs) as a pilot program, with a series of extensions issued by the IRS. The Working Families Tax Relief Act of 2004 provided a final extension for creation of new MSAs through December 31, 2005. New accounts may not be created, but existing accounts can continue, or may choose to roll over into health savings accounts (discussed next).

4. *Health Savings Accounts (HSAs):* HSAs refer to the structure created under Title VII, Section 1201 of The Medicare Prescription Drug, Improvement, and Modernization Act of 2003, which included the following provisions:
   - HSAs may be established January 2004 and thereafter.
   - HSAs must be opened with a companion high-deductible health insurance policy.
   - A high-deductible policy is defined as at least $1,000 for singles and $2,000 for a family, subject to annual cost of living adjustments.
   - A taxpayer must be under 65 years old when opening an account.
   - The taxpayer may take an annual tax write-off equal to the deductible amount of the companion high-deductible plan.

- However, the tax write-off can't exceed certain limits established each year for an individual plan, or for a family plan, again subject to annual cost of living adjustments. As these amounts vary each year, it would be of little value to cite them in this book.
- Contributions may be made for the previous year through April 15.
- Eligible tax-free withdrawals from HSAs include expenditures for: doctors, dentists, and hospitals; artificial limbs; drugs; eyeglasses and contacts; chiropractic; laboratory expenses; nursing home costs; physical therapy; psychoanalysis; x-rays; and nursing home insurance premiums.

At the time of this writing, there is no stipulation that these expenses are limited to domestic providers of services located in the United States and its territories. For more information, review Publication 502 from the Internal Revenue Service (IRS) (also referred to as IRC213D). You may locate this document and download it from the IRS website at www.irs.gov.

MEDICARE AND MEDICAID

Currently, Medicare and Medicaid do not pay for services outside of the United States and its territories. This limitation is incorporated into both Title XVIII and XIX of the U.S. Social Security Act and would take an act of congress to revise.

HEALTH PLANS IN OTHER COUNTRIES

International Private Medical Insurance
International private medical insurance (IPMI) is a type of insurance that expatriates purchase to supplement the basic coverage that is obligatory in other countries. In many cases, the obligatory coverage does not cover private hospital stays, and may be limited to only public health hospitals and clinics. IPMI coverage allows the policy holder a wider selection of providers and richer benefits. It is often very costly to obtain and limits when a policy may be purchased. After that opportunity has passed, a person may or may not be able to take out a policy at a later date.

Statutory Coverage
Statutory coverage in the EU allows for cross border health care (CBHC) under an EU Directive, but only in certain circumstances. This is a developing area and to cover it in detail at this point could prove moot and confusing to the reader in the event of radical changes, which are likely.

TRAVEL ACCIDENT AND MEDICAL ASSISTANCE PLANS

These policies alleviate any travel concerns by insuring your clients' trip against potential setbacks such as trip interruption, lost luggage, emergency medication, unrelated illness or injury, repatriation, or credit card replacement. Sales of these policies are generally limited to licensed agents and authorized brokers and not permitted for sale by medical tourism facilitators who do not have these licenses or authorizations.

MEDICAL TOURISM COMPLICATIONS INSURANCE

This policy alleviates any concerns by insuring medical tourism services against potential complications associated with the care and physical implications associated with long travel, such as deep venous thrombosis. Standard trip or travel medical insurance policies do not provide coverage if one is traveling for the purpose of obtaining medical treatment. These types of insurances are of no help if a medical complication arises and cancel out any travel medical insurance policy. These policies typically feature:

- Medical complications coverage up to U.S. $250,000
- Trip cancellation coverage
- Procedure cancellation fee coverage
- Post-operative remediation of any medical errors
- Home accommodation and adaptive equipment required as a result of a medical mishap
- Medical evacuation coverage
- JCI & non-JCI accredited hospitals accepted
- Coverage worldwide including the United States
- Travel companion coverage
- Repatriation of mortal remains
- Underwritten by several underwriters with excellent reputations and claims management history

Sales of these policies are generally limited to licensed agents and authorized brokers and are not permitted for sale by medical tourism facilitators who do not have these licenses or authorizations.

5 Building Your Product and Inventory

WHAT DO YOU SELL?

Not everyone should coordinate every medical tourism case. For those who have no medical training (anatomy and physiology, terminology and nursing, at a minimum) or have never spent time working in hospitals on direct patient care or haven't had the time to shadow a surgeon in the operating theater and through the pre- and postoperative phases of more complex cases such as transplant, advanced stage cancer care, heart value repair, or replacement, it may be more fitting to coordinate simple, straightforward cases with relatively higher success rates.

If you are a beginner with little to no experience, start on minor cosmetic cases and progress to facial and scalp procedures, the latter being more prone to higher blood loss because of all the little vessels in the face. With orthopedics, first attempt cases with clients who have full mobility, then progress on to cases where mobility is impaired and complex airport transfers won't be as daunting.

With plastic surgery, coordinating a high-mileage trip for clients who have undergone abdominal incisions or pfannenstiel or groin incisions can lead to poor outcomes and dissatisfaction with the entire episode of care if expectations are not managed and follow-up instructions are not followed to the letter. The last thing you want is an upset client Tweeting about their experience with your service because of a bad outcome that was not in your care or control.

Are you planning to specialize in a particular type of medical, dental, or wellness service? For example:

- Orthopedic surgery cases
- Weight loss (bariatric) surgeries and obese traveler considerations
- Cardiac surgery
- Stem cell services
- Oncology (cancer) services
- Plastic and cosmetic surgery
- Gender reassignment (sex change) surgery
- Executive checkup services
- Organ transplantation
- Medical spa and wellness/relaxation services
- Dialysis traveler coordination
- Sight-impaired traveler coordination
- Wheelchair traveler coordination
- Hearing-impaired traveler coordination
- Psychiatric traveler coordination (e.g., schizophrenia, bipolar disorder, obsessive-compulsive disorder)
- Other specialty services

First, each of these specialized areas requires a basic knowledge of your clients' specific traveler needs. At the very minimum, you will need a basic command of medical terminology, anatomy, and physiology as well as dietary, medication management, or other requirements for not only your medical clients, but also for their companions, if applicable.

Second, there may be special rules imposed by airlines as to fitness for travel, dietary accommodations, security considerations in light of the restriction on fluids that can be packed in luggage, and special rules that are established and enforced in consideration of the safety and comfort of other passengers.

You will also need to know about the surgeries that you will coordinate. It may be helpful for you to observe a case from start to finish and note the preoperative and postoperative coordination necessary for a local patient if you have not experienced that particular kind of case. How do you sell your services or product? What makes you different from the rest of the medical tourism facilitators out there? Do you need to be different?

6 The Procedures

As a part of your business planning and preparation, prepare a checklist and operations policy and procedure for each type of surgical procedure conducted by surgeons and by facilities, in consultation with network providers. It should include the following considerations:

Name of the procedure
Surgeon
Facility

- Ideal candidate indications (helpful for marketing the procedures)
- Adverse candidate indications (who should not have the procedure)
- Necessary medical records/diagnostics required prior to acceptance of the case
- Physician-to-client consultation options
- Physician-to-physician consultation options (pre- and postoperative)
- Notes on special techniques and unique surgical approach by the surgeon
- Notes on special capabilities of the facility
- Outcomes statistics by surgeon and by facility
- How long before the procedure the client should arrive
- Concierge services required upon arrival
- Client and companion accommodations available and estimated cost
- Estimated length of stay postoperatively
- Concierge services required prior to departure
- Special travel home considerations
  - Dietary
  - Seating
  - Transfer/mobility assistance
  - Medication/supplies (pain management and wound care, dressing changes)
  - Flight surgeon notifications
- How soon after the procedure aftercare is required in the home city
- Average cost of the procedure at each destination, by surgeon, by facility
- Average cost of the follow-up care upon return home
- A list of surgeons in the United States that will accept the patient after treatment abroad for follow-up
- Your outcomes monitoring plan and method
- Facilitator discharge management plan
- Client relationship termination (unplanned)
- Client relationship termination (at termination of episode of care)

PAPER OR SOFTWARE?

Ideally, you could develop a database with all this information and not keep it on paper. If you are unsure how to go about it, take a course on how to use relational database software or hire a database programmer to build it for you once you know what you want your database to be able to tell you. As a rule, relational databases are built in reverse. You design what you want to be able to search and how the reports will look when the database produces the report for you. That is what you tell your programmer. If you are going to facilitate many cases by many surgeons and many facilities, this will be critical to your efficiency, productivity, and ultimately your success as a facilitator. To my knowledge, no software like this currently exists, although I know of some developers who state that they are working on it. Since they don't know medical tourism or medicine, I am not sure how useful the database tool will be. At the time of this writing, no beta version was available for review. I am afraid they simply don't know what they don't know.

In order to demonstrate a high level of professionalism as a medical tourism or health travel facilitator, it is important that you have complete familiarity with the cases you will coordinate, where and how they are performed, and what happens during the procedure and aftercare.

Ambulatory surgery takes place in a number of settings that can vary by ownership, and control and operation of the outpatient facilities, in addition to local regulations concerning licensing of health care facilities. Procedures that are permitted in the United States in a freestanding ambulatory surgery setting may not be permitted in Mexico, Malaysia, or certain parts of Central Europe in such a setting, but may be performed in an outpatient -department of a full-service hospital. If you don't take time to learn which procedures can and cannot be performed in the countries that you'll work with, and don't verify the credentials, licensure, and limitations of the facilities and privileges of the surgeons, you could easily place your client in harm's way with an overzealous facility or surgeon operating as a maverick for a quick dollar. In Europe and elsewhere, many privately-held ambulatory surgery centers are sometimes here today and gone tomorrow, and have been difficult for government agencies to keep up with, inspect, and shut down for safety reasons.

A large percentage of outpatient surgeries are performed in traditional hospital operating rooms. In many hospitals, outpatients are integrated into the flow of inpatients from the preoperative phase through discharge. At Mercury Healthcare, because we know the procedures from having worked in surgery and have a medical director on staff that understands the complexity of each case we facilitate, we have developed specific infrastructure criteria. Just because a hospital states that it can do a case doesn't mean that we approve that hospital to do that case for our clients. We have determined, through experience, that certain cases require a standard setting, while others require an intermediate or complex staffing, equipment, and setting to expect proper outcomes. The example in Table 6.1 shows the breakdown of our current criteria, by procedure.

To provide a visual framework for classification of surgical procedures by operative complexity category, the following table is included in this document. This chart is included for demonstration purposes. Mercury Healthcare has developed this standard for its clients and its operating policies and procedures. It is strongly suggested that each facilitator create an original.

If you are not familiar with what these cases are and what is involved in them, you probably should enroll in some classes or do some self-study to first understand the terminology, then the nature of the case, its pre- and postoperative course and aftercare implications, as well as travel implications, before you begin sending patients around the world to have procedures done under your brand name.

ANESTHESIA OVERVIEW

No discussion about surgical procedures would be complete without a discussion of anesthesia options and how they relate to your client's other scheduled activities and the untoward side effects and complications that can arise during surgery that may give rise to additional surcharges, interruptions in scheduled itineraries after their procedure, and critical complications that could cause death or debilitation requiring unscheduled, unanticipated medical evacuation and repatriation of your client.

TABLE 6.1
Sampling of Surgical Procedures Identified by Surgical Specialty

	Operative Category		
	Standard	**Intermediate**	**Complex**
Amputation	Amputation, upper extremity, arm, or forearm or hand; amputation, lower extremity, above knee, or below knee or ankle	Amputation, forequarter or hindquarter; disarticulation, hip	
Breast	Aspiration, cyst; drainage, abscess; biopsy or excision, breast lesion; Mastectomy, radical with implant	Mastectomy, complex; reconstruction with muscle flap; malignancy; Chest wall resection or reconstruction	
Cardiac			Coronary artery bypass; cardiac valve replacement; procedures requiring extracorporeal bypass; cardiac electrophysiology (EP) procedures
Ear, nose, and throat (ENT)	Biopsy, soft tissue lesion or lymph node, head and neck; biopsy throat; excision, intranasal polyps or lesions, or turbinates; septoplasty; repair of nasal defects; treatment, nasal fractures; treatment, nosebleeds; sinus surgery; nasal or sinus endoscopy with biopsy, polypectomy, debridement; laryngoscopy with biopsy or foreign body removal; drainage, biopsy, excision, repair of lip or mouth or tongue or gum or salivary, submaxillary, sublingual glands or external ear; excision neck cyst; tonsillectomy; myringotomy; tympanoplasty	Drainage, deep abscess, neck; excision, soft tissue tumors; sinus surgery, obliteration or excision; nasal or sinus endoscopy with resection; laryngoscopy with tumor removal or intervention; construction of tracheoesophageal fistula for speech prosthesis; cleft lip or palate reconstruction; oral vestibuloplasty; partial glossectomy; uvulopalatopharyngoplasty; parotidectomy; esophageal diverticulectomy; thyroidectomy; parathyroidectomy; mastoidectomy; reconstruction of the external ear; tympanic membrane repair; myringoplasty; cochlear implant	Maxillectomy; laryngectomy; tracheal reconstruction; nasal or oral or pharyngeal or laryngeal resection with radical neck dissection; pharyngectomy
Eye	Any procedure except those restricted to "Eye—intermediate," requiring intermediate or advanced infrastructure	Corneal transplant; retinal surgery; exploration, excision, decompression of the orbit	
Facial	Treatment of nasal fracture, closed	Arthrotomy, temporomandibular joint and muscle disorders (TMJ); excision of tumor, benign or malignant, facial bones; preparation, facial prosthesis; maxillofacial fixation; repair or revision or reconstruction, facial bones; treatment of nasal fracture, open; treatment of complex fracture, nasal or maxillary or zygomatic arch or orbit, open or closed; treatment of fracture, palatal or maxillary or mandibular; arthroscopy, jaw; complex surgery, nose	

TABLE 6.1 *(Continued)*
Sampling of Surgical Procedures Identified by Surgical Specialty

	Operative Category		
	Standard	Intermediate	Complex
Foot	Incision; excision; repair; revision; reconstruction; fracture; dislocation; Arthrodesis; or amputation of the foot and ankle		
General surgery (GS)	Biopsy skin or soft tissue or muscle or nerve or lymph nodes; gastrostomy, jejunostomy, open or laparoscopic; appendectomy, open or laparoscopic; liver biopsy; cholecystectomy, open or laparoscopic; diagnostic laparotomy or laparoscopy; lysis of adhesions, open or laparoscopic; hernia repair, inguinal or femoral or ventral or umbilical, open or laparoscopic; drainage, rectal abscess	Complex soft tissue resection; splenectomy, open or laparoscopic; retroperitoneal lymph node dissection, open or laparoscopic; gastroesophageal surgery, subtotal gastric resection, open or laparoscopic; vagotomy and pyloroplasty; gastroenterostomy; small bowel resection, open or laparoscopic; colectomy, open or laparoscopic; proctocolectomy; repair vesicoenteric fistula; proctectomy; repair of rectal prolapse; ablation of liver tumor, open or laparoscopic or percutaneous; common bile duct exploration; cholecystoenterostomy; drainage, pancreatic pseudocyst; pancreatic cyst-enterostomy; abdominal exploration ; drainage, abdominal abscess total gastrectomy; ileo–anal pull through; abdominal perineal resection; proctectomy; bile duct resection; adrenalectomy, open or laparoscopic	Esophagectomy; hepatectomy; total pancreatectomy; bariatric surgery, including laparoscopic bands
General urology (GU)	Kidney biopsy, percutaneous; cystoscopy and renal endoscopy; ureteral endoscopy, procedures or treatment; lithotripsy; placement of suprapubic catheter; urodynamics; cystoscopy, procedures or treatment; transurethral resection prostate; urethral surgery, dilatation or repair or treatment of lesions; biopsy or excision or repair of penis; circumcision; penile prosthesis, placement or removal; orchiectomy; biopsy or exploration or removal of the testes, epididymis, scrotum; vasectomy; hydrocele, drainage or repair or excision prostate, biopsy or ultrasound	Exploration or drainage or resection of the kidney, ureter, open or laparoscopic; kidney biopsy, open; treatment of kidney stones, open or laparoscopic; ureterolysis; urinary diversion; construction of a neobladder; cystectomy; repair of bladder fistula; complex reconstruction of the urethra; prostatectomy, open or laparoscopic; pelvic lymphadenectomy; penectomy	

Gynecology	Incision and drainage (I&D) superficial abscess or lesion; laser or chemical destruction of vulvar lesion; biopsy or excision vulva; repair vagina or perineum; colposcopy or colpotomy; destruction, vaginal lesion; vaginal examination, biopsy or excision or destruction of lesion; examination or treatment of cervix; cervical dilatation; endometrial biopsy or ablation; insertion or removal intrauterine device (IUD); tubal ligation; salpingo-oophorectomy; drainage ovarian cyst or abscess; oophorectomy; repair of vaginal fistula; Removal of cervix; myomectomy; hysterectomy, abdominal or vaginal; surgery, fallopian tube; laparoscopic hysterectomy or myomectomy; hysteroscopy; laparoscopy with adnexal intervention; repair fallopian tubes	Radical vulvectomy; vaginectomy; repair of urethra or bladder or vagina or pelvic floor; resection for ovarian malignancy
Hand	Incision; excision; repair; revision; reconstruction; fracture; dislocation; arthrodesis, forearm or wrist or hand or digits	
Neurosurgery		Twist drill or burr hole for subdural or extradural hematoma; cerebral spinal fluid (CSF) shunts; craniectomy or craniotomy for decompression, biopsy, excision; skull based surgery; twist drill or burr hole for ventricular access or device implantation or biopsy; hypophysectomy, craniectomy or transnasal or transseptal; surgery for aneurysm or arteriovenous malformation or vascular disease; stereotactic surgery; implantation of neurostimulator; neuroendoscopy

TABLE 6.1 (Continued)
Sampling of Surgical Procedures Identified by Surgical Specialty

	Operative Category		
	Standard	Intermediate	Complex
Ortho	Debridement skin or muscle or bone; bone biopsy, open or excisional or percutaneous; injection, tendon or ligament; drainage or injection, joint, bursa; placement or removal, fixation device; removal, implant or wire or pin or rod (except for long bone implants); harvest of tendon or cartilage for transplant; I & D, shoulder: biopsy or excision, soft tissue lesion shoulder; excision or curettage, bone lesion or foreign body; muscle transfer or tenotomy, shoulder; humerus, nailing or plating or pinning or wiring; clavicular fracture, closed treatment; treatment, humerus fracture; treatment shoulder dislocation, closed; surgery of the arm or elbow; surgery of tendons or ligaments, upper extremity; fractures of the upper extremity; soft tissue surgery of the hip; hip dislocation, closed reduction; soft tissue surgery, thigh; surgery knee, not including arthroplasty; curettage, femur; thigh fracture, closed treatment; treatment of patellar and knee fracture; treatment of fracture or dislocation of the leg and ankle; casting or splint	Arthrotomy, shoulder or clavicle; claviculectomy; repair, biceps tendon; shoulder reconstruction; clavicular reconstruction; clavicular fracture, open reduction internal fixation (ORIF); shoulder dislocation, ORIF hip dislocation, ORIF; thigh fracture, ORIF; complex tibia or fibula reconstruction; ostectomy, scapula or humerus or clavicle; shoulder reconstruction; complex reconstruction, humerus or elbow or radius; excision tumor or ostectomy, pelvis or hip or thigh; acetabuloplasty; hip arthroplasty; treatment of pelvic fracture; treatment of thigh fracture; arthrodesis, hip; exploration, reconstruction of the knee; complex reconstruction, leg and ankle; revisional hip arthroplasty; revisional knee arthroplasty	Replantation, arm or hand or foot or digit; bone or osteocutaneous graft, with microvascular anastomosis; jejunal transfer, with microvascular anastomosis; omental flap, intra-abdominal or extra-abdominal, with microvascular anastomosis
Plastic or reconstructive		Fascia or muscle graft for face nerve palsy; excision excessive skin or subcutaneous tissue, face or trunk or extremity, including liposuction; excision coccyx, with or without flap; treatment pressure ulcer, sacrum or ischium or trochanter by excision or ostectomy or closure, Mohs surgery; omental flap, intra-abdominal or extra-abdominal, without microvascular anastomosis; neurorrhaphy, nerve graft, face or arm or leg	

Proctology	Treatment of pilonidal cyst, rectal lesion, rectal abscess, anal fissure, hemorrhoids, anal fistula; anoscopy	
Skin or subcutaneous tissue	Incision, drainage, removal, abscess or pilonidal cyst or foreign body or hematoma; remove mesh, abdominal wall; debridement, skin, subcutaneous tissue, muscle, bone; paring callus; biopsy, skin lesion; remove, skin tags; shave, skin lesions; excision, skin lesion, benign or malignant; excision, hidradenitis, axillary or inguinal or perineal; excision, skin lesion, benign or malignant; surgery of the nails or nail bed; introduction or removal, tissue expanders; insertion or removal, drug delivery system; simple or complex or layer closure, wounds; tissue transfer (Z-plasty, rotation flap, advancement flap); skin grafts, autografts or allografts or xenograft; free flaps; hair transplant; dermabrasion, chemical peel, simple facial plastic surgery; removal excessive skin; destruction lesion, laser or electrosurgery or cryosurgery or chemosurgery; incision, abscess	Complex debridement; complex skin grafts, large surface area or head and neck; skin or deep tissue flaps, face or trunk or arm or leg; destruction malignant lesion, laser or electrosurgery or cryosurgery or chemosurgery
Spine	Incision or drainage, deep abscess, cervical, thoracic, lumbar spine; excision or osteotomy, cervical, thoracic, lumbar spine; spinal fracture, closed or open treatment; vertebroplasty; kyphoplasty; arthrodesis, cervical, thoracic, lumbar spine; laminectomy for exploration or decompression or excision; implantation or removal of spinal catheter or neurostimulator	Complex cervical spine procedures; procedures with open dura
Thoracic	Pericardiectomy; placement or removal of epicardial pacemaker leads; exploration, biopsy, excision of chest wall; repair of pectus or sternal separation; exploration or biopsy of chest, lung, pleura, open, or thoracoscopic; pleurodesis; lobectomy; thoracoscopy, diagnostic, or therapeutic; repair of hiatal or paraesophageal hernia, open or thoracoscopic; esophageal diverticulectomy; thymectomy; pneumonectomy	Completion pneumonectomy; sternal debridement; repair of trachea or bronchus; esophagectomy
	Pacemaker insertion; reposition or repair of lead	

TABLE 6.1 (Continued)
Sampling of Surgical Procedures Identified by Surgical Specialty

	Operative Category		
	Standard	Intermediate	Complex
Tracheostomy	Unrestricted		Kidney transplant; liver transplant; stem cell harvest or transplant; cardiac transplant; lung transplant
Vascular		Carotid endarterectomy; carotid subclavian bypass; upper extremity graft or prosthesis, bypass or interposition; lower extremity graft or prosthesis, bypass, or interposition; infrarenal aortic surgery, bypass, or interposition, open or endovascular; aortic renal or mesenteric, bypass, or interposition; carotid or peripheral endovascular intervention; venous surgery	Thoracoabdominal aortic reconstruction; suprarenal aortic reconstruction
Vascular access	Central venous access; arteriovenous fistula, primary or graft		

Source: ©2010. The Mercury Healthcare Companies. All rights reserved. Used by permission.

GENERAL ANESTHESIA

The types of general anesthesia employed for maintenance are often described as intravenous and inhalational (with a volatile anesthetic agent), or a combination of both intravenous and inhalational anesthetics. Intravenous, or balanced anesthesia, includes the appropriate balance of a hypnotic or amnesic drug (able to produce amnesia), an analgesic agent, and a muscle relaxant.

After arriving in the operating room suite, the patient is identified, the chart is checked for a signed consent or operative permit, and the latest result of any lab tests and diagnostic studies are reviewed once more. Depending on standard operating policy, an intravenous line may be inserted in the preoperative holding area or after the patient is transferred to the operating table.

At induction, the patient is preoxygenated via a mask with 100% oxygen for 3 to 5 minutes. This permits washout of most of the gaseous nitrogen from the body and provides a large reserve supply of oxygen in the lungs should any difficulties be encountered during induction or intubation. As the anesthesia progresses, different agents are used for different purposes. Finally, to facilitate intubation, a laryngoscope is used.

Newer anesthetic agents and better monitoring devices have improved the risks associated with general anesthesia. I have never known a case where there were not expected side effects, but these are not complications, per se; some are minor and temporary. Anesthetic agents cause broad effects on anyone's body. Some of the most common include nausea and vomiting, a sore throat from the intubation procedure, bruising at the injection site, allergic reaction to the drugs used, infection, atelectasis (a condition where the lungs deflate or collapse postoperatively as a complication or as a result of splinting or restricted breathing after chest or abdominal surgery), or malignant hyperthermia syndrome, a rare life-threatening condition characterized by high fever that is triggered by the use of the volatile inhalant agents used in general anesthesia. In malignant hyperthermia, the skeletal muscles are involved and a drastic and uncontrolled increase in oxidative metabolism that overwhelms the body's ability to supply oxygen, remove carbon dioxide (CO_2), and regulate body temperature, eventually leading to circulatory collapse and death if not treated quickly.

A well-trained, well-informed facilitator must know this because, if this happens, the case is interrupted and the patient is transferred to the intensive care unit (ICU) or cardiac care unit (CCU). As a result, all package pricing disclaimers for a simple, straightforward outpatient surgical case will figure prominently. Malignant hyperthermia is generally not the result of malpractice unless the surgeon and anesthesiologist were so negligent as to not inquire about previous experiences with anesthesia and the drugs used in previous cases during their history and physical assessment. Instead, it is a medical condition that arises because of all the volatile inhalants and succinylcholine with associated risks. As an exemplary practice, it is critical that you obtain all past medical records, including operative notes and anesthesia notes whenever possible to forward them to the surgeon and the hospital for prior review when seeking to book a surgical case.

REGIONAL (BLOCK) ANESTHESIA

Regional anesthesia can be accomplished by injecting a local anesthetic anywhere along the peripheral nerve pathways from the spinal cord (spinal anesthesia), epidurally, peripherally, or topically.

SPINAL ANESTHESIA

A local anesthetic (often lidocaine tetracaine or bupivacaine) is injected into the cerebral spinal fluid (CSF) in the subarachnoid space. The anesthetic is generally mixed with a 10% dextrose solution in a total of 1 to 4 mL to make a hyperbaric (heavier than the cerebrospinal fluid) solution. The anesthetic mixture settles in a gravity-dependent place, so by changing the patient's position, the block can be directed up, down, or to one side of the spinal cord.

One of the most frequent postoperative complications following spinal anesthesia is a "postspinal headache." The incidence is greatest in young parturients (women about to give birth) or other patients less than 40 years of age, but even in these patients, it is only about 1% when a certain needle gauge has been used. While rumor has it that this is related to how quickly the patient is ambulated, current science has yet to record statistics to prove this theory. The headache is thought to result from leakage of cerebrospinal fluid through the hole in the dura mater (the tough outermost membrane of the three that cover the brain and spinal cord) and typically occurs when the patient assumes an upright position. The headache usually locates in the occiput (lower back of the head) and generally resolves within 1 to 3 days.

As a medical travel facilitator, you need to understand this because, if it happens, you must first consider if tourism activities may be involved postoperatively. The pain is tantamount to a severe migraine. Also, it could change the price of your package because treatment for this postspinal headache is strict bed rest for 24–48 hours, vigorous hydration, abdominal binders, epidural infusion of saline, and injection of 5 to 10 mL of autologous blood into the epidural space at the puncture site to create a "blood patch." The additional procedures and the extended length of stay may not have been originally calculated into your package price but is indeed medically necessary and, therefore, your client will be at risk for some unanticipated but chargeable expenses.

EPIDURAL AND CAUDAL ANESTHESIA

The epidural space is between the ligamentum flavum and the dura mater and extends from the foramen magnum to the sacrococcygeal membrane. This space is filled with epidural veins, fat, and loose areolar tissue. Now do you understand why it is important to understand anatomy and medical terminology for this profession? For epidural anesthesia, the local anesthetic is usually injected through the intervertebral spaces in the lumbar region, although it can also be injected in the cervical and thoracic regions. The anesthetic spreads both cephalad (toward the head) and caudad (toward the feet) from the site of the injection.

The most frequently used anesthetic is lidocaine (with or without epinephrine), bupivacaine, and chloroprocaine. To help verify that the anesthetic is not being placed incorrectly, a test dose of 3 to 5 mL of lidocaine is injected. If injected intravascularly, the test does cause a transient tachycardia indicating that the injection is placed incorrectly. If injected into the subarachnoid space, it produces the onset of spinal anesthesia. Neurological symptoms have been reported when chloroprocaine was inadvertently injected into the subarachnoid space, and cardiac arrest has occurred when bupivacaine was injected intravascularly.

With epidural anesthesia, several problems can occur:

- Inadvertent puncture of the dura mater with a large epidural needle is called a "wet tap" and can cause a postpuncture headache. This headache is significant in about 50% of patients, and the intensity can be incapacitating. Treatment is essentially the same as a postspinal headache, which can lead to increased expense and extended length of stay for your client.
- If the needle or catheter is unintentionally inserted into the subarachnoid space and the large volume of local anesthetic is injected as a bolus (a rapidly absorbed intravenous injection of a drug), it causes a "total spinal" anesthesia. The anesthetic effect can move all the way to the brain and results in rapid hypotension (low blood pressure) caused by vasodilatation (expansion of a blood vessel), profound bradycardia (low heart rate) as the vagus nerves to the heart are blocked, and a totally paralyzed and anesthetized patient. Treatment includes intubation, control of ventilation and respiratory support, support of blood pressure and the cardiovascular system, and amnesic drugs until the block has worn off. If properly managed, this is not usually life threatening, but use of a test dose usually averts this problem. When a surgeon or hospital describes who will be involved and how the case will be organized, I always like to question who else will be in the room to provide the anesthesia. As you can see, this type of emergency would require all hands on deck to

be ready to act quickly as a team to avoid a disaster. If the case is to be performed in a small ambulatory surgical center by a surgeon and his nurse, I want to be sure that the test dose is a routine standard operating procedure and that there is a nurse anesthetist at minimum to assist in the case of an untoward event. Proper anesthesia procedure is not where corners should be cut in order to reduce costs of a case.

- The local anesthesia may be inadvertently injected into an epidural vein. This can occur with the initial injection or any subsequent dose. In addition to the risks of this happening with bupivacaine, including cardiac arrest and cardiovascular collapse, toxicity from other local anesthetic agents can cause sudden and profound hypotension, convulsions from the effects on the central nervous system, and tachycardia (rapid heartbeat) if the solution contains epinephrine. Use of the test dose with each injection usually prevents these problems.

PERIPHERAL NERVE BLOCK

Many peripheral nerves can be successfully blocked by injecting local anesthetic around them to provide adequate surgical anesthesia. How quickly the anesthesia takes effect and how long it lasts is related to the drug that is used, its concentration and volume, and the addition of epinephrine. Complications are usually caused by inadvertent intravascular injection, an overdose of the local anesthetic, or allergy to the drug. Rarely, nerve damage may also occur.

INTRAVENOUS REGIONAL ANESTHESIA (BIER BLOCK)

This method of anesthesia is most often used on upper extremities. A small intravenous catheter is inserted as distally (far down the arm) as feasible and a single- or double-cuffed pneumatic tourniquet is placed around the limb proximal (toward the head) to the surgical site. The limb is raised and the blood is exsanguinated (removed) from the limb by wrapping it with an Esmarch bandage. The tourniquet is inflated to approximately 100 mm hg above the patient's systolic (the top number in a blood pressure reading) blood pressure and the Esmarch bandage is removed. The anesthesia effect is rapid and lasts until the tourniquet is deflated.

The patient may feel pain from the tourniquet and is often given additional analgesics or sedatives to supplement the Bier block. Problems can arise from overdose, toxicity, or allergic reactions of lidocaine. Another risk of this procedure is that of loss of pneumatic pressure in the tourniquet, which could cause both toxic reactions and loss of anesthesia.

MONITORED ANESTHESIA CARE (MAC) (ANESTHESIA STANDBY)

This popular method of anesthesia is used for both normal, healthy patients as well as sicker, unstable patients who may not tolerate general anesthesia very easily. During MAC the anesthesiologist may supplement a local anesthetic with an intravenous analgesic such as fentanyl and with sedative and amnesic agents such as Midazolam, as necessary. The anesthesiologist or nurse anesthetist carefully monitors the patient's vital signs, respiratory and cardiovascular status, and positioning, and may give supplemental low-flow oxygen. At any time, the anesthesiologist may have to convert to general anesthesia or use another regional technique if greater anesthetic effect is required.

When your client is scheduled for this kind of anesthesia, inquire as to whether or not your patient has any allergy or sensitivity to eggs. Often, Diprivan (marketed under the brand name Propofol) is the drug of choice for MAC. Diprivan contains egg lecithin extracted from the yolk. To the best of my knowledge, there is no official agreement on this, and since the manufacturer still lists an egg allergy warning, the decision about using Diprivan in patients with drug allergies should be done on a case-by-case basis. The main thing is to get the allergy notation on the chart and in front of the surgeon or anesthesiologist and let them take it from there. The patient may not know which part of the egg they are allergic to.

LOCAL ANESTHESIA

In some cases, surgeons may elect to perform their own regional nerve blocks or use an infiltration technique with a local anesthetic in their office or clinic. Others may elect to take the case to an operating room. As a medical travel facilitator, it is prudent to understand the particulars of each surgeon's preference, methodology, rationale, safety record, and outcomes for the cases you entrust to their care. This is all part of your due diligence and research into your product. Your professionalism and domain knowledge will be reflected in how well you prepare yourself to offer a particular service line.

Rarely is an anesthesiologist involved in local anesthesia administration. More often, patient monitoring is performed by a nurse as directed by a physician. The patient is awake during the procedure. Untoward events can occur with local anesthetics if the patient is allergic to the drug.

ACUPUNCTURE AND HYPNOSIS

Acupuncture and hypnosis are rarely used but commonly employed in Asian countries.

Acupuncture is one of the oldest, most commonly used medical procedures in the world and is beneficial in treating a variety of health conditions. Acupuncturists are often licensed in the United States and regulated as a profession by various departments at a state level. Acupuncture is actually a set of procedures involving the stimulation of various anatomical points significant in Asian and traditional Chinese medicine (TCM). In the United States, acupuncture incorporates medical traditions from Japan, Korea, and other countries, not just China.

In terms of pain control, acupuncture treatment encourages the production and liberation of various neuroendocrine and neurochemical substances, which then activate endogenous pain control systems, often providing an effective, nonpharmacologic means to control pain. In fact, the analgesia afforded by acupuncture, especially electro-acupuncture, can be so profound that it has, at times, been used as the sole pain-relieving measure during surgery.

In 1975, the Chinese government created a set of four stamps to commemorate the successful integration of Chinese medicine, including acupuncture, with modern biomedicine.

HYPNOTIC ANESTHESIA

Hypnotic anesthesia has been around longer than any chemical anesthesia. There have been many cases where hypnosis is documented to be useful for anesthesia. For instance, a weak heart, dental procedures where the inhalation mask and induction tubes would be impossible to work around, or cases where lessened anxiety would be beneficial. Sometimes, hypnosis is used in conjunction with other anesthetic agents. An article published in *Lancet*,[*] a respected medical journal, reported that a hypnotic group asked for and was given less medication than a control group. There were fewer problem events with hypnosis, and because of this, procedures took less time. In the case of each variable measured, hypnosis was superior to the attentional (focusing concentration) manipulation, so hypnosis is not only effective but the effects are also due to the hypnosis (not the placebo effect).

One thing to keep in mind about any anesthesia modality: The patient has to believe that it will work for them. Do not try to "convince" your client that one method is more preferable than another. No matter what your personal experience or training, if anything short of a licensed physician, and licensed in the state in which the advice is given, you chance practicing medicine without a license. Leave that task for the physician and measure your words accordingly. I have tried both hypnosis and acupuncture. I came with an open mind and found that neither worked for me, personally. Others swear by these methods.

---

[*] Lang, E. V., Benotsch, E. G., Fick, L. J., Lutgendorf, S., Berbaum, M. L., Berbaum, K. S., Logan, H., and Spiegel, D. (2000). Adjunctive non-pharmacological analgesia for invasive medical procedures: A randomised trial. *Lancet*, 355, 1486–1500.

POSTANESTHESIA RECOVERY

Recovery from anesthesia is often carried out in the postanesthesia recovery unit (PACU) in the surgical suite. The recovery room should be immediately adjacent to the operating room suite (a typical hospital and ambulatory surgical center accreditation standard) for rapid response by the anesthesia team if required. Ideally, I look for a nurse-to-patient ratio of 1:1 and a staff of specially trained nurses with advanced training in surgical recovery. (This should be a question on your facilitator checklist as you interview hospitals prior to engaging in your provider network.)

When coordinating aftercare, you will do well to include reports in a format that is familiar to the hometown surgeon, including operative and recovery reports. The most popular report format for postanesthesia recovery is the postanesthetic recovery score (PARS) originally proposed by Aldrete. It includes a graphic summary of the patient's recovery progress and is used by most institutions.

The Aldrete Score has withstood the changes in anesthesia and surgical care that have developed in the past three decades. Nevertheless, it is imperative that (1) a modification is made to incorporate the most effective monitor of the respiratory and hemodynamic functions, e.g., pulse oximetry; and (2) the five indices previously used be expanded by incorporating five more indices including dressing, pain, ambulation, fasting/feeding, and urine output to evaluate patients undergoing ambulatory surgery and anesthesia. A patient's recovery from anesthesia and surgery, using 10 indices graded 0, 1, or 2, would provide criteria for street fitness and discharge to home when the patient reaches a post-anesthesia recovery score of 18 or higher.

AN OVERVIEW OF MEDICAL PROCEDURES

While a book of this type cannot conceivably cover all the procedures available in modern surgery, this chapter will attempt to describe some of the procedures that are most frequently requested in association with medical travel.

Diagnostic Procedures

Cancer Treatment

Cardiac Surgery

Laryngectomy

A laryngectomy is a surgical procedure performed to remove all or part of the larynx.

Biopsy

A biopsy is an examination of cells or tissues removed from the body of a living person.

Myotomy

A myotomy is a surgical procedure in which a muscle is cut open.

Radiosurgery

Radiosurgery, also known as stereotactic radiotherapy, is a medical procedure that allows noninvasive treatment of benign and malignant conditions, avascular malformations (AVMs), and some functional disorders by means of directed beams of ionizing radiation. The procedure is usually performed by radiation oncologists using linear accelerators, gamma knife, computers, and laser beams. The highly precise irradiation of targets within the brain is planned by the radiation oncologist based on images, such as computed tomography (CT), magnetic resonance imaging (MRI), and angiography of the brain and body. These procedures are great candidates for medical travel to developing nations due to the tremendous cost savings over procedures performed in the United States.

LAPAROSCOPY

A laparoscopy is an examination of the internal organs of the abdomen using a laparoscope.

CAUTERIZATION

Cauterization is a medical term describing the burning of the body to remove or close a part of it. The main forms of cauterization used today are electrocautery and chemical cautery.

PLEURODESIS

Pleurodesis is the artificial obliteration of the pleural space by surgical or chemical means. The procedure is done to prevent the recurrence of pneumothorax or pleural effusion.

GRAFTING

Grafting is a surgical procedure to transplant tissue without a blood supply. Many tissues can be grafted: skin, bone, nerves, tendons, neurons, and cornea are commonly grafted.

HEMORRHOIDECTOMY

A surgical procedure to remove hemorrhoids (one of the most commonly misspelled words in medicine).

FISTULOTOMY

A fistulotomy is the surgical opening or removal of a fistulous tract. A fistula is usually an ulcerous, channel-like formation between two internal organs or between an internal organ and the skin. It may follow a surgical procedure with improper healing, or it may be caused by injury, abscess, or infection with penetration deep enough to reach another organ or the skin. When open at only one end, it is called an incomplete fistula or sinus. The most common sites of fistula are the rectum and the urinary organs, but almost any part of the body may be affected. Rectal fistulas are often associated with colitis, cancer, sexually transmitted diseases, and other disorders. Usually a fistula requires surgery. They can be performed by excision of the tract and surrounding tissue, simple division of the tract, or gradual division and assisted drainage of the tract by means of a seton, a cord passed through the tract in a loop that is slowly tightened over a period of days or weeks. This is often done as an outpatient procedure.

PARATHYROIDECTOMY

A parathyroidectomy is a surgical procedure to remove the parathyroid gland. This procedure is used to remove primary tumors or hyperplasia of the glands, especially when they produce excessive parathyroid hormone.

ANGIOPLASTY

An angioplasty includes any surgical repair of a blood vessel, especially balloon angioplasty or percutaneous transluminal coronary angioplasty (PTCA), a treatment for coronary artery disease. In balloon angioplasty a balloon-tipped catheter is inserted through the skin into a blood vessel and maneuvered to the clogged portion of the artery.

CRICOTHYROTOMY OR CORODOTOMY

A cricothyrotomy (also called thyrocricotomy, cricothyroidotomy, inferior laryngotomy, intercricothyrotomy, coniotomy, or emergency airway puncture) is an incision made through the skin and cricothyroid membrane to establish a patent airway during certain life-threatening situations, such as airway obstruction by a foreign body, angioedema, or massive facial trauma. It is easier and faster to perform than a tracheotomy and often performed by paramedics at an accident scene.

ENDOSCOPIC THORACIC SYMPATHECTOMY

An endoscopic thoracic sympathectomy is a procedure performed to correct or control hyperhidrosis, a dysregulation of the neural sympathetic control of the eccrine sweat glands, which leads to excessive and unpleasant sweating. The thoracic sympathetic chain is involved in the neural control of sweating in hyperhidrosis of the upper limbs. It lies in front of the neck of the thoracic ribs and under the parietal pleura. The procedure is performed through an endoscope as an outpatient.

FRENECTOMY

A frenectomy (also known as a frenulectomy or frenotomy) is the removal of a frenulum, a small fold of tissue that prevents an organ in the body from moving too far. A lingual frenectomy of the tongue is done as a treatment for ankyloglossia, where a partial immobilization of the tongue is required due to shortness of the central fold of the mucous membrane that attaches it to the floor of the mouth.

EYE SURGERY

The eye can have many problems due to injury or illness. Conditions that can affect the whole body can result in eye damage that requires surgery to repair. Some of the surgeries and conditions we will discuss here include: refractive errors, cataracts, retinal detachments, macular degeneration, and glaucoma.

Corneal Transplantation

The cornea is the clear part of the eye in front of the iris and pupil. Corneal transplantation, also known as corneal grafting or penetrating keratoplasty, is a surgical procedure where a damaged or diseased cornea is replaced by donated corneal tissue that has been removed from a recently deceased individual having no known diseases that might affect the viability of the donated tissue.

Refractive Surgery

A refractive error, or refraction error, is an error in the focusing of light by the eye and a frequent reason for reduced visual acuity. Refractive errors have historically been treated with eyeglasses or contact lenses. Contact lenses bend the parallel light rays so that they correct a person's sight. The trend today is to surgically correct the lens of the eye. Incisional radial keratotomy and photorefractive keratectomy (PRK) are surgical procedures used to correct refractive problems. Refractive errors account for the largest number of vision problems, the four most common being myopia, hyperopia, astigmatism, and presbyopia.

> *Myopia* is also called nearsightedness. The eyeball is elongated and images do not reach the retina. It is surgically corrected by flattening the cornea.

Hyperopia is often referred to as farsightedness, indicating that the eyeball is too short from front to back. The images are focused beyond the retina. This is corrected by surgically reshaping the lens into a cone formation.

Astigmatism is an unequalled curvature, or curvatures, in the shape of the cornea. A combination of myopia and hyperopia causing blurred vision. This can be caused by injury, inflammation, and corneal surgery, or may be inherited.

Presbyopia is a decreased ability to focus on close objects causing hyperopia. This loss of elasticity in the lens is often a result of age, affecting those over the age of 40.

The cornea is the clear surface of the outer eye and consists of five layers: epithelium, Bowman's membrane, stroma, Descemet's membrane, and the endothelium layer. The epithelium, first layer, must be removed to permanently alter the shape of the cornea.

There are several commonly prescribed procedural approaches using a surgical incision to the cornea, called a "keratotomy." Incisional radial keratotomy is a process of little slit cuts (incisions) made with a precision-calibrated diamond knife. These incisions are cut deeply into the corneal stroma to be more effective. Arcuate keratotomy (AK) is similar to radial keratotomy and used to correct astigmatism. It is also done with a diamond knife, but in these cases, cuts are made in a circle or "circumferentially," parallel to the edge of the cornea. Healing is very slow and unpredictable, and it can often take years to completely heal. Postoperative infection is also a concern and can occur years after surgery. Side effects of an adverse outcome can include loss of vision at high altitudes and visual starbursts during situations such as night driving.

In laser-assisted in situ keratomileusis (LASIK), a surgical procedure is done to make a tiny flap by cutting the top of the cornea. The underlying corneal tissue is then removed with an excimer laser, and the flap is put back in place. Photorefractive keratectomy (PRK) is also referred to as advanced surface ablation (ASA), subepithelial keratectomy, or laser epithelial keratomileusis (LASEK), in which case the epithelium is loosened, usually with alcohol, and reflected like a LASIK flap and replaced after the excimer laser is applied to reshape the cornea. An explanation of how the excimer laser is created and how it works is a very heady physics discussion and not within the scope of this book. LASEK is a procedure that is similar to LASIK, used mostly for people with thin corneas who are poor candidates for LASIK. In LASEK, the outer layer of the cornea is removed manually and a small amount of tissue is ablated (vaporized). With PRK, the visual recovery time and pain is more than with LASIK, but the structural integrity of the cornea is less altered. "No touch" is a newer form of this type of procedure and uses the excimer laser for the entire surgery.

LASIK is a distinctly different procedure. Laser-assisted in situ keratomileusis creates a permanent flap deep in the layers of the cornea. With the use of a mechanical knife "microkeratome" using a metal blade or a femtosecond microkeratome (the term means a unit of time equal to 0.000,000,000,000,001 seconds and is indicated with symbol "fs"), a laser then corrects the shape of the cornea and the flap is replaced to allow healing. The newest technology of "'wavefront-guide'" LASIK provides a higher quality of vision acuity during night or in high visual demand.

Cataract Surgery

Cataracts cause a lack of visual acuity. Cloudiness develops due to types of proteins (crystallins) forming on the lens; it is painless and can be corrected by having the lens surgically removed. The three types of cataracts are subcapsular, nuclear, and cortical.

Subcapsular cataracts starts at the back of the lens due to diabetes, farsightedness, retinitis pigmentosa, or from taking high doses of steroids.

Nuclear cataracts are the most common form. This cataract forms in the nucleus, or center of the lens, and is due to age.

Cortical cataracts form in the cortex of the lens and gradually extend from the outside of the lens toward the center and are common in persons with diabetes.

Phacoemulsification is a procedure performed using an ultrasound-driven instrument that uses sound waves to "sonically" break up the cloudy lens as it is suctioned (aspirated) out of the eye. Phacofracture is another surgical method where special instruments mechanically break up the cataracts into small pieces that are then removed from the eye through a small incision.

After the removal of the lens, the surgeon inserts a plastic or silicone intraocular lens (IOL or Phakic IOL) inside the eye. This replaces the natural lens that was removed. The lens may be inserted between the cornea and the iris or just behind the iris.

New advances are being made in lenses (multifocal and accommodating IOLs) that make them capable of correcting vision for nearsightedness, farsightedness, and presbyopia. Factors including health of the eye, lifestyle, surgeon and patient preference, and cost will determine what type of IOL is used. Most incisions used for cataract surgery are self-sealing. On occasion, incisions may need to be sutured; however, they rarely need to be removed.

The actual surgery lasts about 10 minutes; the time in an outpatient facility may be more like 90 minutes. A patch is usually worn to protect the eye for the first week, and some bruising under the eye may occur. It is essential that strenuous activity and heavy lifting be avoided (over 25 lbs) along with bending and exercising. The surgeon will provide the details to the patient. As a facilitator, unless you are also a physician and specialize in this subspecialty, the aftercare is here for your own knowledge, and is not intended for you to advise the client. Patients are often advised to also keep water away from the eye while bathing and avoid swimming or hot tubs for at least 2 weeks after surgery. This could have some implications on what activities you might schedule for your client if they are also planning to do some tourist activities near a beach, pool, or spa while recuperating after the surgery.

With cataracts, one eye surgery at a time is done with a waiting period of several days to a few weeks in between. This allows for healing and a re-evaluation before the second procedure is performed.

Complications may include endophthalmitis, an ocular emergency typically caused by an infection from eye surgery or trauma. Symptoms include floaters (little deposits of opaque cell fragments in the eye's vitreous humor), light sensitivity, eye pain or discomfort, a red or pink eye, and vision loss. While rare, complications such as increased intraocular pressure, macular edema, retinal detachment, vitreous loss, bleeding into the interior chamber of the eye (hyphema), inflammation of the internal coats of the eye (endophthalmitis), and bleeding from a ruptured blood vessel (expulsive hemorrhage) may occur.

When evaluating client history for these procedures, keep an eye out for daily medications including alpha blockers such as Flomax, Flomaxtra, and Urimax (Tamulosin) used for prostate patients, which may cause problems associated with intraoperative floppy iris syndrome (IFIS) during cataract surgery. A facilitator should look out for these implications and always remind patients to disclose to their eye surgeon all medications and supplements they are taking before undergoing cataract surgery.

Leading factors of cataracts may include: age, sunlight, diabetes, smoking, steroids, nutritional deficiencies, alcohol consumption, trauma, eye infections, and congenital defects.

Macular Degeneration

Currently in the United States, the leading visual impairment is macular degeneration for those over the age of 50. There are two types of this disease: atrophic (dry) and exudative (wet). The dry form is a slow and progressive loss of central and near vision. The eyes are affected separately and blindness is not total, most patients do not lose peripheral vision. Currently, there is no treatment for the exudative type. The atrophic type is sudden and has the same type of loss as the exudative type. If early diagnosis occurs in the wet type, an argon laser photocoagulation procedure can seal leaking blood vessels. This will leave a small, permanent blind spot and slow the process of vision loss.

Glaucoma

Glaucoma is a dangerous buildup of internal eye pressure also known as *intraocular pressure* (IOP) and *optic neuropathy*. This pressure can cause damage to the eye's optic nerve, which is responsible for transmitting visual information to the brain. Peripheral vision loss occurs first, followed by reduction in the central vision and then eventual blindness.

There are two major types of glaucoma: acute angle-closure and primary open-angle closure. Acute angle-closure glaucoma (AACG) refers to the configuration of the internal eye structure that drains fluids. This type of glaucoma is very painful with a quick onset. Symptoms include headaches, halos around lights, dilated pupils, vision loss, red eyes, nausea and vomiting, which is most often the reason a person seeks medical attention. A surgical procedure called an iridotomy is a laser procedure that creates a hole in the iris to improve the drainage passages blocked by a portion of the iris. The iridectomy is basically the same procedure but actually removes a small piece of the iris. Notice the difference in the suffix terminology, where "-otomy" means to cut into and "-ectomy" means to remove.

With primary open-angle glaucoma (POAG), the IOP remains normal and offers no pain. Permanent damage is caused by the time the person realizes that they have lost peripheral vision. Treatment includes optic drops, oral medication, and/or surgery called laser trabeculoplasty, which can offer a temporary solution. A trabeculectomy creates a "controlled" leak of fluid (aqueous humor) from the eye; a trabeculotomy is the same as a trabeculectomy, except that incisions are made without the removal of tissue.

There are also several different glaucoma drainage implants, or shunts. They are surgically attached to the eye's surface and allow the aqueous fluid to bypass the damaged drainage canals. Some are designed to allow drainage while others close off drainage.

Other types of glaucoma include congenital glaucoma, pigmentary glaucoma, and secondary glaucoma.

A goniotomy surgery is most commonly used to treat congenital (from birth) defects of the eye, typically used for infants and small children, allowing for drainage of fluids. The defect is caused by developmental arrest of some of the structures of the front (anterior) of the eye. The purpose of the procedure is to clear the obstruction to aqueous outflow from the eye, which then lowers the pressure. Ocular syndromes and anomalies that predispose a child to congenital glaucoma include the following: Rieger's anomaly, Peter's anomaly, Axenfeld's syndrome, and Axenfeld-Rieger's syndrome. Systemic (affecting the entire body) disorders that affect the eyes in ways that may lead to glaucoma include Marfan's syndrome, maternal rubella (German measles), neurofibromatosis, juvenile rheumatoid arthritis, and Sturge–Weber syndrome. Since these disorders affect the entire body as well as the eyes, the child's pediatrician or family doctor will help to diagnose and treat these diseases.

Retinal Detachment

This is a separation of the retina from the choroids layer of the eye that allows fluid to enter the space between the layers. Without rapid treatment, the entire retina may become detached and blindness will occur. There are three types of retinal detachment: rhegmatogenous retinal detachments, nonrhegmatogenous retinal detachments, and secondary, or exudative detachments.

Rhegmatogenous retinal detachments are caused by a hole or tear related to degenerative changes, or they might result from moderate trauma such as direct trauma to the eye, weight lifting, or stooping. The incidence of rhegmatogenous retinal detachments increases with age.

Nonrhegmatogenous tractional detachment occurs when fibrous tissue attaches to the retina and pulls it away from its normal position. This may be caused by an injury, inflammation, or neovascularization, and also occurs in persons with sickle cell disease or diabetes mellitus.

Exudative serous, or secondary detachment, occurs when fluid accumulates underneath the retina without a hole, tear, or break and is often seen in conditions such as advanced hypertension, pre-eclampsia (an abnormal state of pregnancy characterized by hypertension, fluid retention, and albumin in the urine), eclampsia (a toxic condition characterized by convulsions and possibly coma during or immediately after pregnancy), and/or intraocular tumors.

Several types of treatment are available to reattach the retina. These procedures include laser photocoagulation, cryosurgery, scleral buckling, and a few nonsurgical treatments.

Laser photocoagulation is used when a small area of the retina is affected. Cryosurgery (freezing) is similar to the laser treatment and used when a larger portion of the retina is detached.

Scleral buckling is used to close a retinal break. A thin silicone band is sewn around the sclera of the eye. Buckles are used to move the eye closer to the retinal hole, thus allowing fluid to flow away from the retina where it has formed. The retina is then able to reattach with the choroid layers. Often buckles are left in place and only removed if complications occur.

Other nonsurgical treatments include electrodiathermy (the same process microwaves use to cook) and pneumatic retinopexy (where the surgeon uses a gas bubble replacement). Silicone oil is used to mechanically hold the retina in place until it reattaches. The oil is clear and remains in the eye approximately a year and is then removed. This procedure is used when damage occurs due to cytomegalovirus (CMV), a herpes virus that affects 50–85 percent of adults in the United States by around age 40 and is most often transmitted to a child before birth. Infectious CMV may be shed in the bodily fluids of any previously infected person, and thus may be found in urine, saliva, blood, tears, semen, and breast milk. The shedding of viruses may take place intermittently, without any detectable signs, and without causing symptoms. It is from person to person and requires close contact. It is often described as a sexually transmitted disease, but as you can see, it doesn't require sexual contact to spread.

Retinal detachment is more common in those with severe nearsightedness (myopia) and can occur more frequently after cataract surgery.

GENITOURINARY SURGERY

Hysterectomy
A surgery performed to remove the uterus.

Oophorectomy
An oophorectomy is a surgical procedure where the ovary is removed. The procedure may be performed as a laparotomy or via laparoscopy.

Episiotomy
An episiotomy is an incision procedure sometimes made to enlarge the vaginal opening in the late stages of labor to prevent tearing and facilitate the birth.

Tubal Ligation
Tubal ligation (informally known as getting one's "tubes tied") is a permanent form of female sterilization, in which the fallopian tubes are severed and sealed or "pinched shut," in order to prevent fertilization.

Tubal Reversal (Tubal Anastomosis)
Tubal reversal—short for tubal sterilization reversal or tubal ligation reversal—is a surgical procedure that restores fertility to women after a tubal ligation. By rejoining the separated segments of fallopian tube, tubal reversal gives women the chance to become pregnant again naturally. This delicate surgery is best performed by a reproductive surgeon with specialized training and experience in the techniques of tubal ligation reversal.

Colporrhaphy
Colporrhaphy is a surgical procedure that repairs a defect in the wall of the vagina. It is the surgical intervention for both cystocele (protrusion of bladder into the vagina) and rectocele (protrusion of rectum into the vagina). This is often performed on morbidly obese women who may experience difficulty in controlling urine on sneezing or exertion.

Lithotripsy

A lithotripsy is the fragmentation of a stone in the urinary system or gallbladder—for example, with ultrasound shock waves—so that the gravel can be passed naturally. It is also performed in the treatment of heel spurs.

Orchidectomy

An orchidectomy is a surgical procedure where the testicles are removed.

Circumcision

A circumcision is an operation to remove the foreskin covering the glans penis. It is often done shortly after birth of a male child, but may also be done to an adult to prevent repeated urinary tract infections.

Foreskin Restoration

Foreskin restoration is the process of expanding the residual skin on the penis, via surgical or non-surgical methods, to create the appearance of a natural foreskin (prepuce) covering the glans penis. Foreskin restoration techniques are most commonly undertaken by men who have been circumcised or who have sustained an injury, but are also used by uncircumcised men who desire a longer foreskin and by men who have phimosis (the inability of the foreskin to loosen). The procedure may be carried out by a urologist but is more often performed by a plastic or reconstructive surgeon.

Penectomy or Peotomy

Penectomy is the practice of surgical removal of the penis for medical reasons, such as cancer, where it is sometimes necessary to remove all or part of the penis.

Genital surgical procedures for transsexual women undergoing sex reassignment surgery do not usually involve the complete removal of the penis. Instead, part or all of the glans are usually kept and reshaped as a clitoris, while the skin of the penile shaft may also be inverted to form the vagina.

Phalloplasty

A phalloplasty is a cosmetic procedure to reshape the glans penis.

Vasectomy

A vasectomy is a procedure for male sterilization by surgical excision of the vas deferens, the thin duct that carries sperm cells from the testicles to the prostate and the penis. It is performed on an outpatient basis.

Prostatectomy

A prostatectomy is the surgical removal of all or part of the prostate gland. There are several forms of the operation and several approaches. In the transurethral resection of the prostate, the surgeon introduces a cystoscope through the shaft of the glans penis, directly. The procedure takes about 45 minutes, and the patient remains in the hospital for a few days postoperatively. The procedure may also be performed using a laparoscope or the Da Vinci robot.

In Vitro Fertilization

In vitro fertilization (IVF) is a process by which egg cells are fertilized by sperm outside the body, in a laboratory setting (*in vitro*). IVF is a major treatment for infertility and belongs to a group of treatments called assisted reproductive therapies (ART).

Gender Reassignment Surgery

Gender reassignment surgery (also known as SRS [sexual reassignment surgery]), genital reconstruction surgery, sex affirmation surgery, sex realignment surgery or sex-change surgery is a term for the surgical procedures by which a person's physical appearance and function of his or her exist-ing sexual characteristics are altered to resemble that of the other sex.

It is part of a treatment for gender identity disorder/gender dysphoria in transsexual and transgen-der people. It may also be performed on intersex babies, often in infancy.

NEUROLOGICAL SURGERY

DISCECTOMY

A discectomy is a surgical procedure in which the central portion of an intervertebral disc, the nucleus pulposus, which is causing pain by stressing the spinal cord or radiating nerves, is removed. Advances in options have produced effective alternatives to traditional discectomy procedures (e.g., a microdiscectomy), which is often performed on an outpatient basis with a small bandage strip closure and one or two sutures.

BILATERAL CINGULOTOMY

Bilateral cingulotomy is a form of psychosurgery, introduced in 1952 as an alternative to lobotomy. Today, it is mainly used as a last resort for the treatment of obsessive–compulsive disorder and chronic pain. The objective of this surgical procedure is the severing of the supracallosal fibers of the cingulum bundle, which pass through the anterior cingulate gyrus.

CORDOTOMY OR CHORDOTOMY

A cordotomy or chordotomy is a surgical procedure that disables selected pain-conducting tracts in the spinal cord, in order to achieve loss of pain and temperature perception. This procedure is commonly performed on patients experiencing severe pain due to cancer or other diseases for which there are currently no cure. Anterolateral cordotomy is effective for relieving unilateral, somatic body pain while bilateral cordotomies may be required for visceral (organ) or bilateral pain.

SPINAL SURGERY

Back pain guidelines are offered from the American Pain Society (APS), which has revised its clinical guidelines for the treatment of lower back pain to emphasize noninvasive methods over the use of invasive diagnostic procedures and treatments such as provocative discography, prolo-therapy, facet joint injection of corticosteroids, and intradiscal corticosteroid injects for patients with nonradicular low-back pain. The guidelines, published in the May 1 issue of the journal *Spine,* also recommend more communication between the surgeon and patient in deciding on treatment options, especially given the benefit/harm tradeoffs of some interventional procedures. "In general, noninvasive therapies supported by evidence showing benefits should be tried before considering interventional therapies or surgery," said Roger Chou, MD, director of the APS Clinical Practice Guideline Program.

ORTHOPEDIC SURGERY

Hand Surgery

Hip Replacement

Patients suffering from joint problems caused by various types of arthritis, fractures of the hip, and bone tumors are potential candidates for hip replacement surgery. While there are investigational therapies to regrow the lost or damaged joint tissue, much of this is dependent on further developments in stem cell research. An estimated 250,000 hip replacement surgeries are performed in the United States each year.

Conventional hip replacement involves cutting a 10- to 12-inch incision, detaching muscles from the bone, and removing the damaged parts of the hip. This is often referred to in clinical circles as lateral, anterolateral, and posterior approaches. Another approach is commonly referred to as the anterior approach. The anterior approach is much less invasive than conventional hip replacement surgery. Anterior hip replacement surgery requires a much smaller incision—only 4 to 5 inches in the front of the hip. Because of the placement of the incision, no muscle is detached from the bone. The damaged parts of the hip are removed and the new parts take their place.

The surgery is most often carried out under general anesthesia. After surgery, patients are in a fair amount of pain. Often a patient-controlled analgesia (PCA) pump is placed via an intravenous line so that the patient may control smaller more frequent doses of pain medication instead of waiting long periods between doses, where peaks and troughs are experienced.

Patients receiving conventional hip replacement surgery require physical therapy to strengthen the muscle and ligaments that were cut from the bone. Slowly rebuilding muscle strength has proven to be less stressful on the recovering patient. Usually within 24 hours, a physical therapist visits to help the patient begin to ambulate with a walker. Walking is often difficult for the first several days following hip replacement surgery. Patients who elect the anterior hip replacement surgery often do not require physical therapy. This is because the muscle was not cut away from the bone during the procedure, so full recovery time is drastically reduced. The anterior approach also usually results in less blood loss during the procedure.

The average hospital stay is generally 3 to 10 days for conventional hip replacement. By comparison, the average hospital stay for patients receiving anterior hip replacement surgery is only 2 to 4 days' time.

After conventional hip replacement, patients must limit flexing the hip to no more than 90 degrees, which makes something as simple as sitting on the toilet a compromising or even painful event. Flying for long transcontinental, transpacific, or transatlantic flights is not encouraged for several weeks postoperatively. Protecting the new hip joint is the top priority. Following the anterior approach, patients may resume normal everyday activities within days as opposed to weeks.

Total recovery time for conventional hip replacement surgery ranges from 2 to 4 months. Typical results vary from patient to patient. Patients who had problems during surgery or extensive immobility before surgery may require more assistance in making a full recovery. With the anterior approach, what would take up to 4 months only takes about 8 weeks to heal, with some patients reporting recovery times as short as 2 to 6 weeks.

With hip replacement surgeries, the risks and side effects may include some lingering pain after full recovery even though all scans are normal. Some of this pain may be due to nerve damage during the replacement procedure. Dislocation of the new joint may occur in about one percent of prosthetic hip patients. There have also been cases where patients have had to undergo surgery again due to normal wear and tear of the prosthetic joint. Postoperative infection may occur in about 1% of hip replacement patients annually.

Hip Resurfacing (Birmingham Hip™)

The Birmingham Hip™ Resurfacing system (BHR) is the global market leading hip resurfacing system with over 70,000 implantations worldwide. While the procedure is new in the United States, it has been performed worldwide since 1997. The procedure was designed using knowledge gained from first generation metal-on-metal total hips and a thorough understanding of hip resurfacing principles.

The typical candidate for this surgery is under 60 years of age with a history of degenerative hip arthritis, hip dysplasia, or avascular necrosis of the hip. In patients over the age of 60, testing must be performed prior to the decision to use this system because the bone quality has to be strong enough to support the implant. Females of child-bearing age are not candidates for the procedure because the effects of metal ion release on the fetus are yet unknown. Patients with renal insufficiency, or those with conditions that could impair renal function, are not likely candidates. Neither are those with AIDS or other immunosuppressive conditions. Patients who are severely overweight as well as those with diabetes and those on high doses of corticosteroids are generally refused the procedure. Still another contraindication is in people who have known or suspected metal sensitivity, as with jewelry.

Surgery is carried out under general anesthesia. The incision is between 6 and 8 inches in length, but some may be smaller, depending on the surgeon's technique.

Postoperatively, after the first year, patients often return to the level of physical activity before the hip pain began to limit activity and mobility. During the first year, low-impact activities like walking, swimming, and cycling are encouraged to strengthen the femoral neck and muscles around the implant.

As with other hip replacement techniques, some of the risks of the procedure include damage to the nerves and muscles around the structures of the hip, nonunion of the implant to the remaining bone, thrombo-embolism (blood clot), and fat embolism, where fat enters the right atrium of the heart after a cemented hip replacement. Other risks include component loosening, a reaction to the bone cement, damage to large blood vessels during surgery, and limb length discrepancy, among others. The surgeon will review all the potential risks and complications with the patient prior to obtaining informed consent for surgery.

Arthrodesis

An arthrodesis, also known as artificial ankylosis or syndesis, is the artificial induction of joint ossification between two bones via surgery. This is done to relieve intractable pain in a joint that cannot be managed by pain medication, splints, or other normally-indicated treatments.

Arthroplasty

An arthroplasty (literally meaning "remodeling of a joint") is an operative procedure of orthopedic surgery performed, in which the arthritic or dysfunctional joint surface is replaced with something better or by remodeling or realigning the joint by osteotomy or some other procedure.

Arthroscopy

An arthroscopy (also called arthroscopic surgery) is a minimally invasive surgical procedure in which an examination and sometimes treatment of damage of the interior of a joint is performed using an arthroscope, a type of endoscope that is inserted into the joint through a small incision. Arthroscopic procedures can be performed either to evaluate or to treat many orthopedic conditions including torn floating cartilage, torn surface cartilage, anterior cruciate ligament (ACL) repair or reconstruction, and trimming damaged cartilage. Arthroscopies may be done on knees, ankles, wrists, elbows, shoulders, hips, toes, and fingers.

Knee Replacement (TKR)

Partial Knee Resurfacing/Unicondylar Knee Arthroplasty (UKA)/Journey Deuce

As an alternative to total knee replacement, a new procedure, called the Journey Deuce bi-compartmental knee system, is an implant that provides a new treatment option specifically designed for about 6% of the reported 70% of patients whose osteoarthritis only afflicts two of the three compartments of the knee. The procedure is also referred to as the unicondylar knee arthroplasty. The procedure is reported to provide more of a natural feeling and stability in the knee, less postoperative pain, less physical therapy, and a shorter recovery, period. By comparison, this procedure removes less bone and ligament than traditional total knee replacement.

Ideal candidates for a Journey Deuce procedure should have degeneration in only the medial and patellofemoral knee compartments, and not the lateral (outside) compartment. They should also have a healthy, functional anterior cruciate ligament (ACL) and posterior cruciate ligament (PCL).

As with other knee replacement surgeries, this is performed under general anesthesia. Most patients can resume normal activities once they have regained adequate strength and flexibility. However, any activity that results in repetitive joint trauma, such as jumping or twisting, should be avoided for most patients. Patients who have recovered from this procedure have returned to such activities as golf, doubles tennis, dancing, swimming, and gardening.

Anterior Cruciate Ligament (ACL) Reconstruction

Surgery for anterior cruciate ligament (ACL) injuries in the knee involves reconstructing or repairing the ACL.

ACL reconstruction surgery uses a graft to replace the ligament. The most common grafts are autografts using part of the patient's own body, such as the tendon attached to the kneecap (patellar tendon) or one of the hamstring tendons. Other good choices include allograft tissue, which is donor material that comes from cadavers. (Muslim clients have to be assured that the donor was a Muslim as well.)

ACL surgery is done by making small incisions in the knee and inserting instruments for surgery through these incisions (arthroscopic surgery) or by cutting a large incision in the knee (open surgery).

SHOULDER RECONSTRUCTION

Acromioplasty

An acromioplasty is a arthroscopic surgical procedure of the acromion in the shoulder. Acrioplasty is the most commonly performed procedure to treat symptoms of impingement in the absence of a full thickness tear of the rotator cuff.

Shoulder Replacement

In shoulder replacement surgery, doctors replace the ends of the damaged upper arm bone (humerus) and usually the shoulder bone (scapula) or cap them with artificial surfaces lined with plastic or metal and plastic.

Shoulder joint components may be held in place with cement, or they may be made with a material that allows new bone to grow into the joint component over time to hold it in place without cement. The choice of the surgical technique is largely dependent on the patient's age and activity level.

FOREARM SURGERY

Ulnar Collateral Ligament (UCL) Reconstruction or Tommy John Procedure

The ulnar collateral ligament reconstruction is a surgical procedure in which a ligament in the medial elbow is replaced with a tendon from elsewhere in the body (often from the forearm, hamstring, knee, or foot of the patient). The procedure is used to repair an injury from repetitive stress injuries common among collegiate and professional athletes who play baseball. It was originally performed at the Jobe Clinic in Los Angeles. Full rehabilitation takes about 1 year for professional athletes.

AMPUTATION

An amputation is removal of all or part of a limb or other body part. The development of sophisticated techniques and antibiotics for treatment and prevention of infection has greatly decreased its necessity. Surgical amputation is currently performed in cases of bone and tissue cancers, gangrene, and uncontrollable cellulitis infections of the arm or leg. An amputation is performed as far above the affected area as is necessary to remove all unhealthy tissue and to leave a portion of sound tissue with which to pad the bone stump. Whenever possible, amputations are performed at points on the limb that permit the fitting of prosthetic devices.

PEDIATRIC SURGERY

Medical tourism for pediatric surgery is rare, but not for the reasons you might think.

Pediatric surgery cases cancel more frequently than adult surgery; most often because the child is too sick to undergo the operation. Usually, it is something minor like a cold or ear infection, but because children receiving eye surgery require general anesthesia delivered by tracheal intubation, the child's airways must be healthy and non-inflamed. Any kind of residual swelling or airway restriction could have devastating consequences.

Every hospital sets its own rules but many require a child to not have any type of upper respiratory infection for 14 days prior to general anesthesia.

The same rules are applied to asthma attacks as well. Fever is generally not the indicator, but instead it is the clarity of the breathing passages.

A child's delicate bronchioles are very sensitive after illness and could go into bronchospasm if challenged by anesthetic agents. Healthy children have died because the anesthesiologist was unaware of a child's recent respiratory illness.

As a medical tourism facilitator, you may decide as a matter of business policy not to accept pediatric cases to avoid these potential liability and high stakes cases.

PLASTIC SURGERY

Rhytidoplasty or Rhytidectomy

Otherwise known as a facelift, technically known as a rhytidectomy (literally, "surgical removal of wrinkles"), the procedure is a type of cosmetic surgery procedure used to give a more youthful appearance. It usually involves the removal of excess facial skin, with or without the tightening of underlying tissues, and the redraping of the skin on the patient's face and neck.

BOTOX® Cosmetic, Dermal Fillers, and Other Wrinkle Treatments

BOTOX® Cosmetic is actually botulinum toxin type A, which is produced by the *Clostridium botulinum* bacterium. It is a simple, nonsurgical, physician-administered treatment, and is the only treatment approved by the U.S. Food and Drug Administration (FDA) for this purpose. It is approved for the temporary treatment of moderate to severe frown lines between the brows in people ages 18–65 by reducing the muscle activity that cause the frown lines between the brows to form over time. One 10-minute treatment and a few tiny injections that are described to feel like a pinprick, or a bee sting, generally produces a noticeable improvement that can last approximately 4 months. Therefore, BOTOX® Cosmetic is not a permanent solution to correcting wrinkles and other conditions. Clients usually opt for a treatment a few days before a special event but some keep up their regimens as a routine, just like a manicure and pedicure. There are other preparations of botulinum toxin type A on the market, but they vary in strength and formulation. There is only one BOTOX® Cosmetic.

Typically, for BOTOX® Cosmetic, there is no anesthesia required, but the physician may use cold packs or anesthetic cream to numb the area if the client complains of discomfort. There is no recovery time needed, but you might caution your client to spend the rest of the day relaxing and save heavy exercise and tourist activities that could produce perspiration for the day after. The most common side effects following injection include temporary eyelid droop and nausea. Localized pain, infection, inflammation, tenderness, swelling, redness, and/or bleeding and bruising may be associated with the injection. Patients with certain neuromuscular disorders such as ALS (Lou Gehrig's Disease), myasthenia gravis, or Lambert–Eaton syndrome, may be at increased risk of serious side effects.

Alpha-hydroxy acids (AHAs) are derived from fruit and dairy products and act as exfoliators and moisturizers. Many dermatologists recommend AHAs to soften rough skin and erase fine lines. The strength of AHAs depends on their acid concentration.

Chemical peeling, also called chemabrasion and dermapeeling, is a facial skin rejuvenation procedure that does what its name implies—it peels the skin. Chemical peels may contain alpha-hydroxy acids or other acids. Peels are typically used to treat wrinkles and pigment changes caused by sun exposure.

Collagen is a fibrous protein substance that is part of all human and animal tissue. Collagen injections typically involve bovine (cow-derived) or human collagen. Collagen injections are used to minimize lines and scars, filling wrinkles between the eyebrows, wrinkles from mouth to nose, and forehead wrinkles. Collagen is typically a dermal filler that offers a partial, short-term approach to fill in and smooth mild lines or folds.

Dermabrasion is a procedure where the surface layer of the skin is removed by high-speed sanding. This technique is used for a wide range of purposes, from removal or reduction of acne and scars to facial skin rejuvenation. Microdermabrasion is a technique that removes less surface skin and is used most often for superficial skin defects.

Laser resurfacing is carried out with a pulsed CO_2 laser. It works best on fine, shallow wrinkles caused by aging or sun damage. Lasers emit a very brief pulse of high-intensity light that is fast enough to limit heat damage in the skin yet strong enough to vaporize tissue cleanly.

Fat implants are used as subdermal fillers. With this procedure, fat is essentially taken from one area (usually the belly, buttocks, or thighs) and put elsewhere—in an area where you want it. The fat is cleansed of blood and other fluids and deposited in laugh lines, frown lines, sunken chins, and hollow cheeks.

On the day of the appointment, the client may meet with the physician, a nurse, an aesthetician, or all three before receiving treatment. The physician generally reviews the potential risks and side effects, and answers questions about prognosis, outcomes, etc. They may also ask questions about allergies and other conditions that might indicate that the client is not a good candidate for the procedure. The nurse may actually be the one to take care of obtaining consent signatures after the physician explains the procedure and risks, and answers any of the client's additional questions. Then, a nurse or aesthetician may clean and prepare the client's face. The client is seated in a reclining chair, similar to that encountered in a facial treatment at a spa. The procedures may be carried out in a clinic or medical spa on an outpatient basis.

In any of the procedures mentioned, the client may be turned away and refused the procedure if they have an active infection in the area where the procedure will be performed. Some physicians may refuse to do the procedure if any infection is present. Another contraindication may be breast feeding or if the client is planning to become pregnant soon.

One key safety issue for you as facilitator is to act as a second set of eyes and ears as an advocate for your client. Be sure to obtain a list of any and all medications and vitamin and herbal supplements being used by your client, as some cause bleeding abnormalities while others may be contraindicated (cannot be used at the same time) altogether.

Breast Augmentation (Implants)

For women who experience sagging of the breast tissue, asymmetry of the breasts, or disproportionate breast size in comparison to the rest of their body, implant surgery may be an option that is not very expensive and is relatively safe. In 1992, silicone implants were banned from the market by the FDA for cosmetic reasons. After years of extensive research, the FDA concluded that silicone breast implants did not cause any kind of disease. Studies showed that there was no greater incidence of any type of disease in women with silicone breast implants compared to the general female population. Silicone implants were determined to be medically safe.

Today, women have a choice of whether to have silicone or saline implants. Silicone tend to have a more natural feel than saline implants, and most surgeons tend to prefer the silicone implant result over the saline. Each case is different and personal.

The average breast augmentation can take approximately 2 hours to complete. Clients should be prepared to restrict regular activities for at least 5 to 7 days.

Before the client has the procedure, certain decisions must be made about the surgical approach and the materials that will be used for the implants. For instance:

- Silicone or saline implants
- The size of the implants
- The shape of the implants (oval or round)
- The surface of the implants (smooth or textured)
- The placement of the implants (over or under the muscle)
- The location of the incision site (inframammary, infra-areolar, and transumbilical breast augmentation (TUBA), or supra-umbilical)
- If they will have a lift with the procedure or only the implant
- Their profile (high profile, or moderate and more natural looking)

Prior to conferring with the selected surgeon, the client should be directed to do some research and write down all their questions and be prepared to discuss the eight points above. The surgeon will also likely ask for photographs depicting the breasts as they currently appear, without clothes or undergarments. This is normal but should be protected as any other medical records, in compliance with HIPAA and other privacy and security measures.

Breast augmentation is often carried out through an infra-areolar incision, where the incision is placed in the bottom half of the nipple area. While the scar is in a noticeable place, it seems to heal well and is less noticeable after about a year postoperatively. Loss of sensation can occur with any approach and has to do with a nerve that comes from the side of the chest wall and goes to the nipple. In rare circumstances, it happens that the nerve is nicked during surgery.

Another approach to breast augmentation is the axillary incision. This is chosen when the patient wants no scar on the breast at all. The incision is made under the armpit and the implant is manipulated through the tissue under the muscle flap in the breast. Some clients complain of pain for days and weeks after the procedure but the pain is usually temporary and subsides with time.

Axillary incisions have a greater chance of becoming infected if the surgical area is not vigilantly kept clean and dry. Underarm perspiration can create a breeding ground for bacteria and promote infection.

The TUBA approach is via an incision through the navel. While a few plastic surgeons have become very proficient at it and love it, many have tried it and don't like to use it. The best feature of this approach is that it doesn't leave a scar on the breast, but it is also far from the breast and the surgeon has less control of the pocket in which the implant will be placed. Most surgeons agree that it is best suited for saline implants.

Each approach offers some benefits; however, it is usually recommended to go under the muscle. Placing the implants under the muscle provides the most natural and long-term result. Additionally, it is usually easier to obtain a mammogram. However, going under the muscle will require a few more days of recovery time.

Prior to surgery, some surgeons prescribe a drug that is often used for seasickness to prevent nausea. This is in the form of a patch that can be worn for up to 3 days. The patch is worn behind the ear and is placed there the night before surgery. It can cause dry mouth and sleepiness. This also helps afterward when the patient is given pain medications as the most frequent side effects from pain medications are nausea and vomiting. Vomiting would not be a good thing after breast surgery for obvious reasons!

During the surgery procedure, short- and long-acting local anesthetic agents are injected after the patient is sedated and before surgery starts. Typically, there is a 15–30 minute delay to make sure that the anesthetic is working. The long-acting anesthetics often last between 12 and 18 hours.

At the conclusion of the case, the surgeon attempts to blunt the pain for the first 24 hours. To do this, often a pain pump is prescribed. This device has two components. The first is a very small catheter. It is placed in the operated area and is brought out through a pinhole-sized opening in the skin. The catheter connects to a reservoir of local anesthetic, which is pumped continuously into the operated area. There are multiple benefits to this. The patient takes fewer pain medications because she feels a lot less pain. There is less nausea. Patients are often offered the opportunity to purchase a pain-management pump, so you should inquire as to whether or not the package price includes the pain pump or not.

Breast Lift (Mastopexy)

Often, a breast augmentation is performed in conjunction with a breast lift or (mastopexy).

Breast Reduction

Breast reduction is a plastic surgery procedure that lifts the breast and makes it smaller. It is often covered by health insurance because the sagging breast tissue may be the cause of symptoms of back pain, neck pain, breast pain, and other medical problems associated with having large breasts, and is therefore considered a reconstructive surgery. Candidates for this surgery often complain that they feel that their breasts are too large or uneven, they are causing back or neck pain, may have a difficult time finding clothes that fit or engaging in fitness activities and playing sports.

The procedure can be performed under general anesthesia or MAC. During the procedure, excess skin and breast tissue are removed. The nipple is left attached to remaining breast tissue and moved to a new position to match the new smaller breast size. They may also minimize the areola, if appropriate.

To close and lift the breast, many surgeons use a vertical technique also referred to as a lollipop incision. Others elect to use an "inverted T" (Weiss pattern) for skin closure. Some surgeons feel that the Weiss pattern underneath the breast is not only unattractive, but that it has a tendency to broaden or become thick and form a keloid, or thick, fibrous scar. This is most often the case in women of olive complexion.

With the vertical incision, there is less scarring and also a more youthful, perkier shape over the long term. The recovery time is generally 1 to 2 weeks. The procedure is usually well-tolerated.

In the United States, the surgeons' fee for breast reduction averages about $3,500 and includes 90 days of postoperative office visits. Additional costs include the hospital charge and post-op medications. In most cases, insurance carriers will reimburse the majority of the cost of the procedure as long as a minimum amount of breast tissue is removed. On average, insurance companies generally approve by medical necessity if the anticipated removal is at least 500 cc of breast tissue from each breast, together with symptoms explained previously, in order to be considered a covered procedure.

Breast Reconstruction

Breast reconstruction includes a series of surgical procedures performed to recreate a breast. It is the second most commonly performed cosmetic surgical procedure practiced on women in the United States. The statistics are readily available from the American Society of Plastic and Reconstructive Surgeons. At the 2008 Medical Tourism Association Congress in San Francisco, the association's president spoke to the audience very negatively about medial tourism and surgery performed outside the United States. He put up lots of sensationalist photos of disfigured patients but did not offer whether or not those cases could also go wrong in the United States. Needless to say, his presentations were unimpressive. Reconstructions are commonly begun after portions of one or both breasts are removed as a treatment for breast cancer. A breast may need to be refashioned for other reasons such as trauma or to correct abnormalities that occur during breast development.

Reconstructive Mammoplasty

For reconstructive mammoplasty, the most common procedure is to stretch the existing skin. An implant is inserted and then, over weeks or months, the implant is injected to attain the correct size. At that time, a permanent implant is inserted and the reconstruction of the nipple and areola can proceed. In some cases, the pectoral muscle may be released along the inferior edge to allow for more expansion of the implant.

Acellular human graft material (sold under many different manufacturer names) and animal dermal grafts have been used with good results. Another option for breast reconstruction is to use one's own tissue and is usually the safer option. In this way, no foreign material is introduced into the body.

Lumpectomy

A lumpectomy is a surgical operation for breast cancer in which the surgery is limited to the removal of the visible and palpable tumor only.

Mammectomy or Mastectomy

A mastectomy is the surgical removal of breast tissue, usually done as treatment for breast cancer.

Flap Procedures

A flap procedure (also called a pedicle graft) can be used. This is an almond-shaped piece of skin with attached muscle tissue. This is taken from under the arm using the latissimus dorsi muscle, or from the abdomen using the rectus abdominus muscle if a larger amount of tissue is needed for the reconstruction.

In general, the latissimus dorsi is only a good option for a woman with small to medium-sized breasts because there is so little body fat in this part of the back. The muscle and skin piece are pulled under the skin to the mastectomy site. The almond-shaped skin is then attached and formed to match the other breast. On the positive side of the latissimus dorsi procedure, many breast surgeons like this procedure because the flap is easily slipped around front through a short tunnel in the skin and put into position. Generally, this procedure produces excellent results with few complications. On the negative side, the skin on one's back has a different color and texture from breast skin. Also, the latissimus dorsi approach results in some back asymmetry (unevenness in the appearance of one's back). Usually, though, back function and strength aren't affected.

When using the transverse rectus abdominis muscle (TRAM) flap, the wall of the abdomen is then weakened. The surgeon may place a piece of surgical mesh to strengthen this area. This offers the same benefit as a tummy tuck; however, the stomach muscle will always be weaker than preoperative. The TRAM flap is not for everyone. Generally, it is held that thin women who don't have enough abdominal tissue, women who smoke and have narrower and less flexible blood vessels, and women who have multiple surgical scars on their abdomens from other surgeries (cesarean-section scars may be okay) are not ideal for this type of procedure. In general, most women are pleased to have a flat belly from the tummy tuck that accompanies the TRAM procedure. This must be weighed against the long scar that will run crosswise from hip to hip between the top of the pubis and the navel.

Perforation techniques are also used such as the deep inferior epigastric perforator (DIEP) flap and the superficial inferior epigastric artery (SIEA) flap. These require precise dissection of small perforating vessels through the rectus muscle. Other locations can be used for the replacement of the breast tissue such as the superior gluteal artery perforator (SGAP) or inferior gluteal artery perforator (IGAP) flaps of the buttocks.

The nipple is also reconstructed and is done so after the reconstructed breast has healed. Taking from the mature breast areola, skin can be used to form a nipple on the reconstructed breast. Another option is to have a small flap produce a mound of skin duplicating the nipple, then tattooed to give color. To simulate the areola, a circular incision can be made, then sewn back again.

An implant may still be an option for appearance and symmetry. In many cases, the mature breast will undergo a mammoplasty, or lift (mastopexy), to offer the best possible outcome. Complications can occur if infection, swelling, or drainage occurs.

Recovery for an implant is shorter than with a flap-type reconstruction, in many cases, taking from 3 to 6 weeks for the breast surgery to heal. Patients will likely return to full activity in several weeks without permanent limitations. There is little information about upper body exercise postmastectomy. Your doctor can inform you of the appropriate exercises and when to begin them.

In 1998, the Women's Health and Cancer Rights Act mandated health care payer coverage for reconstruction of the breast and nipple, contralateral procedures to achieve symmetry, and treatment for the recuperative care after a mastectomy. Additional legislation in 2001 imposed penalties on insurers who were noncompliant. Similar provisions exist in many countries through the national health care programs. While this may be a regulatory matter, the health plan may not approve payment to an international or domestic provider who has not been empanelled into their network.

BUTTOCK AUGMENTATION/BUTTOCK LIFT

This is a relatively new procedure that is often performed independently or as part of an entire body lift. The procedure improves the contour of the buttock. There are two common approaches:

- The first approach is by removing excess skin and tightening the skin above the upper part of the buttocks, which in turn reshapes the contours.
- The second approach is a lift by fat injections or implants. The fat injection approach is often referred to as the Brazilian butt lift. This approach provides more volume and prominence.

Sometimes, if the buttock is very large, the surgeon will also suggest liposuction in conjunction with the lift. After dramatic weight loss, such as that following gastric bypass surgery and successful weight loss, the buttocks may sag. This can be addressed through removal of the excess skin and tightening skin through a procedure known as a "butt wedge" (I know, I know … not the best mental picture!) excision, wherein the tissue is removed at the natural buttock crease. This leaves a relatively unnoticeable scar at the buttock crease. This may also be done in conjunction with liposuction of the hips and thighs.

One consideration for the medical travel facilitator in this approach is the return home. The client may not be able to sit for long transatlantic or transpacific flights, or even transcontinental flights. As you build your database of case information, you will want to review these concerns and logistical issues with the surgeon prior to deciding where to refer the case if the client asks for suggestions. In most cases, the doctor advises the patient not to sit for one week so as not to stress the operated area. The doctor will likely advise your clients that they may return to work in 2 weeks if they do not do a lot of extensive sitting. Therefore, extensive sitting on an airplane is not advised unless they plan to spend their recuperation relaxing by the pool, face up, as sunburn on the postoperative area would also not be a wise decision. The buttock lift is most often carried out under MAC anesthesia or general anesthesia. A good surgeon will hide the scar so that it is not visible when wearing a bathing suit.

In the United States, the cost of the procedure can range from $5,000 to $13,000 depending on the complexity and location in the country where the procedure is carried out.

EYELID SURGERY (BLEPHAROPLASTY)

For clients who complain of always looking tired, having puffy eyes and dark circles under the eyes, and extra skin on their eyelids, eyelid surgery may help. This procedure removes excess skin from the upper and lower eyelids and provides a more youthful look. Sometimes, instead of a blepharoplasty, the client will research and decide upon a brow lift instead. The surgeon should make the decision together with the client to determine which will be the most optimal choice of procedure for the client.

Eyelid surgery is often carried out through a small incision inside the eye (with the eyeball draped and protected). Most of the surgery is carried out on the external eye area.

Healing time is generally about 10 days, and there is some ecchymosis (bruising). Most clients will wear large sunglasses during the 10-day period. Sometimes the residual swelling is longer and is reduced by massage. Most clients report that the most painful part of the procedure is the removal of their sutures after the surgery and healing. A skillful surgeon will place the sutures in such a way that the pain during removal is minimized. Eyelid and brow lift surgery can be carried out under local anesthesia or MAC.

EAR SURGERY (OTOPLASTY)

An otoplasty is a surgery performed to correct prominent or floppy ears. The otoplasty procedure will make the ears have better natural proportion to the head. Prominent ears are often the result of an unusually large cartilage bowl, which is common in people of Irish/Scottish heritage. Lop ears are due to a weakness in the cartilage of the upper earlobe. With lop ears, the upper part flops down instead of lying near to the head. The incisions made to pin the ears back are carefully hidden in the crease behind the ears. Once the ears have healed, it is almost impossible to distinguish them from normal ears. In some cases, patients have both a large cartilage bowl as well as weakness of the cartilage. In this case, the treatment is surgical repair of the deformed cartilage. The procedure is generally performed as an outpatient procedure in the hospital.

The procedure is most often done under monitored anesthesia care (MAC) or general anesthesia. When the procedure is complete, the patient is bandaged. Bandages may be removed in most cases after a week. There are no stitches to remove. Patients are often advised to wear a tennis sweatband for an additional 2 weeks to protect the postoperative area from perspiration that can contaminate the healing surgical wound. The patient may, on average, resume all sports after 6 weeks.

Myringotomy

A myringotomy is a procedure to put a hole in the ear drum. This is done so that fluid trapped in the middle ear can drain out. The fluid may be blood, pus, and/or water. In many cases, a small tube is inserted into the hole in the ear drum. The tube helps to maintain drainage. This surgery is most often done on children. This is an outpatient procedure.

Stapedectomy

Stapedectomy is a procedure to remove the stapes in the ear. The procedure removes the sponge-like bone that prevents the ear from vibrating in response to sound waves. This lack of vibration leads to hearing loss that worsens over time.

Mastoidectomy

A mastoidectomy is a surgical operation to remove part of an infected mastoid process. The mastoid process is a bony protuberance on the skull, found behind the ear.

Adenoidectomy

An adenoidectomy is the surgical removal of the adenoids. They may be removed for several reasons, including impaired breathing through the nose and chronic infections or earaches. The surgery is common. It is most often done on an outpatient basis under general anesthesia during childhood.

Tracheotomy

A tracheotomy is a surgical incision into the trachea, or windpipe. The operation is performed when the windpipe has become blocked by the presence of some foreign object or by swelling of the larynx.

Tracheostomy

A surgical procedure on the trachea where a hole is cut in the trachea to ensure the airway is not blocked or to suction out secretions in a person in a vegetative state.

FRONTALIS LIFT OR FOREHEAD LIFT

A forehead lift, also known as a brow lift or browplasty, is a cosmetic surgery procedure used to elevate a drooping eyebrow that may obstruct vision and/or to remove the deep "worry" lines that run across the forehead and may portray to others anger, sternness, hostility, fatigue, or other unintended emotions.

LIPOSUCTION

Liposuction is one of the most frequently requested plastic surgery procedures. It works well to address areas of slow burning fat bulges from different areas of the body with minimal scarring and quick recovery times. Liposuction is not done to remove weight but the changes in body contour can be dramatic. Once the fat-producing cells in those areas are eliminated or reduced in number, the body starts storing fat in other areas. In this way, the body contour is changed.

Liposuction does not affect muscle tone or skin tone. To change muscle tone, exercise with weights is prescribed. A person with hanging skin is probably a better candidate for dermatolipectomy or a tummy tuck. Targeting these specific areas with liposuction, the surgeon can literally sculpt a figure that is more attractive to the patient. Liposuction is often combined with other procedures.

There are several liposuction techniques. Techniques are based on the amount of anesthetic injected into the tissues (wet, superwet, tumescent), the method used to suction the fat (syringe, power assist, ultrasonic), and the size of the cannulas used (thin, regular).

Liposuction can be done under local anesthesia for small areas. For more extensive areas, MAC or general anesthesia is administered. The patient should expect some bruising after the procedure, and often is prescribed massage therapy to reduce the bruising and improve circulation. Patients often complain of soreness for the first few days following liposuction surgery. Many surgeons recommend that patients be custom fitted with a special garment and padding for at least 10 days following a liposuction procedure.

The cost is highly variable and depends on the areas being treated. In general, the physician's fee per area is $1,500 to $2,000. Other costs include hospital fee and anesthesia. In Thailand, I have seen liposuction advertised in the Bangkok newspaper for around $695 inclusive of surgeon's fee, hospital charge, and anesthesia.

TUMMY TUCK (ABDOMINOPLASTY)

A tummy tuck, or abdominoplasty, is the most effective way to tighten your stomach area. It also gets rid of loose or wrinkled skin. Stretch marks between the belly button and pubic hair are eliminated. Fat tissue in the lower abdomen is removed. The abdominal wall muscles are tightened so that even when sitting down or bending over the abdomen doesn't stick out.

Abdominal wall deformities have four components: loose or wrinkly skin; stretch marks, which can be a result of aging, pregnancy, or marked weight loss; fat tissue, more frequently a problem of the lower abdomen; and muscle separation, which can occur by itself, or as a result of pregnancy. Sit-ups or crunches don't help in this situation, as once the muscles relax, they separate and the tummy bulges out.

While liposuction alone can take care of excess fat tissue, the loose skin and stretch marks must be addressed by one of three routinely available techniques: dermatolipectomy, mini tummy tuck, or full tummy tuck.

The tummy tuck addresses the three components of the abdomen: the skin, fat, and muscle. Part of the procedure is to tighten the abdominal muscles, which will benefit women who want as flat a stomach as possible. A mini tummy tuck is best suited for women who don't have stretch marks or saggy skin but have a pouch below the belly button. It can be done through an incision in the navel or through a C-section scar if the patient elects to have a little excess skin removed. Often, men elect to have this procedure to remove the pouch just above the navel.

For patients who don't have fat that needs to be removed and do not require muscle tightening, a procedure that is designed to only remove the loose skin, called a dermatolipectomy, can help. It benefits most slender women who have wrinkly or excess skin but good muscle tone, and has the same scar as a tummy tuck.

The tummy tuck procedure can be done under general, regional, or MAC anesthesia, depending on individual patient preference and needs. The surgical technique that gives the best aesthetic result is the Lockwood procedure, which has a dramatic reduction in post-op seromas that are seen with the standard tummy tuck procedure.

The first step in the tummy tuck procedure is to cut the skin between the belly button and the top of the pubic hair. Surgeons often make every effort to keep this incision below the panty line. The navel is maintained. The muscles are then tightened from the pubic bone to the ribs. The skin above the navel is then stretched down to the pubic area and stitched in place. Finally, the navel is brought out through the overlying skin to occupy its original position. Often, some liposuction is performed to fine-tune the new shape of the abdomen area.

In the United States, the physician's surgical fee for the three types of tummy tucks range from $3,500 to $5,300. Facility fee and anesthesia are in addition to the physician's fee. When you obtain estimates for a package, always ask if the surgical fee quoted includes the liposuction of the waist, which is sometimes quoted separately.

THIGH LIFT

The thigh lift is a cosmetic surgery procedure designed to tighten the skin of the thigh and reduce sagging in the inner or outer thigh. As a general rule, liposuction is not performed on the inner thigh simultaneously with an inner thigh lift.

Patients with inner thighs that are very big (for example, after significant weight loss such as after gastric bypass surgery), and have a lot of fatty tissue, it might be best to do liposuction first to get rid of as much of the excess tissue as possible. After a few months, the patient is reevaluated to determine if additional improvement can be obtained by an inner thigh lift. If the skin of the inner thigh sags or is droopy, a thigh lift is ideal as it will tighten up the skin and smooth the contour of the inner thigh.

The outer thigh is treated most often by liposuction. When the skin of the outer thigh sags, it is usually in conjunction with the buttocks. In this case, the outer thigh lift may be performed together with a buttocks lift.

Generally, MAC anesthesia or general anesthesia is used for this procedure. The procedure is performed as an outpatient procedure. Most thigh lift patients arrive at the hospital 1½ hours prior to scheduled surgery where the patient undergoes marking in a standing position, by the surgeon. The skin is pinched and elevated toward the groin. An estimate is made of how much skin should be removed. The incisional approach is designed so that the final scar is hidden in the groin crease. Excess skin and fat are removed and the remaining thigh skin is elevated and tightened.

Following surgery, the patient is advised to rest as much as possible to avoid a lot of leg motion, which can affect the scar. Recuperation for thigh lift surgery is usually 1 to 2 weeks. Patients should plan to take 7 to 10 days off from work.

In the United States, the average surgeon's fee for this procedure is around is $3,500 for the inner or outer thighs. The facility fee and medications are additional.

FACELIFT (RHYTIDECTOMY)

Rhytidectomy is one of the world's most popular plastic surgery procedures. The procedure makes the patient look younger by getting rid of the signs of aging. The name facelift is actually a misnomer, as there is no "lift" involved. During the operation, the surgeon will tighten tissue underneath the face. Next, loose skin is smoothed out and extra fat and other tissue is eliminated. The end result is a younger-looking, rejuvenated face. Incisions are made in key areas where tissue can easily be accessed, and cuts are made so that they will not be noticeable after they have healed.

After surgery, some swelling and pain is to be expected. Usually the pain isn't much, but the swelling can last for weeks and is quite noticeable. The surgeon will advise the client how to best deal with it. As with any surgery, there is also a risk of blood clotting, infection, and improper healing as the face and scalp are very vascular and bleed easily.

In the United States, the charge for a rhytidectomy ranges anywhere from $5,000 to $8,000. Popular destinations abroad where this is done with high frequency include Brazil and Thailand.

Thread Facelift

A new procedure called the thread or lunchtime facelift is a less complex and less expensive version of the rhytidectomy. The surgeon does some quick adjustments that can be accomplished in an hour or so under local anesthesia with smaller incisions. There is less scarring and healing time is quicker. The results can be very effective for some. The cost is significantly less. As a medical tourism procedure, it is very popular because the medical traveler can enjoy some touristic activities both before and after their surgery. The cost for the surgery is lower than traditional rhytidectomy both in the United States and abroad.

With either procedure, results are not permanent. Over time, the client will experience some sagging and puffiness as gravity takes over. Most clients don't opt for a second facelift because one works well enough.

The typical client profile for this procedure is someone in the 55-plus age group who finds the surgery most effective, although patients of any age may have one. Many female executives opt for rhytidectomy because they feel more confident about their appearance. Entertainers, speakers, and politicians in the public eye also elect to have this procedure as the camera is often merciless and often exaggerates the effects of aging. Others who will benefit from the surgery include postbariatric surgery patients.

RHINOPLASTY (NOSE SURGERY)

Rhinoplasty is a reshaping of the nose. The reshaping can be done to improve the appearance of an otherwise normal nose, or to reconstruct a damaged nose. It can also be used to restore breathing through the nose. When the rhinoplasty is used to both improve breathing and the appearance of the nose, it is called a septorhinoplasty.

The reshaping of the nose can be divided into procedures that change only the appearance of the tip of the nose (tip-plasty) and those that reshape the bony part of the nose (rhinoplasty).

If the nose has been broken or changed in appearance after an accident, insurance carriers will most likely help pay to help restore a more normal appearance to the nose. For those with breathing problems that can be corrected by pulling on the cheek skin next to your nose, a rhinoplasty with some form of cartilage graft will improve breathing. Breathing problems after an accident or inability to breathe through one side of the nose are more likely corrected by a septoplasty.

Some people find they do not like the way the tip of their nose looks but are otherwise happy with the rest of the nose. The tip of the nose may look too "fat," or their nostrils show too much, or the tip may "stick out too far." A more limited procedure, the "tip-rhinoplasty," will help in these cases.

Other people complain of a "bump" in the nose, or a nose that looks too broad, or like the nose is not "straight." In these cases, a total rhinoplasty is indicated.

Most people are not looking for a dramatic reshaping of the nose but a "refinement" of the nose. African Americans are requesting this procedure more frequently, expressing a desire for reshaping that maintains ethnic character.

The rhinoplasty can be performed under general anesthesia or MAC. It involves reshaping of the bones of the nose, generally making the nose appear thinner and straighter, and if there is a "hump," shaving it down to make the nose appear straight from a side view. The tip of the nose is also reshaped to make it look more refined while at the same time bringing it into harmony with the rest of the nose.

Rhinoplasty is typically an outpatient procedure that takes anywhere from 2 to 4 hours to perform. Immediately after the surgery, the nose may be packed with packing tape. The recovery time generally takes between 1 to 2 weeks. A splint is placed on the nose, which will be removed in one week. Following surgery, several postoperative visits are scheduled during the first 2 weeks. Thereafter, the patient is scheduled to return to the office every 2 to 3 months during the first year and then annually. The nose generally continues to look better during the first year as the swelling and surgical trauma subsides.

In the United States, the physician's surgical fee for rhinoplasty ranges from $2,000 for the tip of the nose, to $4,000 for a full rhinoplasty. Additional charges include hospital fees and anesthesia.

MENTOPLASTY

A mentoplasty is a plastic surgery procedure performed on a chin to alter the shape or size.

PODIATRIC SURGERY

For the most part, podiatric surgery cases include

- Removal of bunions
- Surgery for hammertoes
- Treatment of arch disorders
- Treatment of heel spurs
- Ingrown toenails
- Reconstructive foot surgery
- Trauma and athletic injuries
- Non-surgical treatment for neuromas
- Tendon and joint pain
- Arthritis
- Sports injuries
- Diabetic care
- Infections and ulcerations
- Treatment for burning foot pain
- Removal of warts
- Excision of soft tissue masses and tumors

Usually, with the exception of reconstructive foot surgery, most cases are considered minor office-based procedures and the travel costs would be more than the cost of the procedure performed locally.

REGENERATIVE MEDICINE

Regenerative medicine is the process of creating living, functional tissues to repair or replace tissue or organ function lost due to damage or congenital defects.

Usually this is done by harvesting stem cells or progenitor cells, or through the introduction of biologically active molecules or the transplantation of laboratory grown organs and tissues (known as tissue engineering).

Khyphoplasty

Khyphoplasty is a type of surgery to repair compression fracture to vertebra, usually from osteoporosis. In the procedure, a damaged vertebra is expanded with a balloon-like instrument, and the void that was created is filled with a setting material.

Laminectomy

A laminectomy is a surgical operation to remove one or more sides of the rear arches of a spinal vertebra and gain access to the spinal cord or spinal nerve roots.

Hemicorporectomy

A hemicorporectomy is a rarely performed surgical operation to cut away all of the part of the body below the lower end of the vertebral column, including the pelvis and its contents.

UROLOGICAL SURGERY

Diverticulectomy

A diverticulectomy is the surgical removal of a diverticulum, which is a pouch or sac in the lining of the mucous membrane of a hollow organ, especially one produced in the bowel when the bowel muscle ruptures the bowel wall.

Abdominal Surgery

The term *abdominal surgery* broadly covers surgical procedures that involve opening the abdomen. Surgery of each abdominal organ is dealt with separately in connection with the description of that organ (stomach, kidney, liver, etc.). Diseases affecting the abdominal cavity are dealt with generally under their own names (e.g., appendicitis). The three most common abdominal surgeries are: exploratory laparotomy, appendectomy—surgical opening of the abdominal cavity and removal of the appendix, and laparoscopy—a minimally invasive approach to abdominal surgery.

Splenectomy

A surgical procedure performed to remove a damaged spleen.

Pancreaticoduodenectomy

A pancreaticoduodenectomy, Whipple procedure, or Kausch–Whipple procedure, is a major surgical operation involving the pancreas, duodenum, and other organs. This operation is performed to treat cancerous tumors on the head of the pancreas or cancerous tumors on ducts or vessels near the pancreas.

Kidney Transplantation

This is the transplant of a kidney into a patient with end-stage renal disease. Kidney transplants may either be cadaveric or living-donor, which may refer to related or unrelated donors.

LUNG TRANSPLANTATION

Lung transplantation involves removal of one or both diseased lungs from a patient and the replacement of the lungs with healthy organs from a donor. Lung transplantation may refer to single, double, or even heart-lung transplantation. It is performed to replace a lung that no longer functions due to injury or cancer.

THORACOTOMY

This is an incision into the thorax to access organs underneath the bony rib cage.

THROMBECTOMY

A thrombectomy is the excision of an abnormal or dangerous thrombus (blood clot), usually through the use of a balloon catheter. The procedure can also be used to clear a blockage in an arteriovenous (A/V) fistula used for renal dialysis treatment.

THYMECTOMY

A thymectomy is an operation to remove the thymus gland.

PNEUMONECTOMY OR PNEUMECTOMY

A pneumonectomy is a surgical procedure to remove a lung. Removal of just one lobe of the lung is specifically referred to as a lobectomy, and that of a segment of the lung as a wedge resection (or segmentectomy). The most common cause for a pneumonectomy is to excise tumorous tissue arising from lung cancer.

NEPHRECTOMY

A nephrectomy is a surgical procedure in which a kidney is removed. In some cases, only half of the kidney is removed, which is referred to as a heminephrectomy.

THYROIDECTOMY

A thyroidectomy is an operation to remove the thyroid gland.

HEART TRANSPLANTATION

Heart transplantation or cardiac transplantation, is a surgical procedure performed on patients with end-stage heart failure or severe coronary artery disease. The most common procedure is to take a working heart from a recently deceased organ donor (allograft) and implant it into the patient. The patient's own heart may either be removed (orthotopic procedure) or, less commonly, left in to support the donor heart (heterotopic procedure). The first human-to-human heart transplant was performed in 1967 by Dr. Christiaan Barnard in South Africa. Medical travel to South Africa for this procedure continues to gain in popularity.

HERNIA REPAIR

A hernia repair is a surgical procedure to correct a condition in which part of an internal organ projects through the wall of the cavity that contains it, especially the projection of the intestine from the abdominal cavity. Hernias may be described by their location, including: ventral, inguinal, abdominal, or in the spinal column as in a herniated disc that presses on a spinal nerve.

GASTRECTOMY

A partial or complete gastrectomy is a surgical removal of all or part of the stomach to treat peptic ulcers.

NISSEN FUNDOPLICATION

Nissen fundoplication is a complex surgical procedure to treat gastroesophageal reflux disease (GERD) and hiatal hernia.

CHOLECYSTECTOMY

A cholecystectomy is a removal of the gallbladder. It can be performed as an open surgery with a laparotomy or through the use of an endoscope, or through laparoscopy. The procedure is usually accompanied by a common bile duct exploration.

LAPAROTOMY

A laparotomy is an open surgery in which a surgical incision through the abdominal wall is made to allow investigation of an abdominal organ or diagnosis of an abdominal disorder.

HEPATECTOMY

A hepatectomy is a surgical procedure to remove the liver.

APPENDECTOMY

An appendectomy is the surgical removal of the vermiform appendix. This procedure is normally performed as an emergency procedure, when the patient is suffering from acute appendicitis. In the absence of surgical facilities, intravenous antibiotics are used to delay or avoid the onset of sepsis, but many cases will resolve when treated nonoperatively. In some cases the appendicitis resolves completely; more often, an inflammatory mass forms around the appendix. Appendectomy may be performed by laparoscopic access (this is called "minimally invasive surgery") or by an "open" operation.

CESAREAN SECTION OR C-SECTION

A Cesarean section, also known as C-section, is a form of childbirth in which a surgical incision is made through a mother's abdomen (laparotomy) and uterus (hysterotomy) to deliver one or more babies. It is usually performed when a vaginal delivery would put the baby's or mother's life or health at risk, although in recent times it also has been performed upon request for births that could otherwise have been natural.

COLON RESECTION

A colon resection is a procedure undertaken to remove a portion of the bowel. This can be done to treat an obstruction or to remove a portion of the bowel that may be cancerous or otherwise damaged. Most often it is performed through a laparotomy.

COLOSTOMY

A colostomy is a surgical formation of an artificial anus by making an opening from the colon through the abdominal wall. It may be done to decompress an obstructed colon, to allow excretion when part of the colon must be removed, or to permit healing of the colon. Colostomy may be temporary or permanent.

WEIGHT LOSS SURGERY (BARIATRIC SURGERY)

BARIATRIC SURGERY "LITE"

As a minimally invasive, rapid recovery option for weight loss surgery, laparoscopic adjustable gastric banding has been gaining interest among outpatient surgery facilities seeking to add bariatric services to their lineups. It has been a fairly lucrative procedure, and it does not take much longer than other laparoscopic procedures to complete.

Each of the options for bariatric surgery involve the resizing of the patient's stomach to limit its capacity. While gastric bypass, bilio-pancreatic diversion with duodenal switch, and other procedures accomplish this through the removal of a portion of the stomach (and by attaching the remainder to the middle of the small intestine), gastric banding reshapes the stomach in place. The surgeon laparoscopically wraps a saline-filled silicone ring around the upper part of the stomach to reduce its size. In the months and years following the surgery, this pouch can then be adjusted by adding or removing saline through a subcutaneous port during follow-up visits to the surgeon's office.

In the two years that we have hosted gastric banding, we have had two general surgeons complete about 350 cases. Here is how a successful program was built:

Our multispecialty ASC had been open for about a year when one of our general surgeons, William Neal, MD, FACS, FASMBS, proposed bringing gastric banding to our ORs. He had been routinely performing the surgery at the hospital with which we are joint-ventured, but the schedule there didn't always allow him the time to undertake the volume he wanted. So he met with our then-executive director, Paul Wilkinson, a former administrator at the hospital who had formed a working relationship with Dr. Neal, to discuss the procedure and the possibility of offering it here.

One of Mr. Wilkinson's first concerns was whether the center was sufficiently prepared for gastric banding surgeries. Do we have the space, the staff, and the equipment needed to handle it? He ascertained what Dr. Neal required before he could begin, with one major caveat: He was not going to replace the ORs' surgical tables with heavyweight versions. Dr. Neal agreed that they wouldn't be necessary for the weight-limited patients who would be selected for the procedures.

Our center was already equipped for other laparoscopic procedures, so we already had video towers, scopes, cameras, and related equipment. We had to purchase the specialized instruments required for bariatric surgery, an outlay of about $8,000. Sturdy footboard table attachments were necessary to keep patients from sliding down when the procedure required the table slightly sloped to elevate their heads. We were already purchasing new recliners for post-op, so we made sure they were rated for 475 pounds.

Two companies have the FDA's approval to market the stomach-resizing implants in the United States: Allergan, which offers the Lap-Band, and Ethicon Endo-Surgery, which offers the Realize Band. Dr. Neal purchased those supplies for the procedure. Other than the bands, there is surprisingly little that's needed in the way of supplies. Our surgeons request large-sized thromboembolic deterrent stockings, and we supplied extra-large-sized surgical gowns for patients' modesty and comfort.

We brought our medical director, an anesthesia provider, in on the planning since that is crucial for any ambulatory surgery facility adding services to ensure they will be able to deliver outpatient, not inpatient, anesthesia. A combination of medications that dissipate quickly and minimize, to the extent possible, postoperative nausea and vomiting is ideal.

As with other laparoscopic procedures, gastric banding demands an OR staff that is able to operate the camera and otherwise assist the surgeon. We sent a circulator and scrub tech to observe Dr. Neal doing cases in the hospital OR before we started them here, then asked them what we would need, how the cases proceeded, and how the rooms were set up. At first we trained only selected members of our staff to serve as a consistent team for gastric banding cases, but before long all surgical staffers were able to step in. We kept our pre-op and PACU nurses in the loop about the upcoming new service and its demands, and made sure our central sterile department was up to speed on the proper care and handling of laparoscopic instruments.

Successful gastric banding in an ambulatory setting depends largely on selecting the patients who can be treated most efficiently. By the time a patient reaches the OR, the general surgeon should already be well aware of his health factors. He's completed a history and physical and been screened for comorbidities during the pre-op educational seminars and counseling sessions he and his staff hold in his office.

Dr. Neal and our surgery center set a weight limit of 325 pounds for his outpatient gastric banding patients. It would have been possible for us to handle patients of 350 or even 400 pounds before we were limited by our tables' weight capacities, but Dr. Neal reasoned that beyond 325 pounds we'd be more likely to encounter airway, intubation, and anesthesia management difficulties, issues that can present undue risks in a freestanding surgery center.

This weight limit is also intended to protect the nurses and techs charged with lifting and transporting the patients. We purchased, and we use, patient lift assistance devices, which work wonders. But the potential risk of employee injuries increases as a patient population's weight rises.

We do our own pre-op telephone interviews and physical assessments as well. We can handle patients who suffer from diabetes and other systemic disease processes, but we always exclude patients who have recently suffered myocardial infarctions, who have significant dysrhythmia, whose lungs aren't conducive to lying flat, or who have a difficult intubation history.

Our anesthesia providers were initially very hesitant about the new service, envisioning patients with no necks and impossible airways, and cautiously required every gastric banding patient with a body mass index of greater than 40 to undergo an eyes-on assessment before the day of surgery. As we successfully conducted more and more of the surgeries, however, they quickly realized that body mass index alone was not a rock-solid indicator, and that airway complications could happen to any patient. In fact, our gastric banding patients weren't showing any more problems than our laparoscopic cholecystectomy or septoplasty patients. They still do standard anesthesia reviews, as with all patients, and we avoid taking patients with ASA scores of three or four.

All of our patients are self-paying, which offers the economic advantage of decreasing each case's time in accounts receivable. While most insurance companies' contracts now include provisions for bariatric surgery, their reimbursement is typically geared toward the treatment of patients over a certain weight level and who suffer from defined comorbidities. Medicare, for instance, presently covers patients with a body mass index of 35 or higher who suffer from one or more comorbidity related to obesity (and the facility in which they undergo surgery must be certified by the American College of Surgeons or the American Society for Metabolic and Bariatric Surgery). But those weights and conditions are frequently not conducive to the ambulatory surgery setting.

Our gastric banding patients go from door to door in less than 5 hours. Their OR time typically ranges from 1 hour to 90 minutes. They spend about an hour in phase one recovery and another hour or 90 minutes in phase two recovery. Our average room turnover after a procedure is 14 minutes and no more complex than a turnover for any other general surgery case.

We let Dr. Neal schedule four gastric banding cases during his regular weekly block of 7:30 a.m. to 3 p.m. When we began hosting the surgery, we limited him to two cases in a block to see how well it worked and to avoid overwhelming ourselves. Once we had smoothed out the process, we were able to book more cases per block.

As with any procedure, and as with any patient undergoing surgery in any specialty, the out-patient method is the same: get them into the OR, successfully treat them, ensure their recovery and ambulation, and then get them home. Pre-op is standard operating procedure. We start their IV, administer antibiotics, and conduct a physical assessment. But we also let patients walk from their pre-op bay to the OR, which offers them a bit of motivation. They're not sick, after all, and this helps to reinforce in them the knowledge that they are healthy now, and they are going to be healthy and recovering after the surgery.

In post-op, gastric banding patients require specialized care on account of their reshaped stomachs. We begin their recoveries with intravenous narcotics, but since they are on fluid restrictions, they cannot swallow pills. Our post-op pain management regime is hydrocodone or oxycodone elixirs and ice chips for comfort.

On occasion we've had patients who required transfers to the hospital. Some early cases saw cardiac complications, which were unpredictable, or extreme nausea, which led our anesthesia providers to adapt their methods. But there has been no commonality to our post-gastric banding admissions, and, in fact, they number fewer than our laparoscopic cholecystectomy admissions.

As we've handled more of this type of case, we've come to learn that getting the patients into the post-op recliners as soon as possible helps to speed their recoveries. While most PACU wards reserve recliners for phase two recovery, we move our phase one patients into the chairs if they're alert enough. The earlier you get them into the recliners, the better they do, if only because it motivates them with the confidence that their procedure was a success and so is their recovery.

This confidence is important because we've also found that our gastric banding patients are time-intensive in post-op. As a class, they tend to require more emotional attention than the average patient, and by the end of the day, it can wear out a PACU nurse. Fortunately, however, our general surgeons are very accessible to their patients and have educated them preemptively and thoroughly. In fact, our surgeons have even directed us not to give their patients any specific post-op instructions (other than not to drive themselves home), since they've already given their own.

Laparoscopic adjustable gastric banding has been a good addition to our case mix. I will admit it took a little fine-tuning, and there were a couple of rough patches, but bringing it to our center wasn't nearly as difficult as I'd originally imagined it would be. For most ASCs, a diverse case mix is a lucrative case mix, and this adds to our diversity.

7 Workflows

How you run your business may change over time. At first, take time to ask physicians, surgical schedulers, nurses, case managers, and others what they might offer in terms of advice about organizing your workflows. Understanding the cases you coordinate will help immensely, which is why this section follows the description of the procedures.

INITIAL CONTACT

Often, the prospective client contacts you by phone or e-mail. You will reply to their inquiry as quickly as possible and respond with information about the services you provide and the countries in which your providers are located. It is at this point, and not after, that you will ask the client to execute an engagement agreement that engages you as their facilitator for services rendered. You may wish to charge a percentage or all your services fees at that time. You will need to discuss with your attorney the matter of refundable versus nonrefundable fees and the enforceability of each in your state or the state in which the venue and governing law is cited in the contract.

CONTACTING THE MEDICAL EXPERTS

Once engaged, you will need to contact the medical experts at the destination location who will specify the medical records they will need to provide recommended options for your client. You will submit those records securely, in accordance with all applicable privacy and security regulations, and ensure that they were received and are legible.

REPORTING BACK TO THE CLIENT

Upon receipt of the expert opinions of the providers, you will advise the client of their treatment options, recommendations, anticipated length of stay, and the estimated cost of their package for treatment, travel, and tourism options.

Your client will then select an option for their treatment and other activities, travel class of service, and other logistical decisions so that you can button-up all the details and arrange reservations, deposits, etc. At this point, you may also ask for another portion of your fee for your services rendered as well as payment for all prepaids necessary to book the case and the rest of the arrangements, on their behalf.

Between that date and their departure, you will be in close contact with the client to prepare them for all that lies ahead. For this, you should develop a series of checklists, either computer-based in the form of the previously suggested database, or simply on paper. Consider doing these on a database. Make sure that you have a way to present the client with all their paperwork in a nice, neat package and saved to a CD/DVD or a USB drive (one to keep and one to give to the provider at the destination) that can be carried by them to the destination, just as a backup. It is a good idea to send this via receipted courier services such as FedEx, UPS, or DHL. Also, verify receipt with the client and ask them to open the document to verify that it was not damaged in transit. If your vendors will meet the client on arrival, and you have a photograph of the greeter, include that as a print that can be hand-carried without access to a computer. Also, consider making it a standard practice to have the client greeted by an English-speaking agent who can hand them a mobile phone preprogrammed with vital "survival information" in case they get lost, have to describe where they live to a taxi driver or law enforcement officer, or feel ill while traveling. One other thing that many clients love and comment on all the time is having pictures taken with a cell phone of a glass of water, a toilet, a hamburger, a policeman, a nurse, a doctor, an ambulance, and other such necessities. If they are thirsty but don't know how to say, "Please, I'd like a glass of water," they simply show the picture. Same with a hamburger or pizza slice. It works every time!

DAY BEFORE TRAVEL

Call the client early in the day and review any last-minute questions, checklist items, tips, and updates on travel or safety that may be pertinent. The client's satisfaction is going to be based on service. They are paying you to make sure that the trip goes as easily as possible.

TRAVEL DAY

If you have arranged special accommodations, such as special seating assignments, dietary considerations, wheelchair assistance, etc., call the airline and airport to confirm that everything is arranged and that the client is expected and at what time. If anything is not to your satisfaction, be nice, but be firm. Start early in the morning with these confirmations, and do the same for all downline connections until arrival at the destination.

> PwC (PricewaterhouseCoopers) actually has a Hospitality and Leisure Practice, which monitors not only hotel and travel but now also monitors and consults in the area of medical tourism business development and strategy. I only became aware of this when they began to call me for specific market insight and consulting assistance on various projects.

ON ARRIVAL AT THE DESTINATION

Someone should always be there to greet the client by name, in English if that is their native language. If they are not accustomed to international travel or even cross-country travel, they will be anxious, thirsty, and stiff. Make sure that your greeter has bottled still water for them in the car and that their luggage is handled in its entirety by the greeter. Avoid things like flower greetings as in Hawaii and certain island destinations, as the client may be allergic and that reaction can ruin an otherwise perfect start to their adventure.

If feasible, and if the client is headed to a resort or hotel on arrival, have the driver or greeter point out points of interest and take a drive past the hospital to point it out. This way, the client can begin to assess how much lead time they will need for appointments based on time and distance. Have the greeter orient them as to time if there is a large difference in time zones from where they originally departed. Always have the driver or greeter inquire as to whether or not the client is hungry or wants a coffee before arriving at the hotel. Sometimes, the client may want the reassurance that Starbucks still tastes like Starbucks on arrival into a strange land for the first time. The client may not wish to eat hotel food on arrival—then again, you never know. Prior to booking a client in a hotel, you should have at least visited the hotel and know the quality of the food, the type of menu available, customer service orientation, hours for room service and restaurant operations, foreign language proficiency, including English, etc.

Take care to note any consultations with the surgical care team and/or the facility prior to actual admission for the procedure. These will have to be coordinated with either a driver or a taxi service. If in doubt about taxi quality, hire a private driver and car service. Your client will feel more comfortable if they can become familiar with even one friendly face that speaks their language in a nonmedical setting during their trip.

HOTEL CONSIDERATIONS

Facilitators that work with hotels will find that they must not only concern themselves with health-care quality and pricing, but also hotel room rates, resort fee waivers, booking incentives, and overall negotiating.

While higher costs and lower availability at hotels are not good things for facilitators, there is a positive force behind the trend: Corporate travel is also expected to rebound as companies increase their budgets and send more people out on the road to meet and conduct business.

Consulting houses such as PwC and Smith Travel Research publish information about average daily room rates (ADR). It is important that you follow these reports because as the travel market continues to fluctuate, prices and availability will no doubt impact health travelers. As a facilitator, you will need to exercise some creative strategies at the bargaining table. Don't depend on your hospitals to look out for your best business interests here.

When a seller's market exists, it is because there is generally less availability, with a lot fewer hotel rooms coming online, especially in the upscale hotel segment. Given this scenario, facilitators are wise to book hotel rooms as far in advance as possible. If the hotel will let you, you can plan further out. Most hotel managers negotiate with the current state of the market in mind. If you drive volume to a particular market, book for as far in the future as you can.

Booking a hotel stay far in advance doesn't always guarantee good rates, since some hotels will cancel a reservation outright if they can easily fill rooms with higher-paying business in a group.

Your medical tourism clientele may also not be the most attractive client to them. Think about it. They may have soiled sheets from wound seepage, more service intensity, special requests, and other reasons for not necessarily wanting your business, even if it is a longer stay than most business travelers. If your bookings are no longer good for the hotels, they will want to get a higher rate of return.

SECOND-TIER CITY CONSIDERATIONS

The best chance of finding favorable rates and availability are in second-tier cities (STCs). It is difficult to decide what constitutes a second-tier city, as that is determined by fluctuating markets and economic structures rather than by size. They are generally distinct from large urban metropolises, and are spatially distinct, rather than suburbs of larger metropolitan areas. This is something to think about when considering hospitals and medical spas for your health travel network.

Second-tier cities possess a specialized set of activities (paralleling the cluster concept in economic development), and trade-oriented industries (wealth generation), both of which take root (through attraction and growth) in those communities. The STC designation also doesn't take into account that STCs have comparatively strong growth characteristics in terms of both population and employment. As you seek opportunities to add hospitals and other suppliers in your provider network, keep in mind that government officials will view your expansion into their market quite favorably on a number of fronts—if they are ready for that expansion and can accommodate your clients and take good care of them, bringing honor and economic development to the community.

To narrow the concept down for you, Meeting Planners International (MPI) (which I follow because we facilitate a fair amount of executive health travel and executive checkups paired with strategic planning retreats for corporate executives and their significant others) offers a more practical definition, in which a second-tier city is a city with a population of more than 300,000 and less than one million. This statement highlights that STCs are not just defined as "smaller" but also as "larger." STCs have a significant presence of their own that distinguishes them from small cities, micropolitan areas, and rural towns. So, STCs have a ceiling ("no bigger than") and a floor ("no less than").

A precise definition of an STC can be hard to come by, and will always be subject to debate. In the practice of network providers and site selection, the discussion of a second-tier city usually occurs with large corporate-oriented projects, including headquarters and research and development facilities are nearby. Construction may be newer in the area, and roads may be wider, medians and landscaping to the side of the road more familiar to an American health traveler.

STCs will have many the characteristics that meet the needs of health travelers who are not going for the electricity of the downtown touristic inclusions, while offering a mix of advantages that make them highly competitive with the largest locations. The STC will have what the large cities have, and have more of it (responsive government, labor growth), enough of it (transportation infrastructure, financial services), and less of it (congestion, hotel accommodation costs) in a mix that makes them especially attractive. The fundamental value proposition of STCs for placing your health travel clients is the right size at the right cost.

RevPAR—WATCH OUT FOR "ANCILLARY" FEES

Room rates are far from the only factor to consider when cutting deals with hotels. Hotels focus on RevPAR, an acronym that stands for "revenue per available room." Increasingly, add-on fees, sometimes called "resort fees," for everything from parking to use of the fitness center and even maid service are being added to hotel bills. RevPAR is the strongest indicator of hotel profitability.

Industrywide, hotels are following what the airlines are doing in terms of fees. Depending on the nature of your booking and business volume, and how much it is worth to the hotel, you can negotiate these fees out.

In addition to asking for fees to be waived, as a facilitator, you will need to guard against any new fees that could crop up after your booking is arranged. Contract provisions should protect you from fees being added on later upon guest arrival. Once the contract is signed, you'll need to stay on top of how the hotel implements that contract. They sometimes hand the contracts over to reservations people who don't necessarily read them to see what concessions are in there. You have to follow up or your client satisfaction ratings will drop to damaging levels. Keeping an eye on fees has become a necessary part of the negotiating process. For example, your clients who drive to a particular medical tourism destination could be assessed an unexpected $25 daily parking fee. Once they have arrived, your leverage has essentially disappeared. Nobody is going to start looking for a new hotel room under the stress of impending medical care.

You never know what the next money-grabbing gimmick will be, so you really have to stay ahead of the game. I tell the hotel that I want no hidden fees tacked on to the room rate. When I give people a price for the room, I want that to be the price.

KEEPING THE TERMS OF THE NEGOTIATED RATES IS KEY

Creative long-term negotiating tactics for favorable rates are important, along with traveler compliance to keep costs under control.

When the ADR goes haywire, negotiated rates are used by hoteliers to lock in volume business commitments. You also need to inquire if the companies that your clients work for may have already negotiated savings with certain brands, which can save you and your client money—and help their employer meet volume commitments. Companies forfeit a lot of savings when employees book outside preferred agreements and channels and end up paying consumer rates.

POINTERS ON HOW TO NEGOTIATE

Egencia, a division of Expedia that publishes a Travel Forecast and Annual Hotel Negotiability Index, suggests the following recommendations for how travel managers and facilitators can get the best value from hotels depending on market conditions:

- Negotiating with three- to four-star hotels is likely to be easier than with hotels in the luxury category, when luxury category hotels are "in the money."

- Encourage travelers to book hotels that offer free amenities such as the Internet, shuttle service, breakfast, and evening events.
- Negotiations with specific hotels will yield better results than chainwide negotiations, particularly for business concerns without a high volume or average daily spend.
- Consider independent hotels. Without costly loyalty programs to subsidize, these properties may offer better rates and amenities.
- Negotiate last-room availability clauses. This means that properties must offer negotiated rates even if only one room type is available, resulting in lower ADR (average daily rate) throughout the year. One last word of advice: Always walk through your hotels with the same attention to detail as you walk through your hospitals and clinics. Your clients expect you to be the expert and match up their preferences with the best choice for them, their pocketbook, their comfort, their safety, and their culture. The pretty pictures might not show the typical clientele.

Consider one example I experienced in Malaysia: I had to book an extra night in a hotel to extend my stay. I found a hotel online that had beautiful photos of nice, clean conditions, business travelers, and amenities commensurate with my status as a corporate executive. I prepaid as required, in order to lock in my rate. On arrival, I was the only woman not in head cover, and was stared at my entire time in the lobby, in the restaurant, and by the pool. Even young girls who appeared to be about eight years old were covered in black from head to toe, while swimming in the pool. I was very uncomfortable, but it was only for one night. The food on the buffet was not food I was accustomed to, and there was no menu service on that day, so I didn't really get to eat the meal that was included in my plan—the one that I paid for in my prepaid reservation.

ON THE DAY OF SURGERY OR THE DAY PRIOR TO SURGERY

The client will check into the medical facility and receive the desired medical treatment or procedure. The package may include pre- or postoperative care and accommodations for both the client and a travel companion. It is of extreme importance to know the entire facility, its amenities, the rooms where your clients will stay, etc. On hospital tours arranged to meet the doctors and nurses, the administration and clinicians all make comments to me on how many facilitators wish to recruit them for their networks without ever having visited the premises, the country, or interviewing the physicians and dentists. Know where your clients will reside for their time in-country.

- Are the rooms private or semiprivate? Lie on the bed, test the mattress.
- Does the bed creak and groan? Is it comfortable? Are the patient beds operated by electric controls or hand cranks? How soft are the sheets? Are they scratchy?
- How close is the call bell to summon a nurse? Is it able to be clipped to the bed sheets? Where will the companion sleep? Is that comfortable? Is there enough room for a nurse to get in and out to check patient vitals without having to disturb the companion while sleeping?
- Is there television broadcasting available in their language? How many stations? Can the television be viewed by the companion as easily as by the patient? Are there headphones in case the companion wants to watch television while the patient is asleep?

- Is there a library or reading room?
- Is there an Internet connection or wireless service available? Is the speed fast enough to be able to broadcast back home via a Skype connection and a webcam to set loved ones at ease back home and show that all is going well?
- Can you, as the facilitator, call directly into the patient's room to check on your client? Often, cell phone signals are blocked in areas where the signal and transmissions might interfere with medical technology in use in the room or nearby. Don't count on cell phone access while the patient is in the hospital and don't think that calls to the nursing station will be welcome. The nurses and unit secretaries are busy with their assigned duties. Can you imagine what their day would be like if every facilitator called the nursing station to check on their clients?
- Make it a point to obtain a facility map that shows where your client will be assigned, the number of the telephone extensions in each room, and notations about the regular staff at the nurse's station. Do they speak the language of the client? Will an interpreter be available at all hours? Is there a nutrition station or kitchen nearby where the client or companion can help themselves to coffee, juice, and snacks? What kind of snacks?
- What about safety? Do the windows open to the outside? Could a patient disoriented by medications have an accident and jump or fall out of a window? Are there smoke detectors in the room? Fire sprinklers overhead, a nearby fire extinguisher? How nearby are the pull stations for fire alarms? How is the temperature regulated in the room?

These are all questions to ask oneself.

ON THE DAY OF DISCHARGE

Will a copy of all medical records, in the home language of the patient, be available for records transfer back for the return home? If you provided a USB drive, ask the client to prevail upon the medical records staff to digitize all films and studies, and provide them on a CD/DVD or place them on the USB drive. Request that a release be signed by the client during the initial paperwork that releases a retention copy of their complete medical record for your files as well as for the aftercare provider who will follow up on them upon their return home. Call to answer any questions and be available to address any changes of plans.

If the patient is required to fill medications from written prescriptions not dispensed by the hospital or clinic, ensure that a driver is available to accompany them to the pharmacy or run the errand on their behalf. Ensure that the patient has copies of the written prescriptions for medications purchased outside the United States so that they may provide appropriate documentation to customs authorities who might otherwise confiscate them.

POSTOPERATIVE TOURISM AND LEISURE ACTIVITIES

If the client is up to it, they may elect to take a tour, visit a museum, enjoy the theater, or attend a sporting event. Patients often overestimate the amount of energy they will have after surgery. It's best to plan excursions that can be canceled at the last minute without penalty or postponed for a day or so if need be. Your client may be sleep deprived, as one rarely sleeps well in a hospital with all the paging overhead, equipment noises, interruptions to check vital signs, medication dispensing schedules, pain, etc. They may want nothing more than to sink into a quiet hotel bed and have a massage in their room if not contraindicated by their condition or their physician.

If they are to remain in-country for awhile for follow-up appointments prior to departure, ensure that the driver is available. The more customer service you can provide in this way, the better your reputation and the more enjoyable your client's adventure will be. Clients often want to extend a gratuity to the driver and guide. Educate them on the tipping customs and advise them if the gratuity is already included in the contract rate you have with the driver. They may wish to independently contract with the driver and guide for additional excursions on their own. Explain what is included in your arrangements and what is over and above so there are no misunderstandings.

ON THE DAY OF DEPARTURE

Prior to departure, you should again confirm any special arrangements with the departure airline, airport, and all down-line connections. If necessary, determine how to get word to the physician team that monitors flights so that that physician is not blindsided by an unexpected turn of events or a reaction to medication that was not anticipated. On the day of departure, make arrangements to transfer the client to the airport to arrive not less than 3 hours prior to international flights. Determine if there are departure fees and advise the patient if they need to retain some local currency to pay those fees. If they have done any shopping, ensure that they are educated as to how to claim value added tax (VAT) refunds either prior to departure from their hotel or at the airport. Make any necessary arrangements to be able to whisk them (and their companion, if they are not traveling alone) through customs and airport security in a wheelchair. Their standing tolerance may be surprisingly low.

ON RETURN BACK TO THE CLIENT'S HOME COUNTRY

Just as you arranged a meet-and-greet service for the client at the destination out of their hometown, you should inquire about any needed arrangements to get them through customs and immigration back home, including wheelchair and terminal transfers, and how they will get to their home. Will they need aftercare? Who will transfer the records from the treating provider to the hometown provider? As a professional medical travel facilitator, you are paid a fee for your service. When does that service end? How do both parties know that the obligations on your part have been fulfilled? This must be clearly spelled out in your engagement agreement. If anything, always attempt to promise adequate service and do much more!

To build your business, follow up with a nice welcome-home token gift, which includes your business cards, brochures, and a thank-you note, handwritten, the old-fashioned way. Call to follow up and ask for recommendations, a letter of reference or testimonial, and any client satisfaction survey instrument you may use to track outcomes. If the client had one service that identified the opportunity to be of service again (for instance, bariatric surgery that will result in the need for cosmetic plastic surgery about 18 to 24 months later), don't miss out on that opportunity. Stay in touch. Get them excited about their next medical travel adventure. In fact, you may wish to ask your accountant and your attorney how you might go about establishing an escrow account to enable them to make deposits into the escrow account to pay for that next adventure so that they don't take up with another facilitator.

Create an online newsletter and send it to all previous clients to keep them engaged as your business grows. Holland America Cruise Lines is very savvy about this and sends specials and new announcements about new vessels, new packages, hot dates where they have excess capacity, etc., at least once a month. It costs them very little to maintain this connection, even if a customer has not sailed with them for 9 years. But who are they most likely going to call when they plan to sail again? You got it! They are familiar.

One extreme caution about newsletters: Never, ever, use personally identifiable information to even acknowledge if they are a client without their express written consent, or you may be breaking several laws. Also, while they might not sue you, do so and others will be concerned for their own privacy and security. Always note in a footnote that the patient is identified and written consent and release are on file. Obtain good compliance guidance from your compliance attorney.

TABLE 7.1
Generations Explained

Generation Name	Birth Years	% of Adult Population	% of Internet-Using Population
Gen Y (millennials)	1977–1990	26%	30%
Gen X	1965–1976	20%	23%
Younger Boomers	1955–1964	20%	22%
Older Boomers	1946–1954	13%	13%
Silent Generation	1937–1945	9%	7%
GI Generation	Prior to 1936		

Source: Lenhart, A. Adults and Social Network Websites, Pew Internet & American Life Project, 14 Jan. 2009. http://www. pewinternet.org/Reports/2009/Adults-and-Social-Network-Websites.aspx (accessed September 12, 2011). $N = 2,253$ total adults, and margin of error is ±2%. $N = 1,650$ total Internet users, and margin of error is ±3%.

The study notes that the biggest increase in users comes from the 73-plus age group–as 45% of them are now online, a big jump from the last study (Table 7.1).

CONTRACTING FOR YOUR SERVICES

WORKING UP A PRICE ESTIMATE

DEALING WITH EXTRA CHARGES THAT MAY ARISE

TRAVEL PLANNING

You should have certain tools that you use to streamline the travel planning process for clients. One should be a form that includes all their frequent traveler account information and traveler preferences and should note things like floor preference, smoking preference, allergies to latex (foam pillows), allergies to feathers (pillows), wheelchair access needs, etc.

For your own reference, you should have a database that includes contact information for each airline reservation desk, as well as customs and immigration offices, embassies, passport offices, and even the airline station managers at various airports through which your clients travel. This will make it easy to have telephone numbers at your fingertips if you need something in a hurry.

Also keep a handy reference of websites that will make life easier. One that I like is SeatGuru® (www.seatguru.com) by TripAdvisor. SeatGuru provides detailed seat map graphics, in-depth comments about seats, with limited recline, reduced legroom, and misaligned windows. It color-codes the seats to help identify superior and substandard seats, and shows in-seat power port locations for your clients that will travel with electronic devices like portable DVDs, laptops, and even iPods. It also indicates where the galley, closets, lavatories, and exit rows are located.

Here's another idea and a free software application that can help you organize travel plans for your clients: Go to TripIt and establish an account as a travel arranger. You can do this at www.tripit.com/topic/arranger. TripIt not only helps travelers stay organized on the road. It automates most of the manual work involved, and makes it easy for travelers and their travel planners to share and collaborate on trips, with the traveler always having the latest itinerary online and on their mobile phone.

The steps are easy and you will be instantly productive with this intuitive application. To begin:

1. Set up a free TripIt account in your name.
2. When it's time to arrange client (or your own) travel, you can create a new trip on TripIt, entering just the trip name, primary location, and start/end dates. If arranging for someone other than you, the "I am a traveler on this trip" box needs to be unchecked.
3. Once the itinerary is opened, you can add details by forwarding the client's confirmation e-mails to plans@tripit.com. If you book the travel, these confirmation e-mails may go to the client with a copy to you. If the client books it directly, have the client forward the e-mails to you. The plans in the e-mails will be automatically added to the trip the planner created, based on the start and end date. Always verify their accuracy!
4. You may then customize the TripIt itinerary as needed, adding driving directions, appointments, activities, meetings, restaurant reservations, and more for the client.
5. Once the itinerary is ready, you can share the trip with the traveler, inviting them as a "traveler" and a "collaborator." (Note that if the traveler is not already using TripIt, a free account will be automatically created for them.)
6. The facilitator and the traveler can now both access, update, and track plans using the same master itinerary!

One thing about TripIt that I really like is the fact that all trips are stored for you so that you can refer to them after the trip is over.

PLANNING THE TRAVEL FOR A SURGICAL CLIENT

PLANNING THE TRAVEL FOR A WELLNESS VISIT CLIENT

PLANNING THE TRAVEL FOR A DIAGNOSTIC SERVICES CLIENT

IF THE CLIENT IS UNABLE TO TRAVEL IN COMMERCIAL AIRLINERS

As a facilitator, you may be called upon to facilitate for a client that is too ill, injured, or elderly and frail to travel in a commercial airliner and may require medical escort services, whether for domestic or international travel. The client may require extra medical attention and life support during travel. There are several highly trained medical escorts who can provide in-flight medical monitoring and nursing care, including ventilation, sedation, and pain management. Critical care nurses often staff these flights, and the services may range from helicopter to small fixed-wing aircraft. In other cases, highly trained registered nurses, paramedics, or EMT medical escorts may staff the service. Client capabilities may range from those able to walk, to totally immobile clients needing lifting assistance, to clients unable to care for themselves.

In some cases, they have room for additional passengers, such as a family member who may accompany the client. Most offer total bedside-to-bedside services, as well as handling the details associated with airport check-in, customs, and collaboration with airline and airport personnel to make any special provisions that may be required to deal with a wide variety of unexpected challenges that may arise during medical travel.

You should have collaborative arrangements with these services, at least one for each continent, to arrange for a broad array of coverage to and from many countries and have within your database any quotes on firm, fixed pricing they can give and the parts of the handoff that their flight coordinators will handle for you for that inclusive price.

Some carry intermittent pneumatic compression (IPC) for deep vein thrombosis (DVT), but there are other services that utilize a portable sequential DVT system that increases the speed of venous blood flow and reduces the risk of clot formation. With a portable unit, the company can offer quality but more economical services as the equipment may be transferred from rig to rig instead of having to install one in each aircraft in their fleet.

For clients who require stretcher transport, a medical escort service may save as much as 50% over traditional international air ambulance services. This service is for patients not in need of critical care measures. If a client requires stretcher transport in a commercial airliner, the carrier generally has to remove six seats to fly the client flat. It requires blocking rows of seats to allow an FAA-approved stretcher to be placed on the commercial airline. A curtained area would become the patient's "room." Each airline varies as to where they allow the stretcher installation, and the location of the stretcher varies with each type of aircraft. The price of this service ranges from the purchase of four, full-fare, first-class seats to nine coach seats. International carriers have varying degrees of charges related to oxygen requirements. Although this may sound expensive, it is usually half to a third of the cost of a private air ambulance aircraft. You will either rely upon the company to handle the arrangements or you will have to handle it as the client's facilitator. Often facilitation for these specialized services and arrangement for the accompanying medical staff and equipment are included in the price. Each flight is generally staffed with one to two medical crew members that are advance life support (ALS) equipped. Patients, including ventilator-dependent patients, are transported with complete battery support systems and all necessary backups, Also, tremendous preplanning is necessary as the air carrier does not want to place either the flight crew or flight attendants in a situation where they are ill-equipped to handle an emergency that could arise in-flight. Rather than take a chance, many will simply decline the reservation and the liability that may accompany that passage. The longer the distance, the more "cost-effective" it becomes.

For elderly clients, some services offer a discounted program for transporting clients in coach class unless otherwise specified. This service can assist with a client's relocation and provides a skilled travel escort to accompany the client to any destination in the world. The service is often used for those clients who require minimal medical care including assistance with all transportation, wheelchair assistance at the airport, airport check-in, security checkpoint assistance, bathroom care, and feeding assistance.

PERIOPERATIVE PLANNING

PREOPERATIVE DETAILS AND PREPARATIONS

As you tour the facility and inquire of your surgeons, one item on your checklist should be how they handle operative site markings to indicate the site of the procedure (e.g., right leg versus left leg, etc.). How one marks patients' surgical sites with a purple surgical marker will go a long way toward reducing the risk of and preventing wrong-site surgeries. The following four steps are the minimum answers you are searching for in their policies and procedures.

- Single-use skin markers should be utilized to prevent cross-contamination between patients.
- The prep nurse must draw the mark as close to the surgical site as possible and take care not to smudge or remove it during the prepping process so that it remains visible after draping.
- Markings should be on the operative side only. The opposite body should not be marked with any mark (in some places they draw a "happy face" on the operative site and a frown on the opposite part. The physician performing the procedure should also mark the site, or at least initial to countersign the nurse's markings to confirm the location with the patient or patient's family whenever possible.
- The facility's written, published policy and procedures must specify site-marking require- ments, such as who marks the site, what constitutes a site mark (the initials of the operating physician, for example), the placement of the mark, the timing of site markings (before patients travel to the OR), and acceptable alternatives to established site-marking policies. Other means of site marking (i.e., wristbands or paper documentation when patients refuse

site marking or if it's not possible to mark the site, as in the case of premature infants where marking might risk permanent tattooing of their skin), if it's technically impractical (marking of a tooth), or if the marked site won't be visible due to the required draping technique.

It may sound like a frivolous technicality, but as you inspect your provider hospitals and perform due diligence, you are checking for safety and an orientation to safe, consistent procedures to keep your client safe and thrilled with their medical travel experience.

The Joint Commission International (JCI) has worked diligently to ensure that cultural norms are taken into consideration when hospitals, surgery centers, and other providers obtain informed consent. If you are from the United States and accustomed to informed consent procedures, you may be surprised to know that in some places in the world, the family must give consent, not just the patient. In other cases, the family gives consent "instead" of the patient. If you are working with a JCI hospital, this has previously been reviewed and surveyed for consistency with these standards. If your plans include representation of a nonaccredited hospital, you should ask about the procedure and policies for obtaining surgical consent and consent to treat or examine a patient. In the United States, touching, treating, or operating on a patient without informed consent constitutes battery. The rules may not be the same elsewhere.

You can obtain a copy of the JCI accreditation standards online available for download. You should download them and review them to formulate your own questions and review process. The hospitals and other providers you will include in your network should be able to answer any question related to the standards. You should also note when they are scheduled for their repeat survey and ask if there were any reasons for the JCI or other accrediting body to revisit between surveys to address any issues.

POSTOPERATIVE: IN COUNTRY, PRIOR TO DEPARTURE

POSTOPERATIVE, FOLLOW-UP, AND AFTERCARE

POSTSURGERY

This is the recuperation period after surgery or treatment until your client returns home. Make sure your providers have nurses that can communicate with your client in English. They should receive written discharge instructions that they can understand. If they cannot understand them, patient safety will be at issue, as well as patient satisfaction and overall outcomes.

- Provide the patient a means to transport or transfer medical records securely. Include, by contract, that the fee paid includes a doctor's reports with an admission note, operative report or diagnostic report, any images produced, and a discharge summary, in English or the language of the patient.
- If at all possible, schedule a predischarge case management conference between the attending physician at the destination and the follow-up physician back home. When the two chat physician to physician, both physicians feel more comfortable with participating in the care, and the patient enjoys more continuity of care than if everything happens in "silos."
- Make sure that you have inspected and contracted with a small network of appropriate hotels and recovery retreats that offer the amenities, services, and special needs and/or food and beverage services your client will require. For mobility-challenged or weak patients, ensure that the room assignments for these guests will not be higher than the third floor in case of fire or emergency. (Ladder trucks rarely can reach higher than a standard third floor, and the elevators may not be in service.)

RECUPERATION PERIOD

This is the period of time that occurs after your client returns home. Don't be one of the many facilitators that fails miserably in this important period of aftercare.

Remain in contact with your client by phone a few days after his return home to inquire about his trip and condition.

- Do they have the needed medications to get them through the next few days? How is the wound?
- How is the pain?
- Is there anyone there with them?
- Do they have food, groceries, and pet care if necessary?
- Do they need clean laundry?
- Do they need bandages and supplies for dressing changes?
- Extra linens in case the ones currently on the bed are soiled by wound seepage overnight? If necessary, do they need bathing assistance?
- Do they need home health nursing care or nurses' aide care?

Send them a follow-up e-mail a few days later to request a testimonial and to see if they would like to be used as a referral. Track your clinical and patient-satisfaction outcomes.

8 Spa Tourism

Derek Bryson Hedden

This chapter contains the opinions, analysis, and statements of the author. It is the responsibility of every reader to evaluate the accuracy, completeness, or usefulness of any information, opinion, advice, or other content contained in this chapter.

Spa retreats are a great way for clients to unwind and get some well-needed R and R, as well as tend to several medical needs, such as recovery from surgery or minor medical procedures. International spa retreats are also a great way to package services, such as sightseeing excursions and other travel services. What could be more welcoming than a spa retreat in the scenery of the country that they choose to be surrounded by, while being cared for in a comfortable and relaxing environment? According to the International Spa Association, "spas are devoted to enhancing overall well-being through a variety of professional services that encourage the renewal of mind, body, and spirit."

TARGET MARKET

According to the International Spa Association, Approximately 25% of Americans have visited a spa. The average age of spa visitors is the mid-40s, and most have been going for over one year, but less than nine years. Sixty-nine percent of these visitors are females, but the number of men who visit are on the rise. Most have a household income of over $50,000 annually. Between 2006 and 2007 there was a 25% growth in spa visits (from 110–138 million). These statistics point to a rather large target market of consumers who may be willing to purchase these services, and should not be overlooked as a viable source of income.

Consumers visit spas for three major modes of interest: indulgence, escape, and "work." Work does not refer to occupation in this sense, but rather to working on one's health, both physical and emotional. Many regular spa goers see the experience as vital for one's well-being. Men are said to be driven more by indulgence and escape, while the category of work tends to drive most women. Men are also trending to become more accepting to treatments such as facials and manicures. Visitors also tend to be drawn by

- Gender-neutral interior design
- Customization
- Mother–daughter bonding
- The integration of food
- Treatment before the treatment

GETTING TO KNOW YOUR CLIENT

Travelers who choose to purchase a spa retreat may differ from your usual medical tourism client, in the sense that the purpose of travel may very likely be a much more pleasure-oriented one. Having this in mind, it is important to accommodate them by making every portion of their travel arrangements extra special. Finding ways to personalize their experience is key.

Also, keep in mind that, with destination spas, there is a trending pattern towards more exotic treatments. The purpose of this type of travel is to get an authentic treatment that is true to the culture of the destination. Why travel halfway across the planet to get a vanilla spa treatment that could be found down the street in your hometown? The guest may also want the tranquility and peacefulness of the destination to be incorporated into the experience. This may include things such as outdoor treatments, the sounds of the ocean, or culturally based classes.

Who is your client? Is it a soon-to-be bride who wishes to be pampered with a group of girl-friends before "the big day"? Is it a couple who has already had their big day and wish for a romantic retreat? Is it a business traveler on a "biz-cation" who wishes to have his golf swing analyzed during his downtime? Maybe your client is choosing to recuperate from a more serious procedure, and is using this opportunity to heal in a tranquil environment.

SERVICES

Visitors typically go to indulge the senses. The senses help appeal to a sense of relaxation and retreat. This feeling of retreat leads into getting away from the pressures of life. Taking an international spa vacation also plays into this feeling of "getting away." Work has to do with working on one's self-improvement, whether it is physical or mental.

Spas offer a variety of services, ranging from the basics, such as facials and manicures, to more exotic treatments, such as Russian birch branch beating sessions (exactly what it sounds like), meant to exfoliate the skin. Below is a list of some common spa treatments and terminology that you, as a facilitator, should become familiar with:

- *Acupressure* is the use of finger pressure on points of the body to alleviate muscle tension and other symptoms. The same pressure points are used as in acupuncture, and both are believed to improve energy flow throughout the body.
- *Ayurvedic spas* use natural products and often alternative medicines.
- *Balneotherapy* is the use of thermal water for medical treatments.
- *Behavioral medicine* involves therapy techniques that improve behavior. These techniques include hypnotherapy, relaxation training, and biofeedback. Examples of behaviors that may be treated include overeating and substance abuse.
- *Body wraps* are wraps made of anything from synthetic plastic sheets to mud to reduce cellulite, detoxify the body, and reduce excess water weight.
- *Cellular therapy* involves injecting live embryonic animal cells that are suspended in a physiological serum or are frozen. This treatment is said to reverse aging and improve the immune system.
- *Cognitive training* trains an individual to avoid negative or defeatist ways of thinking.
- *Colonic irrigations* are procedures where an enema or water irrigation is used to cleanse the colon from impurities and toxins.
- *Crenotherapy* is any type of therapy that uses mud, vapors, or water.
- *Crystal therapy* is the use of crystals for treatments that are believed to heal.
- *Destination spas* are set up to teach visitors healthy habits: activities, health and wellness activities, nutrition.
- *Chemical peels* use chemicals (usually hydroxies) to peel off dead skin, which reduces blemishes, bumps, wrinkles, and age spots.
- *Dental spas* combine dental services with the addition of spa services.
- *Electrotherapy* is the use of electric currents. This is a generic term that refers to many different treatments.
- *Fango treatment* is a treatment using mud to detoxify, relieve pain, and improve circulation.
- *Glyco peeling* uses alpha hydroxyl acids to improve the skin's appearance, complexion, and texture.

- *Holistic health* is a nonmedical approach to healing the "whole" person's mental state and create well-being. The theory is that if one aspect is out of sync, the others are affected. Holistic-oriented spas often use Eastern exercises, such yoga combined with Western systems.
- *Homeopathy* uses minute doses of substances that cause symptoms similar to that of the disease so that the body can learn to fight them off.
- *Hydromassages* are just that: massages that use water to massage the body.
- *Hydropathy* is a treatment that uses water inside and outside the body.
- *Hydrotherapy* includes: hydromassages, hot and cold water showers, plunge pools, immersion in mineral baths and jet sprays, etc. These treatments may alleviate muscle and joint pain, as well as circulate the immune system.
- *Immunotherapy* consists of enzymes, cell therapy, and/or vitamins to improve the immune system.
- *Infrared treatment* is used to reduce muscle tension.
- *Inhalation therapy* involves filling a room with vapors, such as sea or mineral water with oils such as eucalyptus, to reduce sinus, pulmonary and respiratory problems.
- *Magnetotherapy* is therapy involving magnets. It is believed to have an effect on blood flow.
- *Manicures* are the hygiene of fingernails, which include the clipping of cuticles and filing and polishing of the fingernails.
- *Medicinal spas* can be bathing establishments that have waters with medicinal benefits, or facilities that offer therapies, such as electrotherapy, hydrotherapy, or mechanotherapy.
- *Microdermabrasion* is the polishing of the skin using microcrystals to exfoliate dead skin.
- *Paraffin treatment* involves brushing warm paraffin wax over the body. When the wax dries, a vacuum is created that sucks out impurities from the skin.
- *Phytotherapy* is therapy involving plants.
- *Pedicures* are hygiene services of the toenails, which include the trimming of cuticles and nails.
- *Personal wellness services* range from hiking to yoga and meditation. These are used to exercise the body and mind, and therefore, increase personal wellness.
- *Resort spas* are vacation destinations that offer services such as golf, tennis, water sports, etc.
- *Saunas* are rooms of extreme, dry heat used to detoxify the body through the pores.
- *Steam rooms* are rooms of extreme, wet heat used to detoxify the body through the pores.
- *Swedish massages* are the most commonly offered type of massage.
- *T'ai Chi* is a martial art that combines meditation with movement.
- *Thalassotherapy* is therapy involving sea water.
- *Thermotherapy* is therapy involving heat.
- *Ultra sounds*, or high-frequency sound waves, may be used to sooth aches and pains.
- *Vegan diets* exclude all animal products.
- *Yoga* is an ancient practice that involves stretching and toning the body through various combinations of poses, stretches, and breathing. It is said to increase one's overall sense of well-being.

TYPES OF SPAS

MEDICAL SPAS

Medical spas differ from traditional spas in the sense that they are under the supervision of a medical expert. Services from minor cosmetic surgeries, such as BOTOX® injections, to traditional treatments, such as massages, may be offered. Some medical spas may tend to have a more "clinical" feel to them, so this is an important thing to keep in mind when planning a trip for your client.

RESORT SPAS

Aside from medical spas, destination spas may be another type of spa that you may book for a client. Resort spas are just that. The resort and spa experience are combined to create a tranquil experience. A large part of their appeal has to do with location. Visitors to destination spas are looking for an exotic, calming retreat to rejuvenate and relax.

Unique, vacation-like activities that clients may not have available at home are usually incorporated into the stay, such as hiking, water activities, etc.

DESTINATION SPAS

The purpose of a destination spa or health spa is to assist clients in healthier living. They offer fitness, relaxation, and renewal. These are usually in the form of educational, exercise, and meal programs combined with spa treatments. Destination spas may also offer detoxification, colonics, and fasting.

HOT SPRINGS

Hot springs are some of the most popular spa destinations. Mineral springs have been used for their healing and therapeutic properties for centuries. Not only are they medically useful, but they also tend to be scenic and connect the visitor with nature. While the water from some hot springs is used in an indoor setting in bathing establishments, some are kept completely natural. Some hot springs have even become home to rehabilitation clinics for their medical properties.

The healing properties from hot springs come from their high mineral content. The water's temperature allows them to hold these levels of minerals.

WEIGHT LOSS SPAS

Weight loss spas are a subcategory of destination spas. Weight loss spas combine several elements to train visitors to keep a healthier daily routine, including customized calorie counts, exercise programs, lifestyle coaching, motivational activities, and even stress management. On-staff nutritionists and exercise physiologists can help customize a routine in one-on-one sessions. There are spas that offer fasting programs, however, the main goal of these spas are detoxification, while weight loss may be a bonus effect.

The days of "fat farms" are said to be over. Losing massive amounts of weight during a stay may be an unrealistic expectation, because now the focus is more on lifestyle management and coaching to help visitors to keep and maintain healthy habits and encourage continuous weight loss as opposed to a quick fix. Rapid reduction in diet may affect the metabolism and cause the patient to gain weight upon the return home, and thus is usually avoided. Some weight loss spas even let patients eat as much as they want (from a selection of low-fat foods, of course).

2010 SPAFINDER READERS' CHOICE TOP 10 WEIGHT LOSS SPAS

1. New Life Hiking Spa (Vermont)
2. Ananda in the Himalayas (India)
3. Golden Door Fitness Resort (California)
4. Gwinganna Lifestyle Retreat (Australia)
5. Hilton Head Health (South Carolina)
6. Kamalaya Koh Samui (Thailand)
7. Kurotel Longevity Center and Spa (Brazil)
8. Pritikin Longevity Center and Spa (Florida)
9. Green Mountain at Fox Run (Vermont)
10. Red Mountain Spa Resort (Utah)

SPA ASSOCIATIONS

The International Medical Spa Association offers conferences, workshops, and classes. Their goal is to bring the health care and spa industries together "in a way that will ensure the quality of care available to consumers. Medical spa industry leaders, including licensed health care professionals, spa owners, spa consultants, medical spa facility designers, and product manufacturers, have come together to form The International Medical Spa Association." More may be found on medicalspaassociation.org.

The International Spa Association also offers similar membership benefits. Their site offers relevant information for any facilitator at experienceispa.com.

Globally Integrated Healthcare, by Design
Mercury Healthcare International
A MERCURY HEALTHCARE COMPANY

DATE: _____ Inspected by: _____

SPA NAME: _____

City: _____ Country: _____

Telephone: _____ Fax: _____

Spa Director: _____

Telephone: _____ Email: _____

Type of Spa: _____

☐ Day Spa ☐ Overnight accommodations: # Rooms ____ # HDCP rooms ____ Flr: _____

☐ Restaurant | Hours _____

Cuisine: ☐Vegan ☐ Kosher ☐ Halal ☐ Diabetic ☐ Low Fat ☐ Wheat Free

☐ Medical Doctor on Staff ☐ Nurse Hours: _____ Charge: _____

High Season _____ Shoulder Season _____ Low Season _____

Copies:	Spa experience:	
❏ License	☐Relaxation area	☐Wellness education
❏ Operating permits	☐Wet area	☐Gardens
❏ Insurance	☐Swimming pool	☐Diet counseling
❏ Staff credentialing and privileging policies	☐Beach access	☐Organic foods
❏ Client rights and responsibilities,	☐Fitness equipment & classes	☐Cooking classes
❏ Appointment cancellation policies	☐Café ☐ Juice bar	☐Hiking
❏ Safety rounding policy	☐Locker room	☐Cycling trails
❏ Accommodation walk policy in the event of overbooking	☐Product amenities	☐Vita course
❏ Restaurant menus	☐ hot tub	☐Massage
❏ CV of medical director	☐Co-ed facilities	☐Healing waters
	☐Retail boutique	☐Sulfur waters
	☐Meditation area	☐Physical Therapy
	☐Steam room	☐Lab testing
	☐Sauna	☐X- ray
		☐
		☐

Globally Integrated Healthcare, by Design
Mercury Healthcare International
A MERCURY HEALTHCARE COMPANY

HUMAN RESOURCES AND STAFF

❑ Spa is compliant with all local, state and federal laws and regulations.

❑ Staff is provided with and/or given access to regularly updated treatment procedures and product manuals for all treatment modalities, including the spa's menu.

How often is staff professional development training offered? _____

❑ All specialized staff, such as fitness instructors, personal trainers, massage therapists, estheticians, nail technicians, hairstylists, nutritionists, physiologists, psychologists and medical technicians, comply with applicable international, federal, state and local regulations with regard to licensing, registration and appropriate certification and education.

Staff English language fluency _____%

❑ Specialized staff have the capability to describe procedures and treatments in English to clients and it is the policy to describe treatments and ingredients being used to clients before application or treatment

❑ At least one scheduled, on-site staff member has current cardiopulmonary resuscitation (CPR) and automatic external defibrillator (AED) certification, as well as first-aid certification during all hours of operation.

❑ Staff is hired without regard to race, color, religion, sex, national origin, age, handicapping condition, marital status or political affiliation.

SAFETY

❑ A first-aid kit is properly stocked and readily available at all times. Staff is aware of first-aid kit locations.

❑ In compliance with international, federal, state and local regulations, fire extinguishers are available. Staff is aware of all extinguisher locations and is trained on their proper use.

❑ A written emergency plan is posted in plain view at all appropriate staff stations. Routine evacuation drills are regularly scheduled. The plan includes standard emergency procedures for specific incidents such as power outages, fire, earthquakes, tornadoes, hurricanes and other natural disasters as well as criminal and/or acts of terror.

❑ Phone numbers of local police, fire and emergency medical assistance are visible and easily accessible.

❑ A safe exit plan from each room is established and posted within full view of all occupants.

❑ All procedures for cleaning and maintenance are in accordance with applicable international, federal, state and local regulations, and complete with appropriate manufacturer's guidelines.

❑ All floor surfaces (e.g., pool areas, wet treatment rooms and locker rooms) are designed and constructed to accommodate the intended activities for each area, and promote safety.

Globally Integrated Healthcare, by Design
Mercury Healthcare International
_____A MERCURY HEALTHCARE COMPANY

❏ Signage is posted to alert and educate guests about possible risks and practices as needed in areas such as: exercise studios, pools, wet areas, saunas, steam rooms, whirlpools, racquet sports courts and any other potentially hazardous area, in local language and in English.

❏ The spa has an ongoing monitoring system for ensuring appropriate control of temperatures in all areas where guests are exposed to high thermal stress (e.g., saunas, steam rooms, whirlpools and exercise rooms).

❏ The spa's facilities and operating procedures are in written form, updated regularly and shared with staff. These procedures comply with all applicable international, federal, state and local regulations.

❏ If the spa includes fitness and weight training equipment, well-trained staff is available to provide assistance and instruction in the proper and effective use of such equipment.

❏ The spa has a current risk management program in place that is communicated to management and staff, and updated on a consistent basis.

❏ The spa has an up-to-date file of all MSDS (Material Safety Data Sheets) for all chemical products used within the spa. This includes cleaning products as well as spa treatment products. The information is readily available to all staff.

❏ It is the responsibility of the spa to provide clean, fresh, healthy water for all guest experiences and to comply with local regulations.

❏ The spa facility is maintained in a clean and sanitary condition to prevent illness and/or disease.

SAFETY - STAFF

❏ During hours of operation and for all physically challenging, supervised activities held both on and off site, it is highly recommended (or as required by local laws) that at least one scheduled staff member has current CPR, AED and first-aid certification.

❏ Staff members who perform advanced techniques and/or use advanced technology are appropriately trained and use equipment in compliance with the manufacturer's instructions and guidelines.

❏ There is appropriate supervision for medical spa procedures in compliance with international, federal, state and local regulations.

❏ Products, equipment and instruments used in spa services and treatments are cleaned, disinfected, stored and used in compliance with the manufacturer's instructions and guidelines. Staff is trained on how to handle products and provide first aid if needed.

❏ MSDS are provided for all treatment and chemical products.

❏ Clean and sanitized equipment, instruments and supplies are provided for each guest (e.g., sheets, towels, etc.).

Globally Integrated Healthcare, by Design
Mercury Healthcare International
A MERCURY HEALTHCARE COMPANY

❑ The spa has a current policy and procedure in place regarding sexual harassment. This includes among staff members and also by guests.

GUEST RELATIONS

❑ Written material is provided that accurately depicts the facility and all its programs as well as rates, deposits, customary tipping and gratuities, cancellation policy and grace period for refunds.

❑ Spa guests are given an orientation and tour of the spa as soon as possible upon arrival.

❑ Guests complete a confidential screening questionnaire and/or have a verbal dialogue with their provider regarding any potential contraindications to services in the language they understand.
☐ A translated version is available in English.

❑ Confidential guest information is filed properly and complies with all international, federal, state and local regulations regarding the storage of such information.

❑ All guest history and information is considered private and confidential, and such information is not disclosed by the spa or its co-workers without the proper consent of the individual, unless such a disclosure is legally required.

❑ Guests are able to express their concerns and suggestions regarding facilities, staff and programming through a feedback system designed to encourage guest feedback (e.g., comment cards). Feedback is regularly analyzed by spa management and used for process improvement.

❑ The spa promptly responds to guest complaints and works to resolve them in as timely and efficiently a manner as possible.

❑ Staff members are able to recommend a home care regimen (products and usage) based on their spa experience, in English.

❑ The spa has current liability insurance or the equivalent for the purpose of guest protection.

❑ Spa programs are flexible to accommodate a variety of individual goals and needs.

❑ Spa programs and menus are designed to encourage health-enhancing activities and wellness while acknowledging the guest's current health status.

❑ Spa facilities and services are accessible to guests with disabilities as appropriate.

SERVICE AND GUEST EXPERIENCE

❑ Staff members are courteous, helpful, knowledgeable and articulate.

❑ Staff is committed to anticipating the guests' needs and serving them.

❑ Staff members guard the guest's privacy and modesty through proper draping techniques during spa treatments, and provide gender-specific changing areas when applicable.

9 Quality and Safety Transparency[*]

Lisa Beichl, Transparent Borders LLC

This chapter contains the opinions, analysis, and statements of the author. It is the responsibility of every reader to evaluate the accuracy, completeness, or usefulness of any information, opinion, advice, or other content contained in this chapter.

Successful business enterprises typically provide smart solutions to fill a market demand. Sustainable solutions not only meet market demand, but also provide high perceived quality. In health care, quality-focused and patient safety practices yielding positive medical outcomes have become the hallmark of successful hospital strategies. As hospitals consider expanding into the medical tourism market, transitioning from a traditional domestic strategy to global outreach requires a fundamental shift from a focus on purely domestic quality agendas to expand and include strategies that proactively address cultural bias, social/psychological preferences, travel constraints, and effective transitions of care to the locally based provider.

Medical tourism is a nascent industry. This chapter will review quality program development and aim to

- Define the different medical tourism groupings and general patient flow
- Identify resulting medical tourism risks (that quality programs seek to manage)
- Highlight the importance of transparency to manage risks
- Outline system-level quality and proposing tools to support quality initiatives
- Suggest medical tourism quality outcomes measures (medical, functional, patient satisfaction), as well as patient preference groupings

To put quality initiatives in context, Figure 9.1 summarizes the general strategic development of a medical tourism strategy.

This chapter does not define market demand assessment, but does outline the two general demand groupings (general and selective medical tourists) and two general venues (domestic and international). It also provides important ideas regarding risk assessment for these groupings and venues, how quality initiatives can mitigate these risks, and the measurement of outcomes (medical, functional, social/psychological). At the end of the chapter are recommended metrics for the industry to begin assessing medical and social outcomes of medical tourism.

TYPES OF MEDICAL TOURISM GROUPS AND VENUES

Medical tourism has existed for a long time. In the United States, there are centers of excellence[†] attracting patients with unusual or complicated medical histories seeking specific treatments. Studies show that there is a relation between select medical specialties and quality outcomes— trained specialists performing a consistent volume of a service yield better quality outcomes than

---

[†] Hospitals that provide specialty services typically are associated with high volume and positive medical outcomes. While the U.S. government has criteria for the term, some hospitals and insurers have created their own criteria for defining a Center of Excellence.

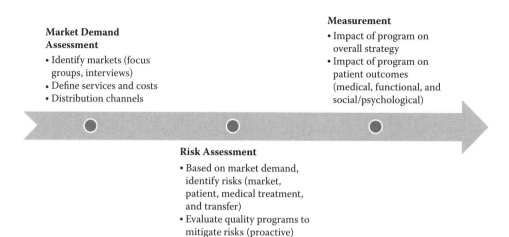

FIGURE 9.1   Main steps in developing a medical tourism strategy.

generalists.[*] Additionally, higher surgeon and hospital volumes are often associated with improved clinical outcomes, in particular for less common and complex operations.[†]

In the United States, hospitals including the Mayo Clinic and Johns Hopkins have international departments designed to manage the medical tourism patient segment. In some markets like Nigeria, a lack of availability of some specialized health care treatments means that patients must travel to neighboring countries for those services. In both of these instances, medical tourism occurs as an "exception," and is termed *selective medical tourism*. Selective medical tourism is driven by specialization, typically at important institutions (centers of excellence) with proven medical quality outcomes.

While the concept of medical care outsourcing for complex cases or selective treatments is not a new idea, the expansion of the concept to attract patients in the general population (general medical tourism) requires a shift in focus. General medical tourism defines those cases where an individual selects an alternative (nonhome-based) venue to receive medical treatment. The general medical tourist typically seeks treatment for a straightforward intervention including elective and cosmetic treatments at a reasonable cost. The medical treatment may take place in a hospital that is not considered a "Center of Excellence." Competition for these services is growing; therefore, cost (rather than specialization) is often an important criterion. Selective medical tourism is a subset of general medical tourism. (See Figure 9.2.)

MEDICAL TOURISM VENUES

The two venues where medical tourism can take place are a domestic or an international medical center. *Domestic medical tourism* refers to medical treatment where travel for care occurs within the boundaries of a state or region. *International medical tourism* refers to movement beyond the national border for health care. While both domestic and international medical tourism are similar and involve travel to another locale for medical treatment, international medical tourism is complicated by involving a foreign marketplace with different regulations, quality standards, culture, communication styles, and so forth.

---

[*] Hagen, T. P., Vaughan-Sarrazin, M. S., Cram, P. "Relation between hospital orthopaedic specialization and outcomes in patients aged 65 and older: Retrospective analysis of U.S. Medicare data," *British Medical Journal*, 2010; 340 doi 10.1136/bmj.c165 (published February 11, 2010).

[†] "Provider volume and clinical outcomes in surgery: Issues and implications." Lee, Clara N., Daly, John M.: June 2002 *Bulletin of the American College of Surgeons*.

FIGURE 9.2   Diagram of the relationship between selective and general medical tourism.

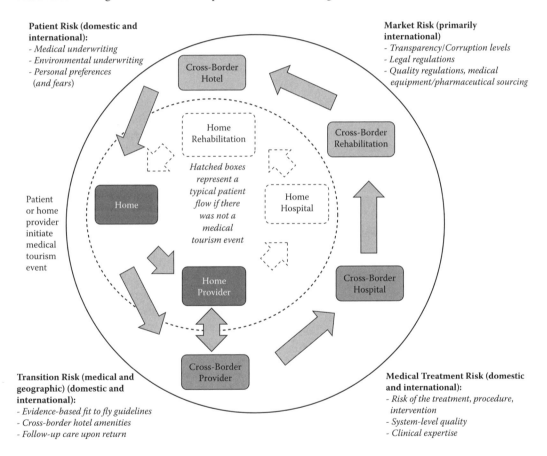

FIGURE 9.3   General relationship between the home and medical tourism event.

GENERAL MEDICAL TOURISM FLOW (DOMESTIC AND INTERNATIONAL)

Figure 9.3 depicts a simple medical tourism event. The internal circle generally depicts a traditional inpatient admission (gray hatch indicate the actions that would happen in the local context). Taken together, the two concentric circles illustrate the patient flow both in the home and medical tourism environments. The dotted edge surrounding the home environment points to the fact that the market in which the medical tourism care is received is expected to be different. Closer inspection of the external circle reveals the two aspects of a medical tourism event:

- Medical treatment/intervention
- Travel, transition of care (medical transition, getting to and from the destination, and fol-low-up care)

Successful management of these aspects increases the likelihood of a positive medical outcome. These two aspects of a medical tourism event are susceptible to four distinct risks: market risk, transition risk, medical treatment risk, and patient risk.[*] Effective identification and management of these risks increases the likelihood of a quality medical outcome.

In a domestic medical tourism event, the market in which the care is received is similar to the home environment, so there are limited compatibility risks. However, when the event is international, there is not only market risk, but the market characteristics influence the other risk groups. (See Figure 9.3.[†])

RISK ASSESSMENTS

Risk assessments[‡] within the medical tourism flow identify quality gaps. Before embarking on a medical tourism strategy, hospitals typically coordinate a thorough demand assessment. Creating quality programs for target markets requires risk assessments of the following categories.

MARKET RISK

Market risk assessment requires a solid understanding of the market elements that could impact a safe patient journey. These include regulations regarding medical device and pharmaceutical importing and the level of health care innovation, as well as the importance of efficiency and effectiveness. For example, if a patient elects to undergo knee replacement surgery in an international market, matching the device regulations to the home market is critical both for follow-up care (a home doctor may refuse to manage a complication on a device that is not accepted in the home market), as well as for a positive medical outcome (if the inserted device fails in a shorter period of time than other options). Another example is Singapore, which has a strong medical quality history, including superior blood management and supply protocols. However, the donor population could potentially be infected with dengue,[§] adding a patient safety issue that might be important to an individual (who may prefer to bring his or her own blood). Finally, matching legal liability differences may also be important to identify, particularly if a patient is receiving care in a market with substantially different malpractice regulations. Market risk affects all other risks (transition, medical treatment, and patient).

TRANSITION RISK

Transition risk refers to both the administrative management of the travel itself, as well as the clinical components of ensuring fitness to fly/travel and coordinating medical follow-up when the patient returns home. For example, a patient seeking bariatric banding may determine that the procedure does not require any follow-up at home. However, both in terms of clinical outcomes and creating

---

[*] Risk groupings taken from the Health Climate Calculator™, from Transparent Borders™ LLC (2010).

[†] The framework is drawn from the Health Climate Calculator™, from Transparent Borders™ LLC (2010).

[‡] The risk assessment methodology is drawn from the Health Climate Calculator™, from Transparent Borders™ LLC (2010).

[§] *Merriam-Webster Unabridged Dictionary,* www.merriam-webster.com/dictionary/dengue. An acute infectious disease caused by a flavivirus (species Dengue virus of the genus *Flavivirus*), transmitted by Aedes mosquitoes, and characterized by headache, severe joint pain, and a rash—also called breakbone fever, dengue fever.

transparency, all treatments are ideally discussed with the home provider to ensure a complete patient history.

An important development in reducing transition risk of a medical tourism event is the advancement of telemedicine. Telemedicine is defined as "the use of medical information exchanged from one site to another via electronic communications for the health and education of the patient or healthcare provider and for the purpose of improving patient care. Telemedicine includes consultative, diagnostic, and treatment services."* Advancing telemedicine techniques will support the globalization of health care by enabling the distant medical provider to follow up with the patient directly rather than solely depending on the home provider.

Medical treatment risk identifies the potential hazards that arise from the treatment and include clinical and facility components. Here are four types of risk typically identified:

- System risk: the chance that a bottleneck in the hospital system will negatively impact patient safety (e.g., patient discharge was delayed due to the attending physician's being on vacation; ensuring equipment use is understood and practiced regularly; use of checklists; practices to manage similar-sounding drug names)
- Medical risk: the hazard of the medical treatment itself (e.g., the chance of a poor medical outcome, impact of comorbid conditions, new and available technology)
- Human management risk: the risk that the clinical expertise or sufficient patient care are not available (e.g., the chance that the attending physician is not apprised of best practices for a new surgery or medical technology)
- Infrastructure risk: the chance that something will go wrong due to poor infrastructure management (e.g., the patient had an adverse outcome because of the lack of necessary equipment such as an MRI machine needed to diagnose a head injury and necessary treatment)

Patient risk for medical tourism treatments includes not only basic medical underwriting (e.g., assessing the individual risk of the treatment due to high body mass index (BMI), smoking history, chronic diseases, etc.), but also environmental underwriting (e.g., risks associated with the home and/or medical tourism venue that could complicate a positive medical outcome including pollution levels, infectious diseases, and food-borne illnesses), and personal preferences (e.g., if the patient feels strongly about the country having a positive human rights track record, or if the person is afraid of being away from family and friends for a long period of time.) All of these issues impact a patient's outcome. With these risks effectively identified, the development of quality and safety transparency begins.

IMPORTANCE OF TRANSPARENCY IN MANAGING RISKS

Merriam-Webster defines transparent as something being free from deceit or pretense, easily detected or seen through, readily understood, characterized by visibility or accessibility of information especially concerning business practices.† The presence of transparency enables a full assessment of issues in the open, so that both problems and successes can be identified and studied. In the medical tourism context, transparency is important at the market level (where the medical tourism event occurs), as well as at the patient level (what and how medical treatments and processes occur).

* Medicine.net website: http://www.medterms.com/script/main/art.asp?articlekey=33620. Extracted November 2010.
† *Merriam-Webster Unabridged Dictionary,* extracted Nov. 15, 2010 www.merriam-webster.com/dictionary/transparent.

TABLE 9.1
Market Transparency and Affect on International Medical Tourism Risk

Risk Category	Some Market Transparency Matching Tasks
Patient	• Identify the difference between the home and medical tourism destination corruption levels for possible communication or behavior concerns
Medical treatment	• Identify differences in hospital and healthcare regulations between the home and medical tourism destination and how market transparency could impact (e.g., counterfeit medicines, using a medical device that is not supported by evidence based medicine, etc.)
	• Map the likelihood of an adverse event based on the identified market differences
Transition (medical and geographic)	• Create a process to identify the impact of corruption on the transition of care including evidence of home provider's willingness to take care of the patient upon return home

IMPORTANCE OF MARKET TRANSPARENCY IN INTERNATIONAL MEDICAL TOURISM

Market transparency in an international context refers to the extent of corruption or the existence of gray markets[*] in a country. Transparency International (www.transparency.org) publishes an annual "Corruptions Perception Index," providing insight into perceived corruption based on analysis of myriad international data sources and opinion surveys from credible country experts and business leaders.[†] Empirical work to quantify the economic extent of corruption in a market has been limited; however, studies show that the more market corruption, the less investment and economic growth in a country.[‡] This suggests that innovation and quality standards are less likely to be present because there is reduced investment initiative. Translated, if health care quality is driven by innovation and competition, a corrupt market could have a more difficult time achieving a sustainable medical tourism strategy. However, there are examples of very successful (quality-focused) medical tourism hospitals operating in corrupt markets. Market transparency, therefore, can be managed. Finally, without a reliable regulatory environment that can be trusted to manage basic services, the quality of infrastructure and services in corrupt markets require additional verification.

Attracting patients from markets with high corruption levels, or seeking medical care in markets with a different corruption level, is ripe for conflict. A critical component of a risk analysis includes understanding the difference between the patient market and the target medical tourism market so that gaps are identified and addressed. Table 9.1 identifies some important issues to consider.

QUALITY AND SAFETY TRANSPARENCY

With a solid understanding of the market demand and associated risks, hospitals can develop quality-focused medical tourism programs. In health care, quality is often the umbrella term for superior outcomes, but the Institute of Medicine (in their publication *Crossing the Quality Chasm: A New Health System for the 21st Century*) expanded the idea by expressing the quality as the "degree to

---

[*] A gray market exists when solutions are created through unofficial means.
[†] Corruptions Perceptions Index 2010, "Short methodological note," http://www.transparency.org/policy_research/surveys_indices/cpi/2010/in_detail#4 (November 18, 2010).
[‡] Mauro, Paolo, "Why Worry about Corruption?" *International Monetary Fund, Economic Issues* (6), 1997.

which health services for individuals and populations increase the likelihood of desired health outcomes and are consistent with current professional knowledge."[*]

As a starting point in the quality discussion, a standard model of health care quality developed by Donabedian focuses on Structure, Process and Outcomes. Specifically, effective structures and processes support positive medical outcomes.[†] This approach also states that the ultimate medical outcome reflects all influences (even external) on the patient journey.

When adapting this concept to the medical tourism market, medical outcome evaluations will have to address specific quality components in transitions of care. This theoretically includes the patient fitness to fly/travel, as well as ensuring that the home physician is willing to provide follow-up care and ways to measure the effectiveness of the process. A positive medical outcome that is compromised through a poor transition plan will emerge as a poor medical outcome in spite of the effective on-site medical treatment. Knowing specifically where the problem occurred (and why) increases the likelihood of resolution.

Furthermore, follow-up of a medical tourism quality program typically includes a longer tail than typically practiced—specifically up to 36 months postdischarge.

ACCREDITATION

Hospital accreditation seeks to improve health care delivery and quality care. The concept is broadly accepted by the international community, including the World Health Organization (WHO) that views accreditation as an important component of health care quality.[‡]

Internationally, there are many hospital credentialing groups, including Trent Accreditation Scheme (UK–Europe), Joint Commission International (JCI; United States), Australian Council for Healthcare Standards International (ACHSI; Australia), and the Canadian Council on Health Services (CCHSA). If your hospital strategy is focused on targeting one specific country, consider the accreditation most closely associated with it.

Additional domestic and international safety standards include ISQua (International Society for Quality Health Care). In 1999 it launched the International Accreditation Programme (IAP), designed to "accredit the accreditors."[§]

PATIENT SAFETY

Patient safety focuses on prevention of errors leading to adverse events. This can include physical patient safety (avoiding slips and falls) and negative medical outcomes such as postsurgical infections. Safety includes continuous identification of potentially harmful issues and methods to measure and manage.

Along with the vast quality credentialing and safety approaches, there are growing information resources on the Internet that offer information on safety issues that potential patients can access. These information sources may create both real and imagined quality obstacles that hospitals should be able to address. Consider the availability of instant online information in the form of "Google Alerts," as well as the impact of country geography (tsunamis, pandemics, etc.). Proactively identify, address, and communicate safety issues that may be present in your environment.

Both hospital and patient safety initiatives primarily work to reduce medical treatment risk.

---

[*] Institute of Medicine, *Crossing the Quality Chasm: A New Health System for the 21st Century,* National Academies Press; 1st edition (July 18, 2001).

[†] Donabedian A, (1988). The quality of care: how can it be assessed? *JAMA* 260, (12): 1743–1748.

[‡] http://www.emro.who.int/mei/HA.htm

[§] ISQua website: http://www.isqua.org/accreditations.htm. Extracted November 21 2010.

QUALITY TOOLS TO PROMOTE TRANSPARENCY

There are international quality tools that support hospital quality and patient safety initiatives. These generally focus on error prevention.

Consider two general types of errors[*]:

- Errors of ignorance: mistakes occurring because there is insufficient knowledge
- Errors of ineptitude: mistakes occurring due to inadequate use of available knowledge

Errors of ignorance can be reduced by research, knowledge sharing, and incentives to use best international evidence-based medicine when treating a patient. Evidence-based medicine development includes identifying clinical information needs, searching published objective literature for findings, and application to a clinical pathway.[†]

Errors of ineptitude can be reduced by adopting best practices through the use of checklists. Checklists, or lists of items that need to be completed before completing a procedure, treatment, or surgery, are a growing source of discussion in the medical field.[‡] Sample surgical checklists (aimed at transparency) collect information confirming patient status, specific steps required in the briefing process, and contingency plans with defined action items listed, as well as a debriefing of the episode postsurgery including counting instruments. The World Health Organization offers a surgical safety checklist and documentation in concert with the Institute for Healthcare Improvement (www.ihi.org).[§]

In both instances, transparency in information (defining the particular best practice), and use of checklists (to identify action items) emerge as consistent with a best medical practice.

RISKS AND REWARDS OF MEDICAL TOURISM

While most agree that quality and safety transparency are critical components of a medical tourism journey, being transparent has benefits as well as drawbacks. Before the medical tourism community commits to providing data on medical outcomes in both the short and the long-term, a first step is to accept relatively basic quality and safety approaches. Returning to the four identified risk groupings that quality initiatives can control, here are some practical recommendations:

Market risk
- Depending on your strategy (general or selective medical tourism; domestic or international patients), identify potential risks and proactively manage.

Transition risk
- Access evidence based guidelines on fitness to fly or travel for medical care.
- Ensure appropriate accommodations, including culture-specific issues (local language television) as well as physical site issues (telephone in the bathroom, wheelchair accommodation).
- Identify potential transition risks including pharmaceutical management (pre- and posttreatment), local regulations regarding durable medical equipment, or medical device sourcing.

---

[*] Gawande, Atul, *The Checklist Manifesto,* Metropolitan Books; 1st ed. (December 22, 2009).

[†] Sackett, D. L., Rosenberg, W. M., Gray, J. A., Haynes, R. B., and Richardson, W. S. (1996). Evidence based medicine: What it is and what it isn't." *British Medical Journal,* 312(7023): 71–72.

[‡] Gawande, Atul, *The Checklist Manifesto,* Metropolitan Books (December 22, 2009).

[§] WHO Surgical Safety Checklist: http://www.ihi.org/IHI/Programs/ImprovementMap/WHOSurgicalSafetyChecklist. htm (extracted November 22, 2010).

- Create a standard process to communicate and confirm follow-up treatment with the local provider, including follow-up assessments up to 36 months postdischarge.
- Create measurements to identify (internally) management of the transition risks (both clinical and geographic).

Medical treatment risk
- If checklists are part of the surgical process, document which were included and had an impact on patient safety; evaluate impact of use on patient outcome.
- Identify best practices for the procedure, treatment, or intervention and the general clinical pathway.
- Create a case management protocol for internal use to identify clinical and social issues potentially impeding a positive medical outcome.

Patient risk
- Identify medical, environmental, and personal preference risks specific to your hospital strategy.

With these four risk groupings evaluated and proactively managed prior to the medical treatment, assess medical outcomes posttreatment.

MEASURING OUTCOMES

Medical approaches are impacted by culture. From the practice of alternative treatments in China, to the aggressive medical treatments in the United States,[*] understanding the medical approach (and managing patient expectations) is important to a long-term positive outcome. While it is difficult to separate the physician from the culture, the impact to outcomes is even less obvious. For this reason, the mapping of both clinical as well as patient satisfaction rates is critical to the growth of the industry.

Overall health outcome measures refer to the impact of the treatment on the patient (all things being equal). For medical tourism treatments for the general population, collect data on three aspects of medical tourism: medical outcomes, patient improvement and functional health, and patient satisfaction.

While each hospital may collect outcomes data on specific issues, for potential comparison purposes in the medical tourism arena, the following medical outcomes data are suggested:

SURGICAL SITE INFECTION RATES

Postoperative infection is a major cause of patient injury, mortality, and health care cost. Specifically, in the United States[†]:

- An estimated 2.6% of 30 million operations are complicated by surgical site infections (SSIs) annually.
- Infection rates up to 11% are reported for certain types of operations.
- Each infection is estimated to increase a hospital stay by an average of 7 days and add over $3,000 in charges (1992 data).
- Appropriate preoperative administration of antibiotics is effective in preventing infection.

---

[*] Payer, L. *Medicine and Culture,* Holt Paperbacks, New York. (November 15, 1996).
[†] Institute for Healthcare Improvement: http://www.ihi.org/IHI/Topics/PatientSafety/SurgicalSiteInfections/ (extracted November 22 2010).

READMISSION RATES

Readmission rates within 7 and 30 days (both for initial diagnosis as well as any other diagnosis). Readmissions are an important quality metric pointing to potential quality issues in the initial patient stay. Categorizing the type of readmission (related and nonrelated to the initial admission) is important to capture as they provide insight into both quality and population characteristics. As an example, the Mayo Clinic defines a hospital readmission as a patient admitted to a hospital within 7 days after being discharged from an earlier hospital stay. The standard benchmark used by the Centers for Medicare and Medicaid (CMS) is the 7-day readmission rate. Rates at the 75th percentile or lower are considered optimal by CMS.[*]

MORTALITY RATES AND DISCHARGE STATUS

These are used to capture patients discharged to their home, or to a hotel or a long-term care facility. Basic discharge status options: discharged to home, discharged to hotel, discharged to rehabilitation, or death.

There are challenges to collecting these data,[†] particularly if hospitals are not required to provide them to a regulatory body. If the results are not audited, assessing validity and reliability can be problematic, particularly in corrupt markets. This could discourage sharing outcomes data publicly. One alternative is to give an international governing group the authority to verify veracity of results, so that there is a perceived fair environment. Alternatively, objective and licensed third party administrators or licensed insurers could also fulfill this role.

Assess patient satisfaction and functional status. For patient improvement and functional status, consider using the Short Form 36 (SF 36) questionnaire (developed by RAND) at both pre- and posttreatments. The SF 36 surveys patient health and is used in economic studies as a variable in the calculation of a Quality Adjusted Life Year (QALY). QALYs are used in studies to measure the cost effectiveness of procedures or treatments.

The original SF 36 was constructed by the RAND Corporation (http://rand.org) and is a multipurpose survey profiling both functional health and well-being. It is a generic measure rather than disease or age specific. The questionnaire has been translated in more than 50 countries as part of the International Quality of Life Assessment (IQOLA) Project.[‡]

The SF survey evaluates patient health from the following perspectives: health perception (and change over time), physical limitations and impact on personal life, personal mental health (feelings of negativity or uselessness), and the individual's perspective on physical impairments.

A critical advantage of the SF approach is that the survey has been tested in multiple languages. This enables the beginning of documentation regarding health improvement (or deterioration) upon completing a medical tourism treatment. This approach, therefore, includes a cultural sensitivity that may be lacking in other methodologies.

PATIENT SATISFACTION

Patient satisfaction surveys should be designed to address the specific medical tourism grouping (general and/or selective) as well as venue (domestic and/or international). Surveys should include satisfaction with the medical treatment, the medical outcome, the provider's capabilities and communication, the hotel or rehabilitation accommodations (functional, social, and longevity), and the ease of transitioning back home to receive follow-up care.

---

[*] Mayo Clinic website: http://www.mayoclinic.org/quality/readmission-rates.html (extracted November 24 2010).
[†] Any analysis of medical outcomes requires a robust assessment of demographics and diagnoses to ensure case mix adjustments accurately reflect population differences.
[‡] SF-36.org, http://www.sf-36.org/tools/sf36.shtml extracted November 15, 2010.

While follow-ups occur after 7 days and 30 days, postdischarge, for the medical tourism patient, perform overall follow-ups for up to 36 months posthospital discharge to ensure solid understanding of issues in health, transitioning care, follow-up treatment, and any personal behavioral changes as a result of the experience.

An additional aspect to medical outcomes analysis particular to medical tourism is to profile the demographics of your patient base. This information enables retrospective review of market characteristics, which can be linked to patient outcomes. Specifically, track the following demographic data:

- Reasons for medical tourism event: Where the medical tourist originated, and the reason this individual chose medical tourism.
- Insurance: Insurance held (or not), including travel insurance.
- Travel history: Passports held, languages spoken, last time on a flight, frequent flyer status, general capability to use Internet to book travel, and so forth.
- Preferences and fears: Country requirements (e.g., human rights or personal safety), personal concerns/fears. Fears are important to identify as they may impede an otherwise healthy medical outcome and include issues such as "I am worried I will not understand my doctor" and "I am fearful of the long flight and of missing my family and friends."

With these cumulative data, hospitals can identify quality gaps and opportunities to proactively address patient concerns and preferences.

MOVEMENT TO STANDARD BEST PRACTICES

As the medical tourism market expands from selective to general medical tourism, hospitals have the opportunity to develop targeted strategies aimed at increasing consumer awareness of both the risks and rewards involved. Proactive development of quality-focused, patient-centered, and transparent processes and results will emphasize the importance of quality medical, transition, and social outcomes, as well as elevate the professionalism of top-tier hospital participants.

Lisa Beichl, MBA, is president and CEO of Transparent Borders™ LLC (www.globalhealthquality.com), a company providing objective cross-border criteria and tools, education, and consulting to increase transparency in the global health care marketplace. Her professional experience spans 20 years across the continuum from broker to (re)insurer in both public and private sectors including the developing health microinsurance segment. It includes leadership positions for multinational (re)insurance organizations including Swiss Re Life and Health (Zurich), as well as completing consulting and educational development projects in global healthcare (medical tourism, microinsurance, and health care strengthening) for public sector organizations including USAID. Her professional health experience includes work in Latin America; North America; the Middle East; Southeast Asia; Western Asia; Central, Western, and Eastern Europe; and Africa.

10 Putting It All Together
Your Provider Network

As you develop your contracts with your suppliers, the following provisions may be helpful to show your attorney in case this person is not a health law specialist. These provisions should not be used verbatim, but the main points of each one should be worked into the understanding between the parties to protect all your hard work and investment into network development.

ANTICIRCUMVENTION

Each Party shall provide adequate legal protection and effective legal remedies against the circumvention of any proprietary or confidentiality measures that are used by, or at the direction of, hospitals, physicians, their officers, directors, agents, and employees for use in connection which are not authorized by the facilitator, their officers, directors, agents, and employees concerned or permitted by law. No person or corporation shall circumvent any provision of this contract that effectively controls access and contractual relationship of the network protected under this agreement.

PROFESSIONAL LIABILITY ISSUES

DISCLAIMER OF LIABILITY

Hospital/provider agrees to indemnify, defend, and hold harmless Facilitator and its officers, directors, agents, heirs, successors, assigns, and employees from and against any and all demands, claims, and damages to persons or property, losses and liabilities, including reasonable attorney's fees, arising out of or caused by hospital/provider's negligence or willful misconduct, malfeasance, neglect, or nonfeasance.

OPTION 2

Each Responsible for Own Acts

Neither party hereto shall be liable for defending or for the expense of defending the other party, its agent, or, employees, against any claim, legal action, dispute resolution or administrative or regulatory proceeding arising out of or related to such other party's actions or omissions under this agreement. Neither party hereto shall be liable for any liability of the other party, its agents, or employees, whether resulting from judgment, settlement, award, fine, or otherwise, which arises out of such other party's actions or omissions under this agreement.

THEORIES OF LIABILITY

Ostensible Liability

This liability focuses on patients' reasonable expectations and beliefs based on the providers' conduct rather than on actual contracts between health care providers. It is common for medical groups who are trying to keep pace with patient demand to bring in an independent contractor to help. It is also common to cut overhead expenses by making space available in the office suite for another physician. The problem is the facilitator can be found liable for any malpractice on the part of independent physicians if patients believe they are members of your network. The same is true for facilitators and the relationships between their contracted providers such as hospitals, drivers, hotels, or other suppliers.

Vicarious Liability

The legal concept of vicarious liability allows liability for a wrongdoing to be extended beyond the original defendant to persons or entities who have not committed a wrong, but on whose behalf the defendant acted. Vicarious liability is based on the historical legal doctrine of respondeat superior: "Let the master answer for the torts (civil wrongs) of his servants."

Shared Liability

According to the doctrine of joint and several liability, defendants found liable in a malpractice lawsuit share among themselves the total amount awarded to the plaintiff. However, since not all parties have the same liability coverage, the defendants with the greatest amounts of insurance—the "deep pockets"—may find themselves paying the most money. When a primary defendant in a lawsuit carries insufficient insurance, other codefendants, even if they're only minimally involved in the case, may be looked upon as "deep pockets" for purposes of claim resolution. Vicarious liability can create situations whereby two or more physicians, each represented by a different medical liability carrier, are named as defendants in a single claim. When this occurs, each carrier's ability to control both the direction and quality of the defense is seriously compromised because there may be competing interests in the case. This can also occur when a physician or hospital is named in a suit with a facilitator, and thus the reason why we ask for Each Responsible for Own Acts provisions.

Assignment of the Contract

Neither party may assign, delegate or transfer this agreement or the rights granted herein without written consent of the other party, which consent shall not be unreasonably withheld.

PROVIDER CREDENTIALING AND PRIVILEGING

Agreement to Accept Hospital's Credentialing

In lieu of requiring provider's physicians to submit to facilitator's credentialing process, facilitator shall rely upon certification from hospital attesting to the fact that hospital's physicians have been properly credentialed in accordance with hospital's credentialing and privileging policies and procedures. In such case, hospital shall provide facilitator with a current description of hospital's credentialing and privileging processes, policies, and procedures. Hospital shall provide to facilitator the names of all physicians who are credentialed and approved in accordance with this paragraph on a continuing basis who will care for facilitator's clients.

Hospital agrees to permit facilitator, during normal business hours or at such other time as may be agreed upon by the parties, to inspect and review a random sample of provider applications and credentialing files to ascertain compliance with facilitator's credentialing and privileging processes, policies, and procedures.

Hospital further agrees that if it revises its credentialing and privileging processes, policies, and procedures, such revisions shall be provided to facilitator at least thirty (30) days prior to their effective date. If facilitator determines that revised processes, policies, and procedures result in the failure of hospital's credentialing and privileging processes, policies, and procedures to meet the credentialing and privileging criteria established by the facilitator, facilitator shall have the right to immediately terminate its acceptance of hospital's credentialing and to require that all participating providers be credentialed in accordance with facilitator's credentialing and privileging processes, policies, and procedures.

Dispute Resolution

Venue is the location where any legal dispute between parties will be carried out. Be forewarned that the majority of international providers will insist that all legal disputes must be settled in their own country with rules of procedure in accordance with their laws and perhaps in their language. There may be little you can leverage to negotiate this to a more mutually beneficial setting. The language is usually similar to that which follows, below:

The parties agree to refer any disputes, controversies, or questions arising under this agreement to either a dispute resolution entity, or to a single arbitrator selected by [name your governing authority], as the parties shall agree within sixty (60) days of the last attempted resolution. The proceeding shall be governed by the rules of the [cite the adopted rules] then in effect, and shall be held in the jurisdiction of the [select facilitator's or provider's] domicile. The compensation and expenses of the arbitrator(s) and any administrative fees or costs associated with the arbitration proceeding shall be borne equally by the parties.

Arbitration shall be the exclusive remedy for the settlement of disputes arising under this Agreement. The decision of the arbitrator(s) shall be final, conclusive and binding, and no action at law or in equity may be instituted by either party other than to enforce the award of the arbitrator(s).

Liquidated Damages

These are damages whose amount is assigned by the parties during the making of the contract for the injured party to be collected as compensation upon a particular breach. Also, if the damages are not predetermined and called upon in advance, then the total amount for the recovery can be determined by the law in the event of the breach.

Reimbursement and Financial Terms

Typically, these terms specify payment conditions for both the provider and the facilitator. You will need to clarify:

Exclusions and Inclusions

What the pricing for the procedure package includes and excludes (for example: doctor fees, surgical room costs, medical supplies, medications, etc.)

What are the terms of the contract and the validity of pricing (how long provider pricing will remain in effect)?

Cancellations and Provider Refund Policies, if Any

What happens if there is some delay or cancellation due to extenuating circumstances, e.g., riots, civil insurrection, fires, floods, storms, or the patient suffering some untoward event during travel that makes surgery impossible?

Commissions

If the facilitator will be paid a commission, the basis for calculating the commission off the revenue of a package price that includes only medical services, or will lodging and other services be included as well? What happens if complications occur and increase the final price? Most hospitals will not want to apply the commission to the charges associated with the revenue for complications.

You may establish a monetary amount you will receive per patient or the wholesale discount from standard charges, so that if you add in a service fee instead of a commission, you will not be disadvantaged from the hospital's usual rates.

Forms or Methods of Payment

There are several choices: Will you take payment, keep the commission, be required to escrow the payment, and send the balance to the hospital, or will the hospital take payment from the patient and send the commission to you?

Revenue Cycle

This is the billing cycle time period for the commission to be sent or the hospital to be paid. Establish whether or not there will be penalties for late payment and if so, how much and what happens if there is no payment of the principle or the penalty within a certain time period. How can one side compel the other side to perform?

Time Period for Provider to Receive Payment

Establish whether or not a deposit is required. If so, when is it due and how much must be paid?

Be sure to negotiate an understanding and include written terms that describe cancellation penalties and any forfeiture of deposits.

Confidentiality

Facilitator and hospital/provider, during and after termination of this Agreement, shall keep confidential all data, including but not limited to quality assurance and utilization management information, all statistical data reports and standards, and all financial information relating to this agreement, and each shall utilize its best efforts to prevent and protect such information from unauthorized disclosure by its agents and employees. Further, during and after termination of this agreement, neither facilitator nor hospital/provider shall use or allow its agents and employees to use any such information to the competitive disadvantage of or in any other way detrimental to the other party. Other than as required by law or a governmental authority, hospital/provider shall not disclose any provision of, nor allow any person to see, read, use, copy, or otherwise have access to this agreement.

PHYSICIAN AND DENTIST AGREEMENTS

CREDENTIALING AND PRIVILEGING

Participating providers shall at all times be subject to, use best efforts to meet, and comply with, facilitator's credentialing policies and procedures.

MALPRACTICE AND PROFESSIONAL LIABILITY

Neither party hereto shall be liable for defending or for the expense of defending the other party, its agent, or, employees, against any claim, legal action, dispute resolution or administrative or regulatory proceeding arising out of or related to such other party's actions or omissions under this agreement. Neither party hereto shall be liable for any liability of the other party, its agents, or employees, whether resulting from judgment, settlement, award, fine, nor otherwise, which arises out of such other party's actions or omissions under this agreement. This provision shall survive the termination of this agreement.

HOTEL AGREEMENTS

Be sure to address the following issues in your negotiations with hotels and then make sure that whatever you negotiated is part of the written agreement.

- Site visits
- Special needs

- Pet accommodations
- Ground transfers
- Special meals
- Special equipment
- Long stay rates

CHAUFFEUR SERVICES

- Insurance
- Meet and greet
- English fluency
- Tour guide services
- Shanghai prevention

Shanghai prevention is a term used to describe a practice in many countries where one hires a tour guide or driver for the day. The driver convinces the passengers that a certain stop is part of the points of interest on the agenda for the day of touring. About midafternoon, the unwitting passengers are taken to some shops or a place where they are cajoled into purchasing trinkets, jewelry, souvenirs, or other wares and the driver often abandons them until the shopkeepers decide that the passengers will buy no more or the efforts are futile. This interruption consumes 2 to 3 hours of the day tour. This occurs in Southeast Asia, South America, and Central America. If this happens to your clients, tell them to call the police or call a taxi and make sure they have the driver's information and name card or business card, as well as their hotel business card on hand and to always have at least three times the typical taxi fare in cash in their possession at all times. They should also not pay the entire tour fee or driver fee if this occurs, and should reserve at least half of the fair for payment at the conclusion of the trip together with any gratuity to ensure proper service.

CONTRACTS, AGREEMENTS, AND FORMS

MARKET RESEARCH

Figure 10.1 shows a sample service survey form.

MEDICAL ASSOCIATION CONTACT INFORMATION

Table 10.1 will help you locate the source for primary source verification of physician credentials in the listed countries. This includes many of the countries that are currently building medical tourism programs.

Procedure or Service Contracted	
Your Name:*	
Your Email Address:*	
Facilitator/Case Manager:	
Destination:	
Departure Date:	
Travel Planner:	
Why did you book with our company? i.e. used XYZ Health Travel before, Colleague or Friend, Advertisement, etc.	
Were your travel arrangements handled promptly and efficiently?	☐ Yes ☐ No
Comments	
Was your in-house XYZ Health Travel Planner knowledgeable and helpful in making your tour a success?	☐ Yes ☐ No
Comments	
If a Destination Manager accompanied you while abroad, was he/she helpful in making your visit a success?	☐ Yes ☐ No
Comments	
Would you use XYZ Health Travel for future health travel arrangements?	☐ Yes ☐ No
Comments	
Name of Destination Manager:	
Were the ground transportation arrangements satisfactory?	☐ Yes ☐ No
Was the vehicle in good condition?	☐ Yes ☐ No
Was your driver friendly and courteous?	☐ Yes ☐ No

FIGURE 10.1   Sample survey form.

Overall comments on Ground Transportation Company	
Name of Airline(s) if applicable:	
Did the aircraft depart on time?	○ Yes ○ No
Did the aircraft arrive on time?	○ Yes ○ No
The inflight service was...	○ Excellent ○ Good ○ Fair ○ Poor
Overall comments on Airline(s)	
Name of Hotel:	
The accommodation was...	○ Excellent ○ Good ○ Fair ○ Poor
The service was...	○ Excellent ○ Good ○ Fair ○ Poor
The food was...	○ Excellent ○ Good ○ Fair ○ Poor
Overall comments on Hotel(s)	

Attractions, Educational aspects such as music venues, language experience (overall impressions):

1: _____   ○ Excellent ○ Good ○ Fair
                    ○ Poor

2: _____   ○ Excellent ○ Good ○ Fair
                    ○ Poor

3: _____   ○ Excellent ○ Good ○ Fair
                    ○ Poor

4: _____   ○ Excellent ○ Good ○ Fair
                    ○ Poor

FIGURE 10.1 *(Continued)*

5: [   ]   ○ Excellent   ○ Good   ○ Fair
                             ○ Poor

6: [   ]   ○ Excellent   ○ Good   ○ Fair
                             ○ Poor

7: [   ]   ○ Excellent   ○ Good   ○ Fair
                             ○ Poor

8: [   ]   ○ Excellent   ○ Good   ○ Fair
                             ○ Poor

9: [   ]   ○ Excellent   ○ Good   ○ Fair
                             ○ Poor

10: [   ]   ○ Excellent   ○ Good   ○ Fair
                             ○ Poor

| If your tour included a "guided" city tour, was your guide well informed and friendly? | ○ Yes   ○ No |

Hospital (overall impression):

1: Hospital Conditions   ○ Excellent   ○ Good   ○ Fair
                               ○ Poor

2: Nursing Care   ○ Excellent   ○ Good   ○ Fair
                               ○ Poor

3: English Language Fluency of Staff   ○ Excellent   ○ Good   ○ Fair
                               ○ Poor

4: Amenities (e.g., Wi-fi, TV Channels, etc.)   ○ Excellent   ○ Good   ○ Fair
                               ○ Poor

5: Explanation of treatments and procedures at a level you could understand   ○ Excellent   ○ Good   ○ Fair
                               ○ Poor

6. The surgeon's bedside manner and patience with your questions and concerns   ○ Excellent   ○ Good   ○ Fair
                               ○ Poor

Overall comments on the hospital: [   ]

FIGURE 10.1 *(Continued)*

Did you enjoy the hospital?	☐ Yes ☐ No
Would you return?	☐ Yes ☐ No
If yes, please comment	
Do you consider this health travel experience good value for the money?	☐ Yes ☐ No
What did you most enjoy about your experience?	
Do you or your family have any future health travel plans?	☐ Yes ☐ No
If yes, where and when:	
Overall comments on your experience with us and our planning:	
May we use your comments for marketing purposes?	☐ Yes ☐ No

FIGURE 10.1 *(Continued)*

TABLE 10.1
Medical Associations by Country

Order of Physicians of Albania (OPA)
Rr. Dibres. Poliklinika Nr.10, Kati 3
Tirana
ALBANIA
Tel/Fax: (355) 4 2340 458
E-mail: albmedorder@albmail.com; e-mail: albmedorder@albmail.com
Website: www.umsh.org

Col'legi de Metges–Andorra
C/Verge del Pilar 5
Edifici Plaza 4t. Despatx 11
500 Andorra La Vella
ANDORRA
Tel: (376) 823 525
Fax: (376) 860 793
Website: www.col-legidemetges.ad; e-mail: coma@andorra.ad

Ordem dos Médicos de Angola (OMA)
Rua Amilcar Cabral 151-153
Luanda
ANGOLA
Tel: (244) 222 39 23 57
Fax: (221) 222 39 16 31
Website: www.ordemmedicosangola.com; e-mail: secretariatdormed@gmail.com

Confederación Médica de la República Argentina
Av. Belgrano 1235
Buenos Aires 1093
ARGENTINA
Tel/Fax: (54-11) 4381-1548/4384-5036
Website: www.comra.health.org.ar; e-mail: comra@confederacionmedica.com.ar

Armenian Medical Association
P.O. Box 143
Yerevan 375 010
REPUBLIC OF ARMENIA
Tel: (3741) 53 58 68
Fax: (3741) 53 48 79
Website: www.armeda.am; e-mail: info@armeda.am

Australian Medical Association
P.O. Box 6090
Kingston, ACT 2604
AUSTRALIA
Tel: (61-2) 6270 5460
Fax: (61-2) 6270 5499
Website: www.ama.com.au; e-mail: ama@ama.com.au

TABLE 10.1 *(Continued)*
Medical Associations by Country

Österreichische Ärztekammer (Austrian Medical Chamber)
Weihburggasse 10-12 – P.O. Box 213
1010 Wien
AUSTRIA
Tel: (43-1) 514 06 64
Fax: (43-1) 514 06 933
Website: www.aerztekammer.at; e-mail: international@aerztekammer.at/
m.reisinger@aerztekammer.at

Azerbaijan Medical Association
P.O. Box 16
AZE 1000, Baku
REPUBLIC OF AZERBAIJAN
Tel: (99 450) 328 18 88
Fax: (99 412) 431 88 66
Website: www.azmed.az; e-mail: info@azmed.az – azerma@hotmail.com

Medical Association of the Bahamas
P.O. Box N-3125
MAB House-6th Terrace Centreville
Nassau,
BAHAMAS
Tel.: (242) 328 1858
Fax: (242) 328 1857
E-mail: medassocbah@gmail.com

Bangladesh Medical Association
BMA Bhaban 5/2 Topkhana Road
Dhaka 1000
BANGLADESH
Tel: (880) 2-9568714/9562527
Fax: (880) 2 9566060/9562527
E-mail: bma@aitlbd.net

Association Belge des Syndicats Médicaux–Belgium
Chaussée de Boondael 6, bte 4
1050 Bruxelles
BELGIUM
Tel: (32-2) 644 12 88
Fax: (32-2) 644 15 27
Website: www.absym-bvas.be; e-mail: absym.bvas@euronet.be

Colegio Médico de Bolivia
Calle Ayacucho 630
Tarija
BOLIVIA
Fax: (591) 4 666 3569
Website: www.colegiomedicodebolivia.org.bo; e-mail: colmedbol_tjo@hotmail.com

TABLE 10.1 *(Continued)*
Medical Associations by Country

Associaçao Médica Brasileira
R. Sao Carlos do Pinhal 324 – Bairro Bela
Vista
Sao Paulo SP – CEP 01333-903
BRAZIL
Tel: (55-11) 3178 6810
Fax: (55-11) 3178 6830
Website: www.amb.org.br; e-mail: presidente@amb.org.br

Bulgarian Medical Association
15, Acad. Ivan Geshov Blvd.
1431 Sofia
BULGARIA
Tel: (359-2) 954 11 81
Fax: (359-2) 954 11 86
Website: www.blsbg.com; e-mail: blsus@mail.bg

Canadian Medical Association
P.O. Box 8650
1867 Alta Vista Drive
Ottawa, Ontario K1G 3Y6
CANADA
Tel: (1-613) 731 8610 ext. 2236
Fax: (1-613) 731 1779
Website: www.cma.ca; e-mail: karen.clark@cma.ca

Ordem Dos Medicos du Cabo Verde (OMCV) Cabo Verde
Avenue OUA N° 6 – B.P. 421
Achada Santo António
Ciadade de Praia-Cabo Verde
CABO VERDE
Tel: (238) 262 2503
Fax: (238) 262 3099
Website: www.ordemdosmedicos.cv; e-mail: omecab@cvtelecom.cv

Colegio Médico de Chile
Esmeralda 678 – Casilla 639
Santiago
CHILE
Tel: (56-2) 4277800
Fax: (56-2) 6330940/6336732
Website: www.colegiomedico.cl; e-mail: rdelcastillo@colegiomedico.cl

TABLE 10.1 *(Continued)*
Medical Associations by Country

Chinese Medical Association
42 Dongsi Xidajie
Beijing 100710
CHINA
Tel: (86-10) 8515 8136
Fax: (86-10) 8515 8551
Website: www.chinamed.com.cn; e-mail: intl@cma.org.cn

Federación Médica Colombiana
Carrera 7 N° 82-66, Oficinas 218/219
Santafé de Bogotá, D.E.
COLOMBIA
Tel./Fax: (57-1) 8050073
Website: www.fmc.encolombia.com; e-mail: federacionmedicacolombiana@encolombia.com

Ordre des Médecins du Zaire
B.P. 4922
Kinshasa – Gombe
DEMOCRATIC REP. OF CONGO
Tel: (243-12) 24589; no e-mail on record

Unión Médica Nacional de Costa Rica
Apartado 5920-1000
San José
COSTA RICA
Tel: (506) 290-5490
Fax: (506) 231-7373
E-mail: unmedica@racsa.co.cr

Croatian Medical Association
Subiceva 9
10000 Zagreb
CROATIA
Tel: (385-1) 46 93 300
Fax: (385-1) 46 55 066
Website: www.hlk.hr/default.asp; e-mail: hlz@email.htnet.hr

Colegio Médico Cubano Libre
P.O. Box 141016
Coral Gables, FL 33114-1016
UNITED STATES
717 Ponce de Leon Boulevard
Coral Gables, FL 33134
Tel: (1-305) 446 9902/445 1429
Fax: (1-305) 4459310; no e-mail on record

TABLE 10.1 *(Continued)*
Medical Associations by Country

Cyprus Medical Association (CyMA)
14 Thasou Street
1087 Nicosia
CYPRUS
Tel: (357) 22 33 16 87
Fax: (357) 22 31 69 37
E-mail: cyma@cytanet.com.cy

Czech Medical Association
J.E. Purkyne
Sokolská 31 – P.O. Box 88
120 26 Prague 2
CZECH REPUBLIC
Tel: (420) 224 266 201-4
Fax: (420) 224 266 212
Website: www.cls.cz; e-mail: czma@cls.cz

Danish Medical Association
9 Trondhjemsgade
2100 Copenhagen 0
DENMARK
Tel: (45) 35 44 82 29
Fax: (45) 35 44 85 05
Website: www.laeger.dk; e-mail: er@dadl.dk, clr@dadl.dk

Egyptian Medical Association "Dar El Hekmah"
42, Kasr El-Eini Street
Cairo
EGYPT
Tel: (20-2) 3543406; no e-mail on record

Colegio Médico de El Salvador
Final Pasaje No. 10
Colonia Miramonte
San Salvador
EL SALVADOR, C.A.
Tel: (503) 260-1111, 260-1112
Fax: (503) 260-0324; e-mail: comcolmed@telesal.net/marnuca@hotmail.com

Estonian Medical Association (EsMA)
Pepleri 32
51010 Tartu
ESTONIA
Tel: (372) 7 420 429
Fax: (372) 7 420 429
Website: www.arstideliit.ee; e-mail: eal@arstideliit.ee

TABLE 10.1 *(Continued)*
Medical Associations by Country

Ethiopian Medical Association
P.O. Box 2179
Addis Ababa
ETHIOPIA
Tel: (251-1) 158174
Fax: (251-1) 533742
Website: www.emaethiopia.org; e-mail: ema.emj@telecom.net.et/ema@eth.healthnet.org

Fiji Medical Association
304 Wainamu Road
G.P.O. Box 1116
Suva
FIJI ISLANDS
Tel: (679) 3315388
Fax: (679) 3315388
E-mail: fma@unwired.com.fj

Finnish Medical Association
P.O. Box 49
00501 Helsinki
FINLAND
Tel: (358-9) 393 091
Fax: (358-9) 393 0794
Website: www.medassoc.fi; e-mail: fma@fimnet.fi

Association Médicale Française
180 Blvd. Haussmann
75389 Paris Cedex 08
FRANCE
Tel: (33) 1 53 89 32 41; e-mail: deletoile.sylvie@cn.medecin.fr

Georgian Medical Association
7 Asatiani Street
0177 Tbilisi
GEORGIA
Tel: (995 32) 398686
Fax: (995 32) 396751/398083
Website: www.gma.ge; e-mail: gma@posta.ge

Bundesärztekammer (German Medical Association)
Herbert-Lewin-Platz 1
10623 Berlin
GERMANY
Tel: (49-30) 4004 56 360
Fax: (49-30) 4004 56 384
Website: www.baek.de; e-mail: international@baek.de

TABLE 10.1 *(Continued)*
Medical Associations by Country

Ghana Medical Association
P.O. Box 1596
Accra
GHANA
Tel: (233-21) 670510/665458
Fax: (233-21) 670511
Website: www.ghanamedassn.org; e-mail: gma@dslghana.com

Association Médicale Haitienne
1 ère
Av. du Travail #33 – Bois Verna
Port-au-Prince
HAITI, W.I.
Tel: (509) 2244 - 32
Fax: (509) 2244 - 50 49
Website: www.amhhaiti.net; e-mail: secretariatamh@gmail.com

Hong Kong Medical Association, China
Duke of Windsor Building
5th Floor
15 Hennessy Road
HONG KONG
Tel: (852) 2527-8285
Fax: (852) 2865-0943
Website: www.hkma.org; e-mail: hkma@hkma.org

Association of Hungarian Medical Societies (MOTESZ)
Nádor u. 36 – PO.Box 145
1051 Budapest
HUNGARY
Tel: (36-1) 312 3807, 312 0066
Fax: (36-1) 383-7918
Website: www.motesz.hu; e-mail: international@motesz.hu

Icelandic Medical Association
Hlidasmari 8
200 Kópavogur
ICELAND
Tel: (354) 864 0478
Fax: (354) 5 644106; e-mail: icemed@icemed.is

Indian Medical Association
Indraprastha Marg
New Delhi 110 002
INDIA
Tel: (91-11) 23370009/23378819/23378680
Fax: (91-11) 23379178/23379470
Website: www.imanational.com; e-mail: imawmaga2009@gmail.com

TABLE 10.1 *(Continued)*
Medical Associations by Country

Indonesian Medical Association
Jl. G.S.S.Y. Ratulangie N° 29 Menteng
Jakarta 10350
INDONESIA
Tel: (62-21) 3150679/3900277
Fax: (62-21) 390 0473
Website:www.idionline.org; e-mail: pbidi@idola.net.id

Irish Medical Organisation
10 Fitzwilliam Place
Dublin 2
IRELAND
Tel: (353-1) 6767273
Fax: (353-1) 662758
Website: www.imo.ie; e-mail: imo@imo.ie

Israel Medical Association
2 Twin Towers, 35 Jabotinsky St.
P.O. Box 3566, Ramat-Gan 52136
ISRAEL
Tel: (972-3) 610 0444
Fax: (972-3) 575 0704
Website: www.ima.org.il; e-mail: michelle@ima.org.il

Ordre National des Médecins de la Côte d'Ivoire (ONMCI)
Cocody Cité des Arts, Bât. U1, Esc.D
RdC, Porte n°1
BP 1584
Abidjan 01
IVORY COAST
Tel: (225) 22 48 61 53 /22 44 30 78/
Tel: (225) 02 02 44 01 /08 14 55 80
Fax: (225) 22 44 30 78
Website: www.onmci.org; e-mail: onmci@yahoo.fr

Japan Medical Association
2-28-16 Honkomagome, Bunkyo-ku
Tokyo 113-8621
JAPAN
Tel: (81-3) 3946 2121/3942 6489
Fax: (81-3) 3946 6295
Website: www.med.or.jp; e-mail: jmaintl@po.med.or.jp

Association of Medical Doctors of Kazakhstan
117/1 Kazybek bi St.
Almaty
KAZAKHSTAN
Tel: (7-327 2) 624301/2629292
Fax: (7-327 2) 623606; e-mail: doktor_sadykova@mail.ru

TABLE 10.1 *(Continued)*
Medical Associations by Country

Korean Medical Association
302-75 Ichon 1-dong, Yongsan-gu
Seoul 140-721
REP. OF KOREA
Tel: (82-2) 794 2474
Fax: (82-2) 793 9190/795 1345
Website: www.kma.org; e-mail: intl@kma.org

Kuwait Medical Association
P.O. Box 1202
Safat 13013
KUWAIT
Tel: (965) 5333278, 5317971
Fax: (965) 5333276
Website: alzeabi@hotmail.com; e-mail: kma@kma.org.kw

Latvian Physicians Association
Skolas Str. 3
Riga 1010
LATVIA
Tel: (371) 67287321/67220661
Fax: (371) 67220657
Website: www.arstubiedriba.lv; e-mail: lab@arstubiedriba.lv

Liechtensteinische Ärztekammer
Postfach 52
9490 Vaduz
LIECHTENSTEIN
Tel: (423) 231 1690
Fax: (423) 231 1691
Website: www.aerzte-net.li; e-mail: offce@aerztekammer.li

Lithuanian Medical Association
Liubarto Str. 2
2004 Vilnius
LITHUANIA
Tel./Fax: (370-5) 2731400
Website: www.lgs.lt; e-mail: lgs@takas.lt

Association des Médecins et Médecins Dentistes du Grand-Duché de Luxembourg (AMMD)
29, rue de Vianden
2680 Luxembourg
LUXEMBOURG
Tel: (352) 44 40 33 1
Fax: (352) 45 83 49
Website: www.ammd.lu; e-mail: secretariat@ammd.lu

TABLE 10.1 *(Continued)*
Medical Associations by Country

Macedonian Medical Association
Dame Gruev St. 3
P.O. Box 174
91000 Skopje
MACEDONIA
Tel: (389-2) 3162 577
Fax: (389-91) 232577
E-mail: mld@unet.com.mk

Society of Medical Doctors of Malawi (SMD)
Post Dot Net, PO Box 387, Crossroads
Lilongwe Malawi
30330 Lilongwe
MALAWI
Website: www.smdmalawi.org; e-mail: dlungu@sdnp.org.mw

Malaysian Medical Association
4th Floor, MMA House
124 Jalan Pahang
53000 Kuala Lumpur
MALAYSIA
Tel: (60-3) 4041 1375
Fax: (60-3) 4041 8187
Website: www.mma.org.my; e-mail: info@mma.org.my/president@mma.org.my

Ordre National des Médecins du Mali (ONMM)
Hôpital Gabriel Touré
Cour du Service d'Hygiène
BP E 674
Bamako
MALI
Tel: (223) 223 03 20/ 222 20 58/
Website: www.keneya.net/cnommali.com; e-mail: cnommali@gmail.com

Medical Association of Malta
The Professional Centre
Sliema Road, Gzira GZR 06
MALTA
Tel: (356) 21312888
Fax: (356) 21331713
Website: www.mam.org.mt; e-mail: martix@maltanet.net

Colegio Medico de Mexico (FENACOME)
Adolfo Prieto #812
Col. Del Valle
D. Benito Juárez
Mexico 03100
MEXICO
Tel: 52 55 5543 8989
Fax: 52 55 5543 1422
Website: www.cmm-fenacome.org; e-mail: fenacome_relint@teyco.com.mx

TABLE 10.1 *(Continued)*
Medical Associations by Country

Medical Association of Namibia
403 Maerua Park, POB 3369
Windhoek
NAMIBIA
Tel: (264) 61 22 4455
Fax: (264) 61 22 4826
E-mail: man.offce@iway.na

Nepal Medical Association
Siddhi Sadan, Post Box 189
Exhibition Road
Katmandu
NEPAL
Tel: (977 1) 4225860, 4231825
Fax: (977 1) 4225300; e-mail: nma@healthnet.org.np

Royal Dutch Medical Association
P.O. Box 20051
3502 LB Utrecht
NETHERLANDS
Tel: (31-30) 282 38 28
Fax: (31-30) 282 33 18
Website: www.artsennet.nl; e-mail: j.bouwman@fed.knmg.nl

New Zealand Medical Association
P.O. Box 156, 26 The Terrace
Wellington 1
NEW ZEALAND
Tel: (64-4) 472 4741
Fax: (64-4) 471 0838
Website: www.nzma.org.nz; e-mail: lianne@nzma.org.nz

Nigerian Medical Association
74, Adeniyi Jones Avenue Ikeja
P.O. Box 1108, Marina
Lagos
NIGERIA
Tel: (234-1) 480 1569, 876 4238
Fax: (234-1) 493 6854
Website: www.nigeriannma.org; e-mail: info@nigeriannma.org

Norwegian Medical Association
P.O.Box 1152 sentrum
0107 Oslo
NORWAY
Tel: (47) 23 10 90 00
Fax: (47) 23 10 90 10
Website: www.legeforeningen.no; e-mail: ellen.pettersen@legeforeningen.no

TABLE 10.1 *(Continued)*
Medical Associations by Country

Asociación Médica Nacional de la República de Panamá
Apartado Postal 2020
Panamá 1
PANAMA
Tel: (507) 263 7622 /263-7758
Fax: (507) 223 1462
Fax modem: (507) 223-5555
E-mail: amenalpa@cwpanama.net

Colegio Médico del Perú
Malecón Armendáriz No. 791
Miraflores
Lima
PERU
Tel: (51-1) 241 75 72
Fax: (51-1) 242 3917
Website: www.cmp.org.pe; e-mail: prensanacional@cmp.org.pe

Philippine Medical Association
2/F Administration Bldg.
PMA Compound, North Avenue
Quezon City 1105
PHILIPPINES
Tel: (63-2) 929-63 66
Fax: (63-2) 929-69 51
Website: www.pma.com.ph; e-mail: philmedas@yahoo.com

Polish Chamber of Physicians and Dentists (Naczelna Izba Lekarska)
110 Jana Sobieskiego
00-764 Warsaw
POLAND
Tel: (48) 22 55 91 300/324
Fax: (48) 22 55 91 323
Website: www.nil.org.pl; e-mail: sekretariat@hipokrates.org

Ordem dos Médicos – Portugal
Av. Almirante Gago Coutinho, 151
1749-084 Lisbon
PORTUGAL
Tel: (351-21) 842 71 00/842 71 11
Fax: (351-21) 842 71 99
Website: www.ordemdosmedicos.pt; e-mail: intl@omcn.pt

Romanian Medical Association
Str. Ionel Perlea, nr 10,
Sect. 1, Bucarest
ROMANIA
Tel: (40-21) 460 08 30
Fax: (40-21) 312 13 57
Website: www.ong.ro/ong/amr/; e-mail: amr@itcnet.ro

TABLE 10.1 *(Continued)*
Medical Associations by Country

Russian Medical Society
Udaltsova Street 85
119607 Moscow
RUSSIA
Tel./Fax: (7-495) 734-12-12
Tel: (7-495) 734-11-00/(7-495)734 11 00
Website: www.russmed.ru/eng/who.htm; e-mail: info@russmed.ru

Samoa Medical Association
Tupua Tamasese Meaole Hospital
Private Bag—National Health Services
Apia
SAMOA
Tel: (685) 778 5858
E-mail: vialil_lameko@yahoo.com

Ordre National des Médecins du Sénégal (ONMS)
Institut d'Hygiène Sociale (Polyclinique)
BP 27115
Dakar
SENEGAL
Tel: (221) 33 822 29 89
Fax: (221) 33 821 11 61
Website: www.ordremedecins.sn; no e-mail listed

Singapore Medical Association (SiMA)
Alumni Medical Centre, Level 2
2 College Road
SINGAPORE 169850
Tel: (65) 6223 1264
Fax: (65) 6224 7827
Website: www.sma.org.sg; e-mail: sma@sma.org.sg

Slovak Medical Association
Cukrova 3
813 22 Bratislava 1
SLOVAK REPUBLIC
Tel: (421) 5292 2020
Fax: (421) 5263 5611
Website: www.sls.sk; e-mail: secretarysma@ba.telecom.sk

Slovenian Medical Association
Komenskega 4
61001 Ljubljana
SLOVENIA
Tel: (386-61) 323 469
Fax: (386-61) 301 955; no e-mail listed

TABLE 10.1 *(Continued)*
Medical Associations by Country

Somali Medical Association
7 Corfe Close
Hayes
Middlesex UB4 0XE
UNITED KINGDOM
E-mail: drdalmar@yahoo.co.uk

The South African Medical Association
P.O. Box 74789, Lynnwood Rydge
0040 Pretoria
SOUTH AFRICA
Tel: (27-12) 481 2045
Fax: (27-12) 481 2100
Website: www.samedical.org; e-mail: sginterim@samedical.org

Consejo General de Colegios Médicos
Plaza de las Cortes 11, 4a
Madrid 28014
SPAIN
Tel: (34-91) 431 77 80
Fax: (34-91) 431 96 20
Website: www.cgcom.es; e-mail: internacional@cgcom.es

Swedish Medical Association
(Villagatan 5)
P.O. Box 5610
SE – 114 86 Stockholm
SWEDEN
Tel: (46-8) 790 35 01
Fax: (46-8) 10 31 44
Website: www.lakarforbundet.se; e-mail: info@slf.se

Fédération des Médecins Suisses (FMH)
Elfenstrasse 18 – C.P. 170
3000 Berne 15
SWITZERLAND
Tel: (41-31) 359 11 11
Fax: (41-31) 359 11 12
Website: www.fmh.ch; e-mail: info@fmh.ch

Taiwan Medical Association
9F, No 29, Sec.1
An-Ho Road
Taipei 10688
TAIWAN
Tel: (886-2) 2752-7286
Fax: (886-2) 2771-8392
Website: www.tma.tw; e-mail: intl@tma.tw

TABLE 10.1 *(Continued)*
Medical Associations by Country

Medical Association of Thailand
2 Soi Soonvijai
New Petchburi Road, Huaykwang Dist.
Bangkok 10310
THAILAND
Tel: (66-2) 314 4333/318-8170
Fax: (66-2) 314 6305
Website: www.medassocthai.org; e-mail: math@loxinfo.co.th

Conseil National de l'Ordre des Médecins de Tunisie
16, rue de Touraine
1002 Tunis
TUNISIA
Tel: (216-71) 792 736/799 041
Fax: (216-71) 788 729
E-mail: cnom@planet.tn

Turkish Medical Association
GMK Bulvari
Sehit Danis Tunaligil Sok. No. 2 Kat 4
Maltepe 06570
Ankara
TURKEY
Tel: (90-312) 231 31 79
Fax: (90-312) 231 19 52
Website: www.ttb.org.tr; e-mail: Ttb@ttb.org.tr

Uganda Medical Association
Plot 8, 41-43 circular rd.
P.O. Box 29874
Kampala
UGANDA
Tel: (256) 41 321795
Fax: (256) 41 345597
E-mail. myers28@hotmail.com

Ukrainian Medical Association (UkMA)
7 Eva Totstoho Street
PO Box 13
Kyiv 01601
UKRAINE
Tel: (380) 50 355 24 25
Fax: (380) 44 501 23 66
Website: www.sfult.org.ua; e-mail: sfult@ukr.net

British Medical Association
BMA House, Tavistock Square
London WC1H 9JP
UNITED KINGDOM
Tel: (44-207) 387-4499
Fax: (44- 207) 383-6400
Website: www.bma.org.uk; no e-mail listed

TABLE 10.1 *(Continued)*
Medical Associations by Country

American Medical Association
515 North State Street
Chicago, Illinois 60654
UNITED STATES
Tel: (1-312) 464 5291/464 5040
Fax: (1-312) 464 5973
Website: www.ama-assn.org; e-mail: ellen.waterman@ama-assn.org

Sindicato Médico del Uruguay
Bulevar Artigas 1515
CP 11200 Montevideo
URUGUAY
Tel: (598-2) 401 47 01
Fax: (598-2) 409 16 03
E-mail: secretaria@smu.org.uy

Associazione Medica del Vaticano
00120 Città del Vaticano
VATICAN STATE
Tel: (39-06) 69879300
Fax: (39-06) 69883328
E-mail: servizi.sanitari@scv.va

Federacion Medica Venezolana
Av. Orinoco con Avenida Perija
Urbanizacion Las Mercedes
Caracas 1060 CP
VENEZUELA
Website: www.federacionmedicavenezolana.org; no e-mail listed

Vietnam Medical Association (VGAMP)
68A Ba Trieu-Street, Hoau Kiem District
Hanoi
VIETNAM
Tel: (84) 4 943 9323
Fax: (84) 4 943 9323
Website: www.masean.org/vietnam; no e-mail listed

Zimbabwe Medical Association
P.O. Box 3671
Harare
ZIMBABWE
Tel: (263-4) 791553
Fax: (263-4) 791561
Website: www.zima.org.zw; e-mail: zima@zol.co.zw

Index